Who Did It First?
A Rowman & Littlefield Music Series

Who Did It First? is a unique series of titles designed to describe for readers and avid music listeners great cover songs by genres. Each volume reveals the unique path many great songs inevitably tread from their first, sometimes little-known or little-recognized, recording to their universal recognition by listeners. It is the ideal companion for music lovers seeking to build or polish their playlists.

Who Did It First? Great Rhythm and Blues Cover Songs and Their Original Artists, by Bob Leszczak, 2013

Who Did It First? Great Pop Cover Songs and Their Original Artists, by Bob Leszczak, 2014

Who Did It First?

Great Pop Cover Songs and Their Original Artists

Bob Leszczak

Who Did It First?

ROWMAN & LITTLEFIELD
Lanham • Boulder • New York • Toronto • Plymouth, UK

Published by Rowman & Littlefield
4501 Forbes Boulevard, Suite 200, Lanham, Maryland 20706
www.rowman.com

10 Thornbury Road, Plymouth PL6 7PP, United Kingdom

British Library Cataloguing in Publication Information Available

Library of Congress Cataloging-in-Publication Data
Leszczak, Bob, 1959– author.
  Who did it first? : great pop cover songs and their original artists / Bob Leszczak.
    pages cm. — (Who did it first?)
  Includes bibliographical references and index.
  ISBN 978-1-4422-3067-5 (cloth : alk. paper) — ISBN 978-1-4422-3068-2 (ebook)
1. Popular music—History and criticism. 2. Popular music—Discography. 3. Cover
versions—Discography. I. Title.
  ML3470.L464 2014
  781.6409—dc23   2013039564

Printed in the United States of America

This book is dedicated to the guy who put the bomp in the "Bomp Buh Bomp Bomp" and megs of ram in the "Rama Lama Ding Dong."

 Contents

List of Illustrations

List of Songs

Acknowledgments

I would like to send sincere, heartfelt thanks to those who made this endeavor such a pleasure. I'm most grateful to all of the extremely talented interviewees who so generously granted their valuable time to supply me with never-before-printed, fun, amazing, anecdotal, behind-the-scenes memories and quotes about their legendary music. Several also graciously offered their own vintage photographs, which are proudly displayed in this volume. In alphabetical order, a fond tip of the hat goes out to Beverly Bremers, Jerry Burgan (of We Five), Kim Carnes, Mel Carter, Gretchen Christopher (of the Fleetwoods), Raoul Cita (of the Harptones), Jimmy Clanton, Buzz Clifford, Paul Evans, Norman Fox (of the Rob Roys), George Galfo (of the Mystics), Buddy Greco, John Claude Gummoe (of the Cascades), Eddie Hodges, Tab Hunter, Brian Hyland, Bob Miranda (of the Happenings), Jay Proctor (of the Techniques), Neil Sedaka, Emil Stucchio (of the Classics), B. J. Thomas, Billy Vera, and Lenny Welch.

Those not quoted but nonetheless very important as cogs in this wheel include Marv Goldberg, Fernando L. Gonzalez, Dennis Ostrom, Steve Propes, Rockin' Richard, David Schwartz, and Vincent Terrace.

Introduction

Everybody has to start somewhere. Businessmen start on the ground floor and try to work their way up the corporate ladder. Baseball players bide their time in the minor leagues wishing for an opportunity to move up and play in the majors. Musical compositions aren't very different—some songs just don't climb the charts the first time they're recorded. However, with perseverance, the ideal singer, the right chemistry, impeccable timing, vigorous promotion, and a little luck, these songs can become very famous.

You'll know most, if not all, of the tunes listed in this book. The songs in this volume began as "pop" songs, but then traveled a circuitous route. In many cases, the familiar hit version you've grown up with, danced with, and romanced with is not the first version, nor the only version. The purpose of this book is to show *who did it first.*

For example, Jackie DeShannon wrote and recorded the original "Bette Davis Eyes" for an album, but the later Kim Carnes mega-hit version is the one everyone knows. Likewise, few recall the original "He's a Rebel" by Vikki Carr, but everyone recalls and can sing along with the number 1 single by the Crystals from Phil Spector's famous "wall of sound." Despite popular belief, Barry Manilow did not "Write the Songs"—that was Bruce Johnston of the Beach Boys, and the original version was recorded by the Captain and Tennille. Did you know that the original "Drift Away" was by John Kurtz, and not Dobie Gray? Would you believe "That's Life" was recorded by Marion Montgomery before Frank Sinatra? It's true. The information contained within these pages will surely shock and awe. You may fancy yourself a music expert, and yet the "oh, wow" factor of discovering *who did it first* will be profound.

Several songs were so good, they became hits three or more times—unforgettable songs such as "Unchained Melody," "Go Away, Little Girl," "I Only

Want to Be with You," "Since I Don't Have You," "Always on My Mind," and "Volare"—but *Who Did It First?*

Several artists had the misfortune of recording several original versions of songs, only to watch as cover artists enjoyed the spoils and achieved the fame. Petula Clark, the Everly Brothers, the Fifth Dimension, Albert Hammond, Neil Sedaka, and B. J. Thomas are just a few of the artists *who did it first* frequently.

Each song in this book, listed alphabetically, consists of information about the original artist and the cover artist, the original record label and the cover version's record label, the record numbers, the years of release, the record speeds (45, 78, LP, even CD), and the chart position each attained. Then read the fascinating history surrounding each song. Within the body of many entries are honorable mentions of still more versions and even "answer records." Many contain quotes and behind-the-scenes information from the artists and songwriters themselves, as well as photographs they've provided. Also included are numerous pictures of key record labels and important songs—all from my own record collection (a lifelong hobby).

This is volume 2 of a three-volume work. This A-to-Z edition's focus is songs that were originally recorded by pop performers and even a few originally by country crossover performers. Volume 1 centered on R&B, and the upcoming volume 3 will focus on rock and roll songs. Your library will not be complete until you have all three.

So, whether you're using this book to quiz your friends at a party, using it to quiz listeners to your radio show, or just satisfying your own insatiable musical curiosity, thank you for having a shared interest in *Who Did It First?*

 # Songs

A

"Abraham, Martin and John"
Composer: Dick Holler
Original Artist: Dion
Label: Laurie Records; *Recording:* Laurie #3464 (45)
Release Year: 1968; *Chart:* #4 *Billboard* Hot 100
Cover Artist: Smokey Robinson and the Miracles
Label: Tamla Records; *Recording:* Tamla #54184 (45)
Release Year: 1969; *Chart:* #33 *Billboard* Hot 100 and #16 R&B

The year 1968 was turbulent in the United States. The unpopular Vietnam War raged on, and both Martin Luther King Jr. and Bobby Kennedy were assassinated. The American melancholy was expressed well in a huge comeback song for Dion Dimucci in that same year. Adding the names of Abraham (for Abraham Lincoln) and John (for John F. Kennedy), the poignant song struck a chord with the record-buying public and sold a million copies. Seemingly out of nowhere (he had been off the charts for four years), Dion was back in the Top 10, and back on the Laurie Records label (which he had left for Columbia years earlier).

"Abraham, Martin and John" became one of those songs that everyone seemed to cover and/or perform on variety programs. Andy Williams, who was one of Bobby Kennedy's close friends, recorded a version on his *Happy Heart* album (Columbia #9844). A few cover versions made the charts. Smokey Robinson and the Miracles reached Top 40 on the Pop charts and Top 20 R&B with their rendition. One of the more unique versions of the song came from stand-up comedienne Moms Mabley (Mercury #72935). It was performed as more of a recitation, and, like Robinson's rendition, reached Top 40.

In 1971, "Abraham, Martin and John" was paired with "What the World Needs Now" and recorded for Motown's Mowest subsidiary label (Mowest #5002). Recorded by Los Angeles disc jockey Tom Clay, the unusual medley was over six minutes in length and briefly hit the Top 10. It receives very little airplay today.

"ACT NATURALLY"
Composers: Johnny Russell and Voni Morrison
Original Artist: Buck Owens
Label: Capitol Records; *Recording:* Capitol #4937 (45)
Release Year: 1963; *Chart:* #1 *Billboard* Country
Cover Artist: the Beatles
Label: Capitol Records; *Recording:* Capitol #5498 (45)
Release Year: 1965; *Chart:* #47 *Billboard* Hot 100

The Buck Owens original version of "Act Naturally." Like the Beatles version, it was also recorded for Capitol.

He made his first records, today categorized as rockabilly, under the name Corky Jones. As Buck Owens, he had his first number 1 country single with a song that no one else wanted to record. "Act Naturally" has many movie and Hollywood-oriented references, but all in all it is a song about loneliness and lost love.

Owens's rendition was on Capitol Records, and so was the cover by the Beatles (a hit on the B-side of "Yesterday"). It's one of the biggest hits with Ringo Starr on lead vocals. It was also very timely, as the Fab Four's fame was spreading to feature films.

In 1989, once again on Capitol Records (#44409), Owens and Starr recorded a duet version of "Act Naturally" and had a Top 30 hit on the Country chart.

"AIN'T NO WOMAN LIKE THE ONE I GOT"
Composers: Dennis Lambert and Brian Potter
Original Artist: Hamilton, Joe Frank and Reynolds
Label: Dunhill Records; *Recording:* Dunhill #50113 (LP)
Release Year: 1972; *Chart:* did not chart
Cover Artist: the Four Tops
Label: Dunhill Records; *Recording:* Dunhill #4339 (45)
Release Year: 1973; *Chart:* #4 *Billboard* Hot 100 and #2 R&B

Recorded very much in a typical Hamilton, Joe Frank and Reynolds pop style, the original "Ain't No Woman Like the One I Got" went relatively unnoticed and underappreciated on their *Hallway Symphony* album in 1972.

There are likely more differences than similarities between their original version and the Top 4 smash by the Four Tops. Some of the lyrics were changed, parts of the melody were altered, and the tempo was slowed down considerably. It was the biggest hit the Four Tops had after leaving Motown, and it sold over a million copies. Both versions of the song were released on Dunhill Records.

"THE AIR THAT I BREATHE"
Composers: Mike Hazlewood and Albert Hammond
Original Artist: Albert Hammond
Label: Mums Records; *Recording:* Mums #31905 (LP)
Release Year: 1972; *Chart:* did not chart.
Cover Artist: the Hollies
Label: Epic Records; *Recording:* Epic #11100 (45)
Release Year: 1974; *Chart:* #6 *Billboard* Hot 100

Singer/songwriter Albert Hammond had a million-selling Top 10 smash in 1972 titled "It Never Rains in Southern California" (Mums #6011). It was also the title cut for Hammond's most successful album. However, on that album was another hit song, "The Air That I Breathe"—a hit for someone else.

Two years after the Hammond version, the Hollies recorded it on a single and sold a million copies. It's a simple song about the simple things in life that we often take for granted, and the lyrics say, "Sometimes, all I need is the air that I breathe and to love you." It was the Hollies' final Top 10 hit.

"ALFIE"
Composers: Burt Bacharach and Hal David
Original Artist: Cilla Black
Label: Capitol Records; *Recording:* Capitol #5674 (45)
Release Year: 1966; *Chart:* #95 *Billboard* Hot 100
Cover Artist: Dionne Warwick
Label: Scepter Records; *Recording:* Scepter #12181 (45)
Release Year: 1967; *Chart:* #15 *Billboard* Hot 100

Paramount Pictures was seeking a title song for its upcoming film about a lothario named *Alfie*, to be portrayed by British actor Michael Caine. The company approached a reluctant Burt Bacharach, who eventually acquiesced. It was thought that, because she was British, Cilla Black would be the best choice for the song. Her version did well in numerous countries, but not in the United States.

A very short time later, "Alfie" was covered by Cher and produced by Sonny Bono. This version (Imperial #66192) fared a bit better in the United States and peaked at number 32. It should be noted that both the Cilla Black and Cher versions were part of the movie soundtrack.

In 1967, Dionne Warwick, for whom Bacharach originally intended the song, recorded it as an afterthought at the end of one of her studio sessions. Even though Warwick's rendition is not in the 1966 movie soundtrack, it is the most familiar version and the biggest one in the United States.

Stevie Wonder recorded a version of the song on the Gordy Records label (#7076) in 1968. The artist on the label was listed as Eivets Rednow, which is Stevie Wonder spelled backward.

The motion picture was a success on its first go-round, but a 2004 remake starring Jude Law was much less so. Joss Stone sings the title song in the updated version.

"ALL I HAVE TO DO IS DREAM"
Composers: Felice and Boudleaux Bryant
Original Artist: the Everly Brothers
Label: Cadence Records; *Recording:* Cadence #1348 (45 and 78)
Release Year: 1958; *Chart:* #1 *Billboard* Hot 100
Cover Artist: Richard Chamberlain
Label: MGM Records; *Recording:* MGM #13121 (45)
Release Year: 1963; *Chart:* #14 *Billboard* Hot 100

The husband-and-wife songwriting team of Felice and Boudleaux Bryant had their biggest successes when their songs were recorded by the Everly Brothers. They wrote "Bye Bye Love," and they wrote this number 1 classic. It should be noted that the up-tempo B-side, "Claudette," also made Top 30 and was written by an up-and-coming Roy Orbison. "All I Have to Do Is Dream" charted again three years later when Cadence rereleased it as a single (number 96 in 1961).

In 1963, while enjoying success as TV's *Dr. Kildare*, Richard Chamberlain recorded "All I Have to Do Is Dream" and suddenly the song was back in the Top 20.

Others who have covered this timeless song include the duos Glen Campbell and Bobbie Gentry, and Andy Gibb and Victoria Principal.

"ALL THROUGH THE NIGHT"
Composer: Jules Shear
Original Artist: Jules Shear
Label: EMI America Records; *Recording:* EMI America #17092 (LP)
Release Year: 1983; *Chart:* did not chart
Cover Artist: Cyndi Lauper
Label: Portrait Records; *Recording:* Portrait #04639 (45)
Release Year: 1984; *Chart:* #5 *Billboard* Hot 100

"All through the Night" began its life as a cut on the Jules Shear album titled *Watch Dog* in 1983. Shear wrote the song, but the album didn't chart and thus most people didn't get to hear the song.

However, Cyndi Lauper was listening and decided to record the song on her 1983 album, *She's So Unusual*. Shear's original version had a pop flavor to it and a medium tempo, but Lauper opted to reinvent the song as a ballad. It became the fourth Top 10 hit from that multiplatinum album late in 1984.

"ALLEY OOP"
Composer: Dallas Frazier
Original Artist: the Hollywood Argyles
Label: Lute Records; *Recording:* Lute #5905 (45)
Release Year: 1960; *Chart:* #1 *Billboard* Hot 100
Cover Artist: Dante and the Evergreens
Label: Madison Records; *Recording:* Madison #130 (45)
Release Year: 1960; *Chart:* #15 *Billboard* Hot 100

Inspired by the popular V. T. Hamlin comic strip *Alley Oop*, the song was a huge million-selling number 1 novelty hit in 1960 by Gary Paxton under the name the Hollywood Argyles on the tiny Lute Records label. Paxton had previously been Flip of Skip and Flip, and when this record became such a smash, he had to scramble to assemble a group for live performances and TV engagements. Two cover versions quickly charted—one by the R&B group called the Dyna-Sores (Rendezvous #120), and another by a doo-wop group called Dante and the Evergreens. The latter became a Top 20 hit.

A similar-sounding novelty record titled "Yogi" by the Ivy Three (Shell #720), also inspired by a comic strip and cartoon character, made Top 10, albeit very briefly, in 1960.

The composer of "Alley Oop," Dallas Frazier, also composed and performed the original version of "Elvira," made famous by the Oak Ridge Boys (see the entry for that song).

Gary Paxton eventually founded his own Garpax Records label, most famous for the monster hit titled "The Monster Mash."

Years later, *alley oop* became a basketball term for an offensive play in which one player throws the ball close to the basket to a teammate who leaps, catches the ball, and slam dunks it.

"ALONE (WHY MUST I BE ALONE?)"
Composers: Morty Craft and Selma Craft
Original Artist: the Shepherd Sisters
Label: Lance Records; *Recording:* Lance #125 (45 and 78)
Release Year: 1957; *Chart:* #18 *Billboard* Hot 100
Cover Artist: the Four Seasons
Label: Vee Jay Records; *Recording:* Vee Jay #597 (45)
Release Year: 1964; *Chart:* #28 *Billboard* Hot 100

This bouncy tune was a Top 20 hit, originally by the Shepherd Sisters in 1957 on Morty Craft's short-lived Lance Records label. It's a song about forgiving and forgetting, but once you've heard the melody, you can never forget it. It became the only hit for a family quartet from Ohio—Mary Lou, Gayle, Judy, and Martha Shepherd.

The song was remade by another quartet—the Four Seasons—in 1964, and once again the song became a fair-sized hit on the Pop charts. The tune was a great vehicle for Frankie Valli's famous falsetto, and like the original it featured a whistling verse. This version was simply titled "Alone" without the question in parentheses.

"ALWAYS ON MY MIND"
Composers: Wayne Carson, Mark James, and Johnny Christopher
Original Artist: Brenda Lee
Label: Decca Records; *Recording:* Decca #32975 (45)
Release Year: 1972; *Chart:* #45 *Billboard* Country

The Shepherd Sisters sang "Alone" long before the Four Seasons.

Cover Artist: Willie Nelson
Label: Columbia Records; *Recording:* Columbia #02741 (45)
Release Year: 1982; *Chart:* #5 *Billboard* Hot 100

"Little Miss Dynamite," Brenda Lee, recorded a lot of very famous songs. One of them, "Always on My Mind," became bigger hits for a few other artists who recorded it. Elvis Presley remade it late in 1972 on the B-side of "Separate Ways" (RCA Victor #74-0815), and it reached Top 20 on the Country chart but didn't crack the Pop charts.

It took a decade and Willie Nelson to finally put the song over. Nelson's 1982 rendition reached number 5 on the Pop charts, sold over a million copies, and was inducted into the Grammy Hall of Fame in 2008.

But, living up to its title, "Always on My Mind" became a hit yet again in 1988 when it was remade by Neil Tennant and Chris Lowe—the Pet Shop Boys (EMI Manhattan #50123). This rendition peaked at number 4 on the Hot 100—the highest position of any artist thus far.

"AND I LOVE YOU SO"
Composer: Don McLean
Original Artist: Don McLean
Label: United Artists Records; *Recording:* United Artists #5522 (LP)
Release Year: 1971; *Chart:* did not chart
Cover Artist: Perry Como
Label: RCA Victor Records; *Recording:* RCA Victor #0906 (45)
Release Year: 1973; *Chart:* #29 *Billboard* Hot 100

Before "American Pie," Don McLean released an album titled *Tapestry.* It's very interesting that he was permitted to use that title after the meteoric success of the Carole King album of that same name. On this mildly successful United Artists LP was a ballad written by McLean titled "And I Love You So." It was not released as a single, but it certainly was not forgotten.

Cover versions abound. Bobby Vinton, Elvis Presley, Bobby Goldsboro, Glen Campbell, Johnny Mathis, and Helen Reddy are among the many who tried to make this song a hit. Surprisingly, out of nowhere Perry Como's version usurped all others and became the definitive hit. It peaked at number 29 on the Pop charts, but reached number 1 on the Adult Contemporary chart. It became the final Top 40 hit in Como's long, storied career.

"AND THAT REMINDS ME"
Composers: Camillo Bargoni, Al Stillman, and Paul Siegel
Original Artist: Della Reese
Label: Jubilee Records; *Recording:* Jubilee #5292 (45 and 78)
Release Year: 1957; *Chart:* #12 *Billboard* Hot 100
Cover Artist: the Four Seasons
Label: Crewe Records; *Recording:* Crewe #333 (45)
Release Year: 1969; *Chart:* #45 *Billboard* Hot 100

Sometimes called "My Heart Reminds Me," this hauntingly beautiful melody was originally written as an instrumental called "Autumn Concerto." The lyrics were added by Al Stillman and Paul Siegel, and the first version with those lyrics was recorded by Della Reese—indeed, the same Della Reese who years later starred in *Touched by an Angel* on CBS. She also costarred in (and delivered the most memorable line from) the 1989 Richard Pryor movie *Harlem Nights.*

There were numerous cover versions by famous names such as Kay Starr, Jane Morgan, Dean Martin, and Vikki Carr, but the most innovative rendition by far came from the Four Seasons. This well-produced interpretation just missed the Top 40 in 1969.

"AND WHEN I DIE"
Composer: Laura Nyro
Original Artist: Peter, Paul and Mary
Label: Warner Brothers Records; *Recording:* Warner Brothers #1648 (LP)
Release Year: 1966; *Chart:* did not chart
Cover Artist: Blood, Sweat and Tears
Label: Columbia Records; *Recording:* Columbia #45008 (45)
Release Year: 1969; *Chart:* #2 *Billboard* Hot 100

In a very short life, Laura Nyro wrote many very memorable songs for artists such as Three Dog Night, Barbra Streisand, and the Fifth Dimension. She also wrote a song called "And When I Die," which took a while to catch on. Peter, Paul and Mary recorded it first on *The Peter, Paul and Mary Album* in 1966.

Nyro recorded her own version in 1967 on her *More Than a New Discovery* album (Rev-Ola #233), but the best was yet to come. A 1969 rendition by David Clayton-Thomas and Blood, Sweat and Tears became the big hit—kept out of the number 1 spot by the Beatles' "Come Together."

Sadly, the lyrics to "And When I Die" today seem prophetic, as Laura Nyro died at the young age of forty-nine in 1997.

"ANGEL BABY"
Composer: David Ponci
Original Artist: Rosie and the Originals
Label: Highland Records; *Recording:* Highland #1011 (45)
Release Year: 1960; *Chart:* #5 *Billboard* Hot 100
Cover Artist: Angelica
Label: Quality/Ultra Records; *Recording:* Quality/Ultra #15171 (CD)
Release Year: 1991; *Chart:* #29 *Billboard* Hot 100

What this original version lacks in polish it more than makes up for in charm. It was recorded when lead singer Rosie Hamlin was in her teens. The master tape was shopped around, but initially no record labels were interested because of its rawness. The tiny Highland label of Southern California took a chance on "Angel Baby," and the ballad surprisingly became a Top 5 smash.

The tune has been covered dozens of times. A version by Vicki Vote (Imperial #66377) in 1969 resembled the original Rosie and the Originals version (with a bit more polish). Even John Lennon recorded a version (produced by Phil Spector), released on his posthumous *Menlove Ave* album in 1986 (Capitol #12533) on which he pays homage to Rosie in the intro.

The biggest remake came in a 1991 version by Angelica, who sang part of the song in Spanish. Much like the original, this rendition is fraught with imperfections, and yet it became a Top 30 hit.

"ANGEL OF THE MORNING"
Composer: Chip Taylor
Original Artist: Evie Sands
Label: Cameo Parkway Records; *Recording:* Cameo Parkway #475 (45)
Release Year: 1967; *Chart:* did not chart
Cover Artist: Merrilee Rush and the Turnabouts
Label: Bell Records; *Recording:* Bell #705 (45)
Release Year: 1968; *Chart:* #7 *Billboard* Hot 100

Because of the subject matter in this song, some recording artists turned it down. Written by Chip Taylor, the song told the story of a woman who "spent the night." Remember, this was 1967 and this kind of thing could still raise some eyebrows. The first released version by Evie Sands was on Philadelphia's Cameo Parkway label. Cameo Parkway was having financial difficulties at this time in its history and likely the record received very little promotion.

Opportunity then knocked for a Seattle-area artist named Merrilee Rush and her group, the Turnabouts. Their version was recorded in Memphis with Chips Moman at the helm, and on the Bell Records label, it became the group's only Top 10 hit.

However, that wasn't the end of the story. Capitol recording artist Juice Newton remade the song (Capitol #4976) in 1981, and once again the song attained Top 10 status. The only difference—this time, the subject matter was a nonissue. Years later, the song was sampled in the 2001 R&B hit "Angel" by Shaggy featuring Rayvon (MCA #155811).

"APPLES, PEACHES, PUMPKIN PIE"
Composer: Maurice Irby Jr.
Original Artist: Sam the Sham and the Pharaohs
Label: MGM Records; *Recording:* MGM #4422 (LP)
Release Year: 1966; *Chart:* did not chart
Cover Artist: Jay and the Techniques
Label: Smash Records; *Recording:* Smash #2086 (45)
Release Year: 1967; *Chart:* #6 *Billboard* Hot 100 and #8 R&B

Originally titled "Ready or Not," the song was first recorded by Sam the Sham and the Pharaohs on *The Best of Sam the Sham and the Pharaohs* album in 1966. This version was not issued as a single and it was not a hit.

Jay Proctor, lead singer of Allentown, Pennsylvania's, Jay and the Techniques said, "I wasn't even aware of Sam the Sham's version. My group got the song because Bobby Hebb, of 'Sunny' fame, turned it down—he didn't like it. What's interesting is that I was always a bass singer. I was the bass for a doo-wop group known as the Sinceres ['You're Too Young/Forbidden Love' on Jordan #117], but producer Jerry Ross wanted me to sing lead. The arrangers on the record were Denny Randell and Sandy Linzer who had worked extensively with the Four Seasons."

The tune was now titled "Apples, Peaches, Pumpkin Pie," and it was a Top 10 smash on the Pop and R&B charts. Proctor added, "We tried to get the Tastykake Company to use our song in their TV commercials, but our efforts were in vain. We gave it the old college try."

The group's follow-up, "Keep the Ball Rolling" (Smash #2124), became a Top 20 hit and was later used as the theme song for the long-running game show *Bowling for Dollars.*

"ARE YOU LONESOME, TONIGHT?"

Composers: Lou Handman and Roy Turk
Original Artist: Charles Hart
Label: Harmony Records; *Recording:* Harmony #431 (78)
Release Year: 1927; *Chart:* did not chart
Cover Artist: Elvis Presley
Label: RCA Victor Records; *Recording:* RCA Victor #7777 (45)
Release Year: 1960; *Chart:* #1 *Billboard* Hot 100

Many versions of "Are You Lonesome, Tonight?" emerged in 1927, but by only a few weeks, Charles Hart is credited with the very first release. Hart's version was a waltz and had a circus carousel feel to it. The first hit rendition was by singer Vaughn DeLeath and it reached number 4 on the charts. DeLeath's release is on one of those very thick, fragile, and noisy Edison 78s.

"Are You Lonesome, Tonight?" made a very important transition in 1950 when it was recorded by Blue Barron on the MGM label (#10628)—it included a talking bridge derived from William Shakespeare's *As You Like It.* That's the version "the King of Rock and Roll," Elvis Presley, remade a decade later. Released only about six months after his return from his army hitch, Presley's "Are You Lonesome, Tonight?" soared to number 1 and remained there for six consecutive weeks. It was so big that several answer records were made by female singers, such as Dodie Stevens (Dot #16167). The title of Stevens's Top 60 release was "Yes, I'm Lonesome Tonight."

Stand-up comic Sam Kinison made the song his own years later. Kinison performed the song totally straight until he got to the spoken bridge and then absolutely cut loose into a hilarious, screaming tirade about a painful breakup (he performed it once on *The Tonight Show with Johnny Carson* and made Johnny laugh).

"AT LAST"

Composers: Harry Warren and Mack Gordon
Original Artist: Glenn Miller
Label: RCA Victor Records; *Recording:* RCA Victor #27934 (78)
Release Year: 1942; *Chart:* #14 *Billboard* Music Hit Parade
Cover Artist: Etta James
Label: Argo Records; *Recording:* Argo #5380 (45)
Release Year: 1961; *Chart:* #47 *Billboard* Hot 100 and #2 R&B

This beautiful song was written for the musical motion picture *Orchestra Wives* in 1941. The hit version by Glenn Miller and His Orchestra the following year was a lesser hit on the flip side of "I've Got a Gal in Kalamazoo."

"At Last" has been covered dozens upon dozens of times since that first pressing by Glenn Miller, but none is more beloved than the rendition by Etta James. This exquisitely produced 45 was not a big hit on the pop charts in 1961—in fact, it barely made Top 50 (but it did conquer the Top 3 on the R&B charts). The postchart life of "At Last," however, is staggering. This romantic song has been utilized as the wedding song for countless happy couples. It has also been included in numerous movie soundtracks and TV commercials—its status almost mythic. It was inducted into the Grammy Hall of Fame in 1999.

Beyoncé performed the song in the Chess Records/Etta James biopic *Cadillac Records* in 2008. Etta James passed away just a few days short of her seventy-fifth birthday on January 20, 2012, after a long illness. Her legacy and her amazing music live on.

"AT THIS MOMENT"

Composer: Billy Vera
Original Artist: Billy Vera and the Beaters
Label: Alfa Records; *Recording:* Alfa #7005 (45)
Release Year: 1981; *Chart:* #79 *Billboard* Hot 100
Cover Artist: Billy Vera and the Beaters
Label: Rhino Records; *Recording:* Rhino #74403 (45)
Release Year: 1986; *Chart:* #1 *Billboard* Hot 100

This beautiful ballad titled "At This Moment" was written by Billy Vera, who has had a long and diverse career. Talent ran in his family—his dad, Bill McCord, was an announcer on TV for *Concentration*, *21*, and *Tic Tac Dough*; his

A "moment" with Billy Vera. Photograph taken by Barry Druxman. *Courtesy of Billy Vera*

mom, Ann Ryan, was one of the regular background singers on *The Perry Como Show*. Son Billy exhibited the most diverse talents—actor/singer/songwriter/musician/arranger.

Besides many songs he'd written for others, Vera had numerous Top 40 hits of his own, such as "With Pen in Hand" and "Country Girl–City Man" for Atlantic Records. In the early 1980s, Vera landed at the short-lived Alfa Records label (on which Lulu was also recording). Now using the moniker Billy Vera and the Beaters, the group returned to the Top 40 with "I Can Take Care of Myself" (Alfa #7002). However, it was another song the group released on the label for which they'd garner a gold record—it just took a little patience.

Vera recalled,

> After our second LP for Alfa, the label folded. I continued performing, however (while also playing bit parts in movies and on TV). "At This Moment" had been a minor hit on the charts in 1981, and I continued to perform it on a regular basis. Several years later, a guy named Michael Whitehorn heard us sing it live and thought it would be perfect for NBC's *Family Ties*. I told him to license the song from my publisher, Warner Brothers Music, and it was used a few times on the show. America went berserk and the show received an historic amount of letters. We just couldn't find anyone to rerelease the record. Finally Richard Foos of Rhino Records made that happen and we leaped right over Madonna to number 1 and sold over a million copies in 1987.

"At This Moment" is the gift that keeps on giving. A new version of the song was included on the 2009 Michael Bublé album titled *Crazy Love* (143 Records #520733) that reached number 1, went platinum, and remained on the charts for eons.

B

"BABY SITTIN' BOOGIE"
Composer: Johnny Parker
Original Artist: Buzz Clifford
Label: Columbia Records; *Recording:* Columbia #41876 (45)
Release Year: 1961; *Chart:* #6 *Billboard* Hot 100
Cover Artist: Ralf Bendix and Klein Elisabeth
Label: ABC-Paramount Records; *Recording:* ABC-Paramount #10340 (45)
Release Year: 1962; *Chart:* did not chart

Reese Francis Clifford III was better known on record as Buzz Clifford, and he had a very fun smash hit in 1961 called "Baby Sittin' Boogie." Clifford said, "I

The original "Baby Sittin' Boogie" created a "buzz" overseas.

want to put to rest any rumors about Ralf Bendix once and for all. I did the song first and had the biggest hit with it on Columbia Records. Anything to the contrary is total B.S. A lot of artists in foreign countries covered the song, and I wasn't too happy about that."

Among those cover versions is one in German by Ralf Bendix and Little Elizabeth (Klein Elisabeth), released in the United States on ABC-Paramount. That version was not released until 1962—a full year after Clifford's original version sold a million copies. Clifford definitely had the original version of the song, and now hopefully that old myth has been effectively debunked.

Clifford recalled, "On its way down the charts, 'Baby Sittin' Boogie' suddenly started moving back up. The nice ballad on the flip side, 'Driftwood,' started to take off. It took Columbia quite by surprise—they weren't prepared. Had they pressed up more copies of the record and promoted it a little better, I would definitely have had a two-sided Top 10 hit. I was very disappointed about that."

By the way, the baby's voice on the Buzz Clifford original was the baby son of the composer, Johnny Parker. Like the baby in the song, in closing, might I say, "Boogoo Boogoo Boogoo, all gone."

"Baby Talk"

Composer: Melvin Schwartz
Original Artist: the Laurels
Label: Spring Records; *Recording:* Spring #1112 (45)
Release Year: 1959; *Chart:* did not chart
Cover Artist: Jan and Dean
Label: Dore Records; *Recording:* Dore #522 (45)
Release Year: 1959; *Chart:* #10 *Billboard* Hot 100

Roy Robinson and the Laurels released the first version of "Baby Talk" in 1959. Released on the tiny Spring label, distribution and promotion were a big problem.

The Laurels original didn't go unnoticed, however. It was covered by and became the first Top 10 hit for Jan and Dean—a duo who later competed for surf turf with the Beach Boys. Some rare early copies were erroneously released as by Jan and Arnie (the name used on Jan's first hit, "Jennie Lee"), but that was quickly corrected by the Dore record label, and this song, which featured a memorable a cappella "bah bah bah bah bah oom da oom da oom mah wah wah" in the beginning, became a Top 10 smash.

"Ballad of Davy Crockett"

Composers: George Bruns and Thomas Blackburn
Original Artist: Bill Hayes
Label: Cadence Records; *Recording:* Cadence #1256 (45 and 78)
Release Year: 1955; *Chart:* #1 *Billboard* Hot 100
Cover Artist: Fess Parker
Label: Columbia Records; *Recording:* Columbia #40449 (45 and 78)
Release Year: 1955; *Chart:* #5 *Billboard* Hot 100

Based on the adventures of the real Davy Crockett, an ABC series titled *Disneyland* featured weekly visits to either Fantasyland, Adventureland, Tomorrowland, or Frontierland. From the latter came the *Davy Crockett* episodes that starred Fess Parker. The theme song from those TV episodes became one of the biggest hits of 1955 and immortalized "the king of the wild frontier."

It was first released as a single by actor/singer Bill Hayes (later of *Days of Our Lives*). His version was number 1 on the Pop charts for five weeks. However, there were numerous cover versions all vying for a piece of the pop pie. Fess Parker himself came out with his own version on Columbia Records and had a Top 5 hit. Then Tennessee Ernie Ford (Capitol #3058) jumped on the Conestoga wagon and his rendition also made Top 5. Between these and still more cover versions, the song sold well over 10 million copies.

Fess Parker went on to star in the sitcom *Mr. Smith Goes to Washington* and later the long-running *Daniel Boone* series on NBC from 1964 to 1970.

"THE BANANA BOAT SONG"

Composers: Alan Arkin, Bob Carey, Erik Darling, Harry Belafonte, Lord Burgess, and William Attaway
Original Artist: Harry Belafonte
Label: RCA Victor Records; *Recording:* RCA Victor #1248 (LP)
Release Year: 1956; *Chart:* #5 *Billboard* Hot 100
Cover Artist: the Tarriers
Label: Glory Records; *Recording:* Glory #249 (45 and 78)
Release Year: 1956; *Chart:* #4 *Billboard* Hot 100

"The Banana Boat Song," also known as "Day-O," has a long and varied history. It was a Jamaican work song that originated from banana laborers near the end of their long shift. The first known recorded version was by an artist from Trinidad named Edric Connor circa 1952. In 1956, a rewritten rendition of the song, first performed on NBC's *Colgate Comedy Hour*, was introduced on Harry Belafonte's *Calypso* album, which attained the top spot on the Album chart.

However, the first single version was by the Tarriers very late in 1956 on the Glory Records label. They beat out RCA's choice to release Belafonte's version on a 45 by a matter of weeks. The Tarriers' version boasts different writers—Carey, Darling, and Arkin. Those names coincide with the members of the Tarriers—Bob Carey, Erik Darling, and Alan Arkin. Indeed, the same Alan Arkin who became an Oscar winner years later. The Belafonte rendition lists the composers as Belafonte, Burgess and Attaway—Harry Belafonte, Lord Burgess (sometimes listed as Irving Burgie), and William Attaway. Both versions made Top 5, and several others made Top 20 (by the Fontane Sisters, Steve Lawrence, and Sarah Vaughan).

Even with all of those hit versions competing for a piece of the banana pie, the song to this day is most associated with Harry Belafonte. New interest in the song was incited by its inclusion in the soundtrack for the 1988 Michael Keaton motion picture *Beetlejuice*. The a cappella "Day-O" line from the song is often played between batters at Major League Baseball games.

"BAND OF GOLD"

Composers: Bob Musel and Jack Taylor
Original Artist: Kit Carson

Label: Capitol Records; *Recording:* Capitol #3082 (45 and 78)
Release Year: 1955; *Chart:* #11 *Billboard* Hot 100
Cover Artist: Don Cherry
Label: Columbia Records; *Recording:* Columbia #40597 (45 and 78)
Release Year: 1955; *Chart:* #4 *Billboard* Hot 100

Not to be confused with the 1970 Freda Payne hit of the same name, this "Band of Gold" had its origins in 1955. A female singer named Kit Carson (sharing a name with the famous frontiersman) had the song out first late in 1955. Her version, which eventually made the Top 20, was covered almost instantly by Don Cherry (who was also quite a proficient amateur golfer). Cherry was soon on top and had the bigger hit, reaching number 4 on the Pop charts.

There were a couple of noteworthy versions in the 1960s—a popular doo-wop version by the Roommates in 1961 (Valmor #10) and a Top 40 remake by the great Mel Carter in 1966 (Imperial #66165).

"THE BATTLE OF NEW ORLEANS"
Composer: Jimmie Driftwood
Original Artist: Jimmie Driftwood
Label: RCA Victor Records; *Recording:* RCA Victor #7534 (45)
Release Year: 1958; *Chart:* did not chart
Cover Artist: Johnny Horton
Label: Columbia Records; *Recording:* Columbia #41339 (45)
Release Year: 1959; *Chart:* #1 *Billboard* Hot 100

Jimmie Driftwood was a schoolteacher who found a unique way to maintain his pupils' interest in history—he wrote clever songs about historic events. Among the best was "The Battle of New Orleans" about the final battle in the War of 1812, which took place on January 8, 1815. Country music star Porter Wagoner got wind of the many songs of Jimmie Driftwood and brought him to RCA Victor. Produced by Chet Atkins, Driftwood recorded that and other songs he had written, but nothing much happened with his album or 45 releases. That is, until "The Battle of New Orleans" was covered by Johnny Horton for Columbia.

This time around, the song was gigantic, and remained at number 1 on the Pop charts for a stellar six weeks. Very quickly, RCA had Driftwood record a song titled "The Answer to the Battle of New Orleans" (RCA #7971), but it wasn't a hit.

A parody of "The Battle of New Orleans" called "The Battle of Kookamonga" by Homer and Jethro (RCA Victor #7585) just missed the Top 10 late in 1959.

"BAZOOM (I NEED YOUR LOVING)"
Composers: Jerry Leiber and Mike Stoller
Original Artist: the Cheers

Label: Capitol Records; *Recording:* Capitol #2921 (45 and 78)
Release Year: 1954; *Chart:* did not chart
Cover Artist: the Charms
Label: Deluxe Records; *Recording:* Deluxe #6076 (45 and 78)
Release Year: 1955; *Chart:* #15 *Billboard* R&B

In rock and roll's early days, it was usually the R&B artist who had the original version, which was then covered for the Pop charts by a white artist. The song "Bazoom (I Need Your Loving)" was a definite anomaly because the reverse occurred.

Written by Jerry Leiber and Mike Stoller, a white group known as the Cheers, with a very young Bert Convy, recorded it for Capitol Records. It got some airplay and sold pretty well, but not well enough to make the charts. It took a cover version by an African American group called the Charms (known mostly for their cover records) to make it a hit. In fact, both sides of the record made the R&B Top 20 ("Ling Ting Tong," another cover, was on the flip).

The Cheers had their day in the sun, however. Another Leiber and Stoller composition titled "Black Denim Trousers and Motorcycle Boots" (Capitol #3219) became a Top 10 smash for the group late in 1955. Bert Convy went on to a successful run hosting game shows such as *Tattletales*, *Win Lose or Draw*, and *Super Password*.

"Before the Next Teardrop Falls"
Composers: Ben Peters and Vivian Keith
Original Artist: Duane Dee
Label: Capitol Records; *Recording:* Capitol #5986 (45)
Release Year: 1968; *Chart:* did not chart
Cover Artist: Freddy Fender
Label: ABC Records; *Recording:* ABC #17540 (45)
Release Year: 1975; *Chart:* #1 *Billboard* Hot 100

Here's yet another song that wasn't an overnight success. It took a few years, and it took the right sound. Country artist Duane Dee was the first to record "Before the Next Teardrop Falls"—a song about a man waiting in line for the girl he loves. That love is unrequited, but he resolutely continues his pursuit undaunted. This version and a cover by Jerry Lee Lewis failed to chart.

Then, late in 1974, a Latino recording artist named Freddy Fender recorded a bilingual version (mostly in English, partly in Spanish). Fender had been recording with marginal success since the 1950s, but at this same time, another Latino Freddie (Prinze) became a star because of a sitcom called *Chico and the Man*. The timing was right for Freddy Fender, and "Before the Next Teardrop Falls" became a number 1 hit on the Pop and Country charts. Almost overnight,

Fender was a guest on every TV talk and variety show. Two more Top 20 hits followed ("Wasted Days and Wasted Nights" and "Secret Love"—see the entries for those songs).

"BEGGIN'"

Composers: Bob Gaudio and Peggy Farina
Original Artist: the Four Seasons
Label: Philips Records; *Recording:* Philips #40433 (45)
Release Year: 1967; *Chart:* #16 *Billboard* Hot 100
Cover Artist: Madcon
Label: Bonnier Amigo/Columbia Records; *Recording:* Bonnier Amigo/Columbia #88697286652 (CD)
Release Year: 2008; *Chart:* #79 *Billboard* Hot 100

"Beggin'" by the Four Seasons had quite an abundance of hooks. It was written by Bob Gaudio and Peggy Farina (a.k.a. Peggy Santiglia of the "My Boyfriend's Back" Angels). This version contains a very powerful and dramatic opening with Frankie Valli saying, "Mm mm mm. Put your loving hand out—I'm beggin'."

"Beggin'" wasn't the biggest hit for the Four Seasons, but it did lead to numerous cover versions—especially after the turn of the century. One version by a Norwegian group known as Madcon became a huge international hit, but only reached number 79 on the Pop charts.

Another rendition by a soulful female group known as the Saturdays in 2008 kept "Beggin'" top of mind.

"BEND ME, SHAPE ME"

Composers: Lawrence Weiss and Scott English
Original Artist: the Outsiders
Label: Capitol Records; *Recording:* Capitol #2636 (LP)
Release Year: 1966; *Chart:* did not chart
Cover Artist: the American Breed
Label: Acta Records; *Recording:* Acta #811 (45)
Release Year: 1967; *Chart:* #5 *Billboard* Hot 100

This was a song in which the girl in the relationship wanted to change her guy and mold him as if he were clay. However, the guy is perfectly OK with this scenario and says, "As long as you love me, it's alright"—thus the title, "Bend Me, Shape Me (Any Way You Want Me)."

Sonny Geraci and the Outsiders had the first version on *The Outsiders In* album. It never became a single. The next version was the first 45 version and the most unique version. It was recorded by a female psychedelic rock band called the Models on MGM Records (#13375). This version also failed to catch on.

It took a group from Cicero, Illinois, named the American Breed in 1967 to make the song a hit. It became the group's only Top 10 hit and only million-seller. However, the American Breed was not done. Some of the members of the band evolved into the group Rufus of Rufus and Chaka Khan fame.

"Bend Me, Shape Me" was used in TV commercials for the clothing store called the Gap in 2003.

"BETTE DAVIS EYES"

Composers: Donna Weiss and Jackie DeShannon
Original Artist: Jackie DeShannon
Label: Columbia Records; *Recording:* Columbia #33500 (LP)
Release Year: 1975; *Chart:* did not chart
Cover Artist: Kim Carnes
Label: EMI America Records; *Recording:* EMI America #8077 (45)
Release Year: 1981; *Chart:* #1 *Billboard* Hot 100

The transformation of "Bette Davis Eyes" from the original to the hit version is truly "eye-opening." The song was co-written by Jackie DeShannon, and her original 1975 version had kind of a swing or Broadway flavor to it. It was included on DeShannon's *New Arrangement* LP and never released as a single.

The tune didn't go unnoticed, however. Kim Carnes recalled,

> I expressed interest in recording the song to the other co-writer, Donna Weiss. I knew it had to be updated and changed, but initially I was unsure what to do with it. My band and I changed the chords to minor after Bill Cuomo came up with that hypnotic synth lick. He found just the right sound with a magical synthesizer called a Prophet. A second keyboard lick was inspired by Gary Numan's hit, "Cars," and it was played by my other keyboard player named Goldie. It all sounded so good and so different. We cut it the very next day at Val Garay's studio and take number two was the one. You just know when it's right. We all knew we had something very special—my band, Val Garay my producer and I knew it was a big record and we begged the label to put it out as the first single from the *Mistaken Identity* LP [EMI America #17052]. I won two Grammys for it. It was number 1 in the US for ten weeks, and, in fact it was number 1 in most countries of the world. It really opened up Europe and South America for me. I still love to perform there.

Did Carnes ever get to meet Bette Davis? "Bette and I became wonderful friends. In fact, she wrote me a letter and said the song made her a hero in her grandson's eyes. I have a wonderful photograph with Bette. She was so generous to me. She had some great stories about the film studios."

Bruce "Baby Man" Baum with Little Roger and the Goosebumps released a parody of the song called "Marty Feldman Eyes" (Horn #11) in 1981.

"BEYOND THE SEA"
Composers: Jack Lawrence and Charles Trenet
Original Version: Charles Trenet
Label: Columbia Records; *Recording:* Columbia BF-156 (French 78)
Release Year: 1945; *Chart:* did not chart
Cover Artist: Bobby Darin
Label: Atco Records; *Recording:* Atco #6158 (45)
Release Year: 1960; *Chart:* #6 *Billboard* Hot 100

This song was originally written by Charles Trenet as "La Mer," which translates to simply "the sea." Trenet had the original release in 1945 in France.

While it was still known as "La Mer," there were several more instrumental versions of the song that made Top 30 by artists such as Benny Goodman and His Orchestra in 1948, and Roger Williams in 1955.

It was lyricist Jack Lawrence who was responsible for "La Mer" becoming "Beyond the Sea." Under this title with the English lyrics, Bobby Darin made the song his own, as a huge follow-up to the million-selling "Mack the Knife." *Beyond the Sea* was chosen as the title for the Lion's Gate 2004 biopic loosely based on Darin's life.

Darin fan George Benson recorded his own version of "Beyond the Sea" in 1985 on the *20/20* album (Warner Brothers #25178).

"BIG YELLOW TAXI"
Composer: Joni Mitchell
Original Artist: the Neighborhood
Label: Big Tree Records; *Recording:* Big Tree #102 (45)
Release Year: 1970; *Chart:* #29 *Billboard* Hot 100
Cover Artist: Joni Mitchell
Label: Reprise Records; *Recording:* Reprise #0906 (45)
Release Year: 1970; *Chart:* #67 *Billboard* Hot 100

Even though this song was penned by Joni Mitchell, her 1970 version was not the first and certainly not the biggest. That honor belongs to a one-hit-wonder group known as the Neighborhood, which consisted of nine members. Mitchell's version that year barely cracked the Top 70.

Early in 1975, Mitchell tried again—this time with a live version of "Big Yellow Taxi"—and almost made Top 20.

The taxi picked up many more fares over the years—Amy Grant took a ride in 1995 (A & M #0976), Janet Jackson and Q-Tip sampled it in 1997 in

The Neighborhood hailed the "Big Yellow Taxi" before Joni Mitchell.

"Got 'Til It's Gone" (Virgin #44762), and Counting Crows featuring Vanessa Carlton remade it in 2002 (Geffen #831). Even though the song has dated lyrics (the mention of the long-gone pesticide DDT), its message favoring nature over progress is timeless.

"BILLY, DON'T BE A HERO"
Composers: Mitch Murray and Peter Callander
Original Artist: Paper Lace
Label: Mercury Records; *Recording:* Mercury #73479 (45)
Release Year: 1974; *Chart:* #96 *Billboard* Hot 100
Cover Artist: Bo Donaldson and the Heywoods
Label: ABC Records; *Recording:* ABC #11435 (45)
Release Year: 1974; *Chart:* #1 *Billboard* Hot 100

Lingering antiwar sentiment in 1974 may have helped popularize "Billy, Don't Be a Hero." Despite the warnings in the lyrics, Billy was killed in action. Paper Lace had the original release and it became a number 1 hit in the United Kingdom. However, it was barely noticed in the United States.

The popular version in the States was recorded by a Cincinnati group known as Bo Donaldson and the Heywoods.

Even though Paper Lace missed out having the U.S. hit that time around, they did indeed score their own number 1 hit with "The Night Chicago Died" (Mercury #73492) only months later.

"BLACK DENIM TROUSERS AND MOTORCYCLE BOOTS"
Composers: Jerry Leiber and Mike Stoller
Original Artist: the Cheers
Label: Capitol Records; *Recording:* Capitol #3219 (45 and 78)
Release Year: 1955; *Chart:* #6 *Billboard* Hot 100
Cover Artist: Vaughn Monroe
Label: RCA Victor Records; *Recording:* RCA Victor #6260 (45 and 78)
Release Year: 1955; *Chart:* #38 *Billboard* Hot 100

For the Cheers, this was the biggest of a string of Jerry Leiber and Mike Stoller compositions they recorded for Capitol Records. The song cashed in on the growing popularity of leather jackets and motorcycles among teenagers. It should be noted that within the Cheers was future actor/game show host Bert Convy.

Even though this recording was more pop than rock and roll (especially with Les Baxter and his orchestra providing the accompaniment), it was still cooler than the cover version. Baritone Vaughn Monroe was well into his forties by the time he recorded this song, and his considerable vocal talents were just ill suited for this kind of material. Monroe's version barely cracked the Top 40.

Another cover by the Diamonds (Coral #61502) did not chart.

"BLOODSHOT EYES"
Composers: Hank Penny and Ruth Hall
Original Artist: Hank Penny
Label: King Records; *Recording:* King #828 (78)
Release Year: 1949; *Chart:* #4 *Billboard* Country
Cover Artist: Wynonie Harris
Label: King Records; *Recording:* King #4461 (45 and 78)
Release Year: 1951; *Chart:* #6 *Billboard* R&B

"Bloodshot Eyes" is a song about a lying, cheating woman who returns to an old love looking for sympathy after her new love didn't work out. This clever and humorous song was penned by Hank Penny, a western swing artist and banjo player who recorded the first version.

Just two years after the original, the song was covered for the burgeoning R&B market by "Mr. Blues," Wynonie Harris. Like the original version, it too was on the King Records label. This very popular and seminal jump tune became the fourteenth of fifteen Top 10 R&B hits for Harris.

"BLOWIN' IN THE WIND"
Composer: Bob Dylan
Original Artist: Bob Dylan
Label: Columbia Records; *Recording:* Columbia #1986 (LP)
Release Year: 1963; *Chart:* did not chart
Cover Artist: Peter, Paul and Mary
Label: Warner Brothers Records; *Recording:* Warner Brothers #5368 (45)
Release Year: 1963; *Chart:* #2 *Billboard* Hot 100

The Freewheelin' Bob Dylan album was released in May of 1963 but didn't make the charts until much later that year. Still, the version of "Blowin' in the Wind" on the album was the first release (and was recorded in 1962).

About a month later, Peter, Paul and Mary released their rendition of the song on a Warner Brothers 45 and reached number 2 on the Pop charts—kept out of number 1 by "Fingertips, Part 2" (Tamla #54080) by Stevie Wonder. Interestingly enough, Wonder had a Top 10 remake of "Blowin' in the Wind" (Tamla #54136) during the summer of 1966.

By the way, Bob Dylan's unsuccessful 1963 45 rpm release of "Blowin' in the Wind" (Columbia #42856) has been known to fetch a few hundred bucks in mint condition.

"BLUE BAYOU"
Composers: Roy Orbison and Joe Melson
Original Artist: Roy Orbison
Label: Monument Records; *Recording:* Monument #824 (45)
Release Year: 1963; *Chart:* #29 *Billboard* Hot 100
Cover Artist: Linda Ronstadt
Label: Asylum Records; *Recording:* Asylum #45431 (45)
Release Year: 1977; *Chart:* #3 *Billboard* Hot 100

Roy Orbison recorded "Blue Bayou" in 1961, but it wasn't released as a single until 1963—as the B-side of the Top 5 smash "Mean Woman Blues." The B-side made Top 30 in the United States, but fared much better in the United Kingdom and several other countries. It was included on Orbison's 1963 *In Dreams* album (Monument #18003).

A 1977 remake by Linda Ronstadt, who was famous for her cover versions, was a platinum smash. It hit number 3 on the Pop charts and remained on the charts for almost half a year. Don Henley provided background vocals, and "Blue Bayou" was included on the *Simple Dreams* album (Asylum #104). The album was number 1 for five weeks.

Sadly, Ronstadt was diagnosed with Parkinson's disease in 2013, and she will likely never perform again.

"BLUE MOON"
Composers: Richard Rodgers and Lorenz Hart
Original Artist: Connie Boswell with the Victor Young Orchestra
Label: Brunswick Records; *Recording:* Brunswick #7363 (78)

A doo-wop rendition of "Blue Moon" by the Emanons, which preceded the Marcels' number 1 smash.

Release Year: 1935; *Chart:* did not chart
Cover Artist: the Marcels
Label: Colpix Records; *Recording:* Colpix #186 (45)
Release Year: 1961; *Chart:* #1 *Billboard* Hot 100 and #1 R&B

The rare occurrence of two full moons within the same month renders the second one a blue moon, thus the phrase "once in a blue moon." "Blue Moon" was also a song that Rodgers and Hart wrote and rewrote numerous times until they got it "just right." It first appeared in the motion picture *Manhattan Melodrama* under its original title, "The Bad in Every Man," and a bevy of hit versions began to surface in 1935. Just two weeks into that year, Connie Boswell released what is thought to be the first recorded rendition of the ballad on the Brunswick label. Glen Gray and the Casa Loma Orchestra (Decca #312) had a number 1 hit with the song later that same year.

Mel Torme had a hit with a remake in 1949 (Capitol #15428), which reached the Top 20. One of the more unusual covers came from Elvis Presley in 1956 (RCA #6640). This very quiet, spare recording, buried in echo, featured a few unusual falsetto parts and just missed the Top 50. It was one of three Presley 45s with "Blue Moon" in the title (the others being "Blue Moon of Kentucky" and "When My Blue Moon Turns to Gold Again").

"Blue Moon" also enjoyed quite a resurgence because of the doo-wop world. The first time it was performed in an up-tempo fashion was when it was recorded by the Emanons (the No Names spelled backward) on the JOZ (Josie) Records label (#801) in 1956. Five years later, a group from Pittsburgh called the Marcels truly made the song their own, and reached number 1 on both the Pop and R&B charts. Two other versions in 1961 cracked the Top 60 (the Ventures on Dolton #47 and Herb Lance and the Classics on Promo #1010).

Three versions of "Blue Moon" (Bobby Vinton, Sam Cooke, and, of course, the Marcels) are included in the soundtrack for the 1981 Universal motion picture *An American Werewolf in London.* The Vinton and Cooke renditions never charted.

"BLUE MOON OF KENTUCKY"
Composer: Bill Monroe
Original Artist: Bill Monroe and the Blue Grass Boys
Label: Columbia Records; *Recording:* Columbia #37888 (78)
Release Year: 1947; *Chart:* did not chart
Cover Artist: Elvis Presley
Label: Sun Records; *Recording:* Sun #209 (45 and 78)
Release Year: 1954; *Chart:* did not chart

Written and originally performed in a waltz tempo, "Blue Moon of Kentucky" made quite a lasting impression. It has become the state song of Kentucky, and in 2002, the original Bill Monroe version was included in the Library of Congress's National Recording Registry.

Most importantly, the tune made an impression upon Elvis Presley. Changed from a waltz to 4/4 time, "Blue Moon of Kentucky" was selected as the B-side of what would be Presley's historic first 45 (and 78) on the legendary Sun Records label. After Presley signed with RCA Victor, it was rereleased as RCA number 6380.

Steve Martin and John Candy sang the song in the hit 1987 Thanksgiving comedy classic *Planes, Trains and Automobiles*.

"BLUE VELVET"
Composers: Bernie Wayne and Lee Morris
Original Artist: Tony Bennett
Label: Columbia Records; *Recording:* Columbia #39555 (45 and 78)
Release Year: 1951; *Chart:* #16 *Billboard* Hot 100
Cover Artist: the Clovers
Label: Atlantic Records; *Recording:* Atlantic #1052 (45 and 78)
Release Year: 1955; *Chart:* #14 *Billboard* R&B

Tony Bennett got the ball rolling for the beautiful and oft-recorded ballad "Blue Velvet" in 1951 for the Columbia label.

In 1955, Buddy Bailey and the Clovers recorded a smooth and romantic version on Atlantic Records. It became a Top 20 hit on the R&B charts, and it demonstrated how perfect a fit the tune was for doo-wop vocal groups. It was then remade by the Velours, the Moonglows, the Statues, Little Duck and the Drakes, and the Paragons, to name a few.

However, no version was bigger or more famous than the one by the gentleman who was later dubbed "the Polish Prince," Bobby Vinton. His Epic 45 of "Blue Velvet" (#9614) was indeed epic. It became Vinton's second of four number 1 hits, and it remained at number 1 for three weeks in 1963.

The Bobby Vinton rendition was the title cut for David Lynch's very dark 1986 motion picture starring Dennis Hopper and Kyle MacLachlan.

"BLUEBIRDS OVER THE MOUNTAIN"
Composer: Ersel Hickey
Original Artist: Ersel Hickey
Label: Epic Records; *Recording:* Epic #9263 (45 and 78)
Release Year: 1958; *Chart:* #75 *Billboard* Hot 100
Cover Artist: the Beach Boys
Label: Capitol Records; *Recording:* Capitol #2360 (45)
Release Year: 1968; *Chart:* #61 *Billboard* Hot 100

Rockabilly singer Ersel Hickey was expected to become a big rock and roll star. It never really happened, even though Hickey released many good records. He wrote his best-known song, the very short "Bluebirds over the Mountain," which barely dented the Hot 100. However, it was covered by some famous people.

Ritchie Valens recorded a cover of the song for his *Ritchie Valens* album (Del-Fi #1201), and the Beach Boys released their take on the song on their *20/20* album (Capitol #133) and it was also a marginally successful single.

"Boogie Woogie Bugle Boy"

Composers: Don Raye and Hughie Prince
Original Artist: the Andrews Sisters
Label: Decca Records; *Recording:* Decca #3598 (78)
Release Year: 1941; *Chart:* #15 *Billboard* Music Hit Parade
Cover Artist: Bette Midler
Label: Atlantic Records; *Recording:* Atlantic #2964 (45)
Release Year: 1973; *Chart:* #8 *Billboard* Hot 100

This World War II song told the story of a boogie woogie bugler who was drafted and then had to settle for blowing "Reveille" for Company B. It was actually written and recorded before U.S. involvement in the war. It was introduced in the Abbott and Costello film *Buck Privates.* The Andrews Sisters reached number 15 with their version in 1941.

In 1973, Bette Midler did Patty, Maxine, and LaVerne Andrews proud with her remake. It introduced the song to a whole new generation and became Midler's very first Top 10 hit. It was included on *The Divine Miss M* album (Atlantic #7238). The LP made the Top 10 and went platinum.

"Bottle of Wine"

Composer: Tom Paxton
Original Artist: Judy Collins
Label: Elektra Records; *Recording:* Elektra #7280 (LP)
Release Year: 1964; *Chart:* did not chart
Cover Artist: the Fireballs
Label: Atco Records; *Recording:* Atco #6491 (45)
Release Year: 1967; *Chart:* #9 *Billboard* Hot 100

The first version of this Tom Paxton composition appeared on a live Judy Collins album titled *The Judy Collins Concert* released late in 1964. It was recorded at Town Hall in New York City on West Forty-third Street. It's an upbeat, lighthearted song about how difficult it can be to stay "on the wagon."

Collins did not have a hit with the song, but her version was an inspiration for a 1967 remake by Jimmy Gilmer and the Fireballs. This time around the song became a memorable Top 10 hit. It should be noted that Gilmer and his Fireballs had a major hit four years earlier with "Sugar Shack"—a song about a romance in a coffee house. "Sugar Shack" was the biggest hit of 1963, and the espresso coffee mentioned in the lyrics of the song would have made for a great remedy for the poor sot in the "Bottle of Wine" song.

"BREAK IT TO ME GENTLY"

Composers: Joe Seneca and Diane Lampert
Original Artist: Brenda Lee
Label: Decca Records; *Recording:* Decca #31348 (45)
Release Year: 1962; *Chart:* #4 *Billboard* Hot 100
Cover Artist: Juice Newton
Label: Capitol Records; *Recording:* Capitol #5148 (45)
Release Year: 1982; *Chart:* #11 *Billboard* Hot 100

Co-written by actor/singer/songwriter Joe Seneca, this is a tune in which the singer knows that bad news is imminent, but asks to be told that news in a gentle fashion. It was just one in a long string of emotional hit ballad singles by "Little Miss Dynamite," Brenda Lee. The flip side, "So Deep," also made the charts.

Twenty years later, Judy Kay Newton, better known as Juice Newton, rerecorded "Break It to Me Gently" and introduced it to an entirely new generation. It was included on her *Quiet Lies* album (Capitol #12210), which also spawned "Love's Been a Little Bit Hard on Me" (Capitol #5120).

The Brenda Lee original was used in an episode of AMC's hit series *Mad Men*.

"BREAKING UP IS HARD TO DO"

Composers: Neil Sedaka and Howard Greenfield
Original Artist: Neil Sedaka
Label: RCA Victor Records; *Recording:* RCA Victor #8046 (45)
Release Year: 1962; *Chart:* #1 *Billboard* Hot 100
Cover Artist: Neil Sedaka
Label: Rocket Records; *Recording:* Rocket #40500 (45)
Release Year: 1975; *Chart:* #8 *Billboard* Hot 100

By 1962, Neil Sedaka's presence in the Top 10 was almost a given. However, up to this point none of his hits had attained the number 1 spot on the Pop charts. It took a song titled "Breaking Up Is Hard to Do" to exorcise that demon. Initially, those in Sedaka's inner circle weren't too keen on the song, and instead suggested that "King of Clowns" was the better song to release. "King of Clowns" only reached number 45 on the charts. Inspired by the beat of "It Will Stand" by the Showmen (Minit #632), "Breaking Up Is Hard to Do" resonated with teenagers during the summer of 1962 and propelled the song to number 1.

The slow Lenny Welch version of "Breaking Up Is Hard to Do" inspired Neil Sedaka's remake.

A singer named Tina Powers quickly released an answer song titled "Making Up Is Fun to Do" (Parkway #847), but it wasn't a hit.

Numerous cover versions emerged over the years from groups such as the Partridge Family and the Happenings. Bob Miranda of the Happenings remembered,

> Neil Sedaka used to come to the Tokens' office pretty often to play us his new compositions with hopes that we'd record his songs. "Breaking Up Is Hard to Do" was brought up and, even though it's a great record and a great song, it might have been too soon after the original version. It wasn't ready to be redone yet—it wasn't our biggest hit. And yet, on a recent trip to the Philippines, that was the song they most wanted to hear. Apparently our albums got a lot of airplay in

Manilla. They were also asking for songs such as "Girl on a Swing" and more—songs we hadn't been asked about for years. That was great. Our music is international.

Then Lenny Welch recorded "Breaking Up Is Hard to Do" as a ballad in 1970. Welch recalled,

I was visiting California but living in New York at that time. I got a phone call from songwriters Helen Miller and Rosemarie McCoy who told me, "We have your next hit when you come back home." It was "Breaking Up Is Hard to Do" done as a ballad in a manner similar to my biggest hit, "Since I Fell for You." It was released on the Commonwealth United [#3004] label and I had Neil's blessing. In fact, Neil called me regularly to see what number the song had reached on the charts that week. It was a Top 40 hit. Years later, when Neil enjoyed his huge comeback, he patterned the ballad version of "Breaking Up Is Hard to Do" after mine.

Sedaka rereleased the song very late in 1975, and by 1976, he, like the Dells ("Oh, What a Night") and Tommy Edwards ("It's All in the Game"), became one of very few recording artists to have a Top 10 hit with two totally different versions of the same song.

"BRIDGE OVER TROUBLED WATER"
Composer: Paul Simon
Original Artist: Simon and Garfunkel
Label: Columbia Records; *Recording:* Columbia #45079 (45)
Release Year: 1970; *Chart:* #1 *Billboard* Hot 100
Cover Artist: Aretha Franklin
Label: Atlantic Records; *Recording:* Atlantic #2796 (45)
Release Year: 1971; *Chart:* #6 *Billboard* Hot 100 and #1 R&B

Paul Simon wrote this song expressly for Art Garfunkel's lead vocals. Yes, it said Simon and Garfunkel on the label, but Simon accepted second banana status on this one. At the time, it was one of the longest records on the radio at just under five minutes in length. *Bridge over Troubled Water* was also used as the title of their next album (Columbia #9914). The single was number 1 for five weeks, the album for ten weeks. It was a double Grammy winner for Record of the Year and Song of the Year in 1971.

We hadn't yet had enough of the tune in 1971. A remake by Aretha Franklin also became a major hit. It's interesting to note that Franklin's rendition was a lot shorter—just over three minutes in length. She also won a "Bridge over Troubled Water" Grammy for Best Female Rhythm and Blues Performance in 1972.

Also noteworthy—the 1970 Elvis Presley version from his *Elvis—That's the Way It Is* Album (RCA Victor #4445). He kept the song as part of his Las Vegas act for several years.

"BUSTED"

Composer: Harlan Howard
Original Artist: Johnny Cash
Label: Columbia Records; *Recording:* Columbia #8730 (LP)
Release Year: 1963; *Chart:* #13 *Billboard* Country
Cover Artist: Ray Charles
Label: ABC-Paramount Records; *Recording:* ABC-Paramount #10481 (45)
Release Year: 1963; *Chart:* #4 *Billboard* Hot 100 and #3 R&B

A clever song about a reversal of fortune, "Busted" was written by Harlan Howard, who had also written "Heartaches by the Number" for Guy Mitchell and "I Fall to Pieces" for Patsy Cline. Johnny Cash included "Busted" on his *Blood, Sweat and Tears* album, and it eventually became a Top 20 hit on the Country charts when released as a single. At just about the same time, Burl Ives released a version of the song on his *Burl* album (Decca #4361).

The biggest version, however, came later in 1963 by Ray Charles on ABC-Paramount. It was also included on his *Ingredients in a Recipe for Soul* album (ABC-Paramount #465). Charles's rendition of "Busted" won a Grammy for Best Rhythm and Blues Recording for 1963.

Paying homage to "the Genius of Soul," a commemorative Ray Charles postage stamp was issued on September 23, 2013.

"BUTTERFLY"

Composers: Bernie Lowe and Kal Mann
Original Artist: Charlie Gracie
Label: Cameo Records; *Recording:* Cameo #105 (45 and 78)
Release Year: 1957; *Chart:* #1 *Billboard* Hot 100
Cover Artist: Andy Williams
Label: Cadence Records; *Recording:* Cadence #1308 (45 and 78)
Release Year: 1957; *Chart:* #1 *Billboard* Hot 100

It was good to be a British musician in 1964, and it was almost as good to be a recording artist in Philadelphia in the late 1950s and early 1960s because of the proximity of *American Bandstand*. The latter was the case for Charlie Gracie whose first single, "Butterfly," became a number 1 smash hit and sold over a million copies.

Jumping quickly on the bandwagon, Andy Williams recorded his own version of the song for Archie Bleyer's Cadence Records label, and it, too, made it to number 1.

Yet another rendition by Bob Carroll (Bally #1028) reached number 61 in that same year. Just like the lyrics say, the record buying public was "crazy about you, you Butterfly."

"BY THE TIME I GET TO PHOENIX"
Composer: Jimmy Webb
Original Artist: Johnny Rivers
Label: Imperial Records; *Recording:* Imperial #12334 (LP)
Release Year: 1966; *Chart:* did not chart
Cover Artist: Glen Campbell
Label: Capitol Records; *Recording:* Capitol #2015 (45)
Release Year: 1967; *Chart:* #26 *Billboard* Hot 100

This song about a breakup was inspired by a real breakup. The guy in the song has written a letter of goodbye to his girlfriend or wife, and envisions what she will be doing by the time he reaches different cities as he passes through them. Johnny Rivers recorded it first on his *Changes* album in 1966.

However, it would take Glen Campbell to make the song a hit. Campbell and compositions by Jimmy Webb went especially well together. Not only did he make Webb's "By the Time I Get to Phoenix" a hit, but also "Galveston," "Honey Come Back," and "Wichita Lineman." Campbell won two Grammys for the song—Best Contemporary Male Solo Vocal Performance and Best Vocal Performance, Male.

A rendition by Isaac Hayes also made the Top 40 in 1969 (Enterprise #9003).

C

"CALL ME"
Composer: Tony Hatch
Original Artist: Petula Clark
Label: Pye Records; *Recording:* Pye # 24237 (EP)
Release Year: 1965; *Chart:* did not chart
Cover Artist: Chris Montez
Label: A & M Records; *Recording:* A & M #780 (45)
Release Year: 1966; *Chart:* #22 *Billboard* Hot 100

"Call Me" was written by Tony Hatch—writer of many of Petula Clark's big hits. Clark's version of the song was released as the title cut of a 1965 EP (extended play) 45 in the United Kingdom.

"Call Me" by Petula Clark was not a hit in the United States, but it was when covered by Chris Montez. Montez previously had one big hit titled "Let's Dance" (Monogram #505), later used in TV commercials for Designer Shoe Warehouse. Montez made a comeback after signing with Herb Alpert and Jerry

Moss's A & M label, and his rendition of "Call Me" made Top 30 on the Pop charts and number 2 on the Easy Listening chart.

Petula Clark's "Call Me" was finally released in the United States on her *Greatest Hits, Volume 1* album (Warner Brothers #1765) in 1968.

"CANADIAN SUNSET"

Composers: Eddie Heywood and Norman Gimbel
Original Artist: Hugo Winterhalter and Eddie Heywood
Label: RCA Victor Records; *Recording:* RCA Victor #6537 (45 and 78)
Release Year: 1956; *Chart:* #2 *Billboard* Hot 100 and #7 R&B
Cover Artist: Andy Williams
Label: Cadence Records; *Recording:* Cadence #1297 (45 and 78)
Release Year: 1956; *Chart:* #7 *Billboard* Hot 100

The first hit version of "Canadian Sunset" was an instrumental by Hugo Winterhalter with Eddie Heywood in 1956. Later that same year, with lyrics from Norman Gimbel, "Canadian Sunset" was a Top 10 hit again—this time by Andy Williams.

Numerous other versions followed, including one from Etta Jones (Prestige #191) and Sounds Orchestral (Parkway #958). There was even a hit doo-wop rendition by the Impacts (RCA Victor #7609) in 1959, produced by Hugo Peretti and Luigi Creatore.

"CAN'T HELP FALLING IN LOVE"

Composers: Hugo Peretti, Luigi Creatore, and George Weiss
Original Artist: Elvis Presley
Label: RCA Victor Records; *Recording:* RCA Victor #7968 (45)
Release Year: 1961; *Chart:* #2 *Billboard* Hot 100
Cover Artist: UB40
Label: Virgin Records; *Recording:* Virgin #12653 (CD)
Release Year: 1993; *Chart:* #1 *Billboard* Hot 100

Elvis Presley's most successful motion picture, *Blue Hawaii*, was released in 1961, and Presley portrayed Chad Gates. Among those in the cast was future *Murder, She Wrote* star Angela Lansbury.

The film spawned a huge hit ballad titled "Can't Help Falling in Love," often mistakenly called "Wise Men Say." The song made it to number 2 on the Pop charts and was kept out of number 1 by "The Peppermint Twist" from Joey Dee and the Starliters. The flip side of Presley's single, "Rock-a-Hula Baby," was also part of the movie soundtrack.

"Can't Help Falling in Love" was a Top 30 hit again in 1987 when covered by Canadian hit maker Corey Hart (EMI America #8368), but there was still more to come.

In 1993, the song was included in the soundtrack for the motion picture *Sliver*, which starred Sharon Stone and William Baldwin. This time around, the artist was UB40, and this time around the song made it to number 1. This updated version consisted of an a cappella open, and once the instrumentation kicked in, a reggae beat.

"Can't Smile without You"
Composers: David Martin, Christian Arnold, and Geoff Morrow
Original Artist: the Carpenters
Label: A & M Records; *Recording:* A & M #1978 (45)
Release Year: 1977; *Chart:* did not chart
Cover Artist: Barry Manilow
Label: Arista Records; *Recording:* Arista #0305 (45)
Release Year: 1978; *Chart:* #3 *Billboard* Hot 100

Karen and Richard Carpenter recorded the first version of "Can't Smile without You," and it was placed on the B-side of one of their less successful singles— "Calling Occupants of Interplanetary Craft."

The Carpenters' rendition of the tune was quite a bit slower than the version made famous by Barry Manilow in 1978. A whistler was added in the Manilow version in the opening. It became a million-seller.

Curiously, with all the hits in the Barry Manilow songbook, only four of them made Top 5—"Mandy," "I Write the Songs," "Looks Like We Made It," and "Can't Smile without You."

Years later, George Michael was initially accused of plagiarizing "Can't Smile without You" on his seasonal hit "Last Christmas," but was later cleared of all charges.

"Can't You Hear My Heartbeat"
Composers: John Carter and Ken Lewis
Original Artist: Goldie and the Gingerbreads
Label: British Decca Records; *Recording:* British Decca #12070 (45)
Release Year: 1964; *Chart:* did not chart
Cover Artist: Herman's Hermits
Label: MGM Records; *Recording:* MGM #13310 (45)
Release Year: 1965; *Chart:* #2 *Billboard* Hot 100

The Goldie in Goldie and the Gingerbreads was Goldie Zelkowitz. She and her girl group recorded the first version of "Can't You Hear My Heartbeat" in 1964. It caught on in the United Kingdom, and, almost overnight, it was covered by Peter Noone and Herman's Hermits.

In the United States, Herman's Hermits were already established as hit makers and their version caught on first—Goldie and the Gingerbreads simply could not compete. They did, however, continue to perform in the United Kingdom throughout most of the 1960s.

After a string of eighteen Top 40 hits in the United States, Peter Noone went on to host VH1's *My Generation* from 1989 to 1993.

"CARA MIA"
Composers: Tulio Trapani and Lee Lange
Original Artist: David Whitfield
Label: London Records; *Recording:* London #1486 (45 and 78)
Release Year: 1954; *Chart:* #10 *Billboard* Hot 100
Cover Artist: Jay and the Americans
Label: United Artists Records; *Recording:* United Artists #881 (45)
Release Year: 1965; *Chart:* #4 *Billboard* Hot 100

The original version of this song by David Whitfield had a very operatic flair to it. Mantovani with His Orchestra and Chorus accompanied the record, which made Top 10 in the United States and number 1 in the United Kingdom, and sold well over a million copies.

"Cara Mia" was not a song one would expect to be covered during the rock era, but Jay and the Americans surprised us with their update in 1965 and had a Top 5 smash. Consistent with the original was the operatic voice of Jay Black, but this new version took on a Latin beat and male background vocals. It was included on the group's *Blockbusters* album (United Artists #6417) and was an audience favorite in live performances for decades.

"CAST YOUR FATE TO THE WIND"
Composer: Vince Guaraldi
Original Artist: the Vince Guaraldi Trio
Label: Fantasy Records; *Recording:* Fantasy #563 (45)
Release Year: 1962; *Chart:* #22 *Billboard* Hot 100
Cover Artist: Sounds Orchestral
Label: Parkway Records; *Recording:* Parkway #942 (45)
Release Year: 1965; *Chart:* #10 *Billboard* Hot 100

Along with all of his great music included in those *Peanuts* TV specials, Vince Guaraldi composed and recorded the original version of "Cast Your Fate to the Wind." It became a Top 30 instrumental hit and won a Grammy for Best Original Jazz Composition in 1963. It was included on his album titled *Jazz Impressions of Black Orpheus* (Fantasy #3337).

A cover version by a British instrumental group known as Sounds Orchestral made number 10 on the Pop charts in 1965. This sound was an anomaly for the Cameo Parkway Records label—they were famous mostly for dance crazes and rock and roll. Their follow-up was a cover version of "Canadian Sunset" (see the entry for that song).

Sounds Orchestral's rendition of the song was included in the soundtrack for the 1987 Touchstone motion picture *Good Morning, Vietnam.*

"CAT'S IN THE CRADLE"
Composers: Harry and Sandy Chapin
Original Artist: Harry Chapin
Label: Elektra Records; *Recording:* Elektra #45203 (45)
Release Year: 1974; *Chart:* #1 *Billboard* Hot 100
Cover Artist: Ugly Kid Joe
Label: Stardog Records; *Recording:* Stardog #864888 (CD)
Release Year: 1993; *Chart:* #6 *Billboard* Hot 100

This sad song began as a poem by Harry Chapin's wife, Sandy. It's the story of a strained relationship between a father and son, as well as a story of karma. The patriarch of the family never seemed to have time for his son as he grew into an adult. As an adult, the son had grown up much the same and never found time for his dad. "Cat's in the Cradle" became a number 1 hit late in 1974 and was produced by Paul Leka, who earlier had been in the studio group known as Steam who recorded "Na Na Hey Hey (Kiss Him Goodbye)" in 1969 (Fontana #1667—see the entry for that song). Chapin's song title later inspired an episode of *CSI* that aired April 25, 2002.

A remake in 1993 by a California group named Ugly Kid Joe had a slightly more rock-infused feel to it. Once again the song was a hit, and although this time it didn't hit number 1, it did sell well over a million copies. It also incited new interest in Chapin, who had perished in an automobile accident in 1981. Chapin also sang the theme song for the short-lived 1970s sitcom called *Ball Four.*

"CHANGING PARTNERS"
Composers: Larry Coleman and Joe Darion
Original Artist: Patti Page
Label: Mercury Records; *Recording:* Mercury #70260 (45 and 78)
Release Year: 1953; *Chart:* #3 *Billboard* Hot 100
Cover Artist: Dinah Shore
Label: RCA Victor Records; *Recording:* RCA Victor #5515 (45 and 78)
Release Year: 1953; *Chart:* #12 *Billboard* Hot 100

Set to a waltz tempo, "Changing Partners" is a song about love at first sight. It tells the tale of a woman at a dance who meets the man of her dreams and dances with him for a brief while until someone shouts "change partners," and he waltzes into someone else's arms. She then ponders the odds of reconnecting with the guy.

The original version of the song by Patti Page was the biggest, but there was a lot of competition. Dinah Shore's rendition just missed the Top 10, and versions by Kay Starr and Bing Crosby also charted in the Top 20. There was even an R&B version by Dean Barlow and the Crickets on the Jay Dee Record label (#785) out of New York.

Patti Page died on January 1, 2013, at the age of eighty-five.

"CHERISH"
Composer: Terry Kirkman
Original Artist: the Association
Label: Valiant Records; *Recording:* Valiant #747 (45)
Release Year: 1966; *Chart:* #1 *Billboard* Hot 100
Cover Artist: David Cassidy
Label: Bell Records; *Recording:* Bell #150 (45)
Release Year: 1971; *Chart:* #9 *Billboard* Hot 100

In other songs we were told that "The Bird Is the Word" and "Grease Is the Word," but in this one "Cherish" was the word. "Cherish" was written by Terry Kirkman, and he and his pop group known as the Association made it a number 1 hit. It was included on the *Then along Comes the Association* album (Valiant #5002) in 1966.

A cover version from 1971 brought the pop ballad back into the Top 10. The artist on the label was listed solely as David Cassidy and not the Partridge Family. It was a million-seller.

This "Cherish" has no relation to the Kool and the Gang or Madonna songs of the same name.

"CHERRY PINK (AND APPLE BLOSSOM WHITE)"
Composers: Louiguy and Mack David
Original Artist: Perez "Prez" Prado and His Orchestra
Label: RCA Victor Records; *Recording:* RCA Victor #5965 (45 and 78)
Release Year: 1955; *Chart:* #1 *Billboard* Hot 100
Cover Artist: Alan Dale
Label: Coral Records; *Recording:* Coral #61373 (45 and 78)
Release Year: 1955; *Chart:* #14 *Billboard* Hot 100

"Cherry Pink (and Apple Blossom White)" originated as a French song in 1950, but in 1955 the first version in the United States came from Perez Prado, "the King of the Mambo," featuring a very famous elongated, emphatic trumpet solo from Billy Regis. This instrumental rendition had previously been included in the soundtrack for the RKO Pictures Jane Russell film *Underwater!* in 1954. The single was a huge success and hit number 1 on the Pop charts, where it remained for ten weeks.

A vocal version, utilizing the lyrics of Mack David, was recorded by Brooklyn native Alan Dale on the Coral Records label. Although not as big as Prado's monster-hit version, Dale just missed Top 10 with this release. He did reach Top 10 with his next single—"Sweet and Gentle" (Coral #61435).

Alan Dale's cover of the "Prez" Prado classic. Dale's version had lyrics.

"CHIRPY CHIRPY CHEEP CHEEP"
Composer: Lally Stott
Original Artist: Lally Stott
Label: Philips Records; *Recording:* Philips #40695 (45)
Release Year: 1971; *Chart:* #92 *Billboard* Hot 100
Cover Artist: Mac and Katie Kissoon
Label: ABC Records; *Recording:* ABC #11306 (45)
Release Year: 1971; *Chart:* #20 *Billboard* Hot 100

The happy, sing-along melody of "Chirpy Chirpy Cheep Cheep" defies the sad lyrics—"Where's your papa gone?" and "Woke up this morning and my mama was gone." It was written and originally performed by male vocalist Lally Stott. His version was a big hit in France, but barely dented the Pop charts in the United States.

Several months later, a brother-and-sister act known as Mac and Katie Kissoon recorded a cover version. It was very similar to the Lally Stott original, but it caught on in a big way and made Top 20 in the United States. It's interesting to note that the writer's credits on the Kissoon 45 mistakenly credit the composer as Scott instead of Stott.

"THE CHOKIN' KIND"
Composer: Harlan Howard
Original Artist: Waylon Jennings and the Waylords
Label: RCA Victor Records; *Recording:* RCA Victor #9259 (45)
Release Year: 1967; *Chart:* #8 *Billboard* Country
Cover Artist: Joe Simon
Label: Sound Stage 7; *Recording:* Sound Stage 7 #2628 (45)
Release Year: 1969; *Chart:* #13 *Billboard* Hot 100 and #1 R&B

Joe Simon won a Grammy for his remake of Waylon Jennings's "The Chokin' Kind."

This versatile song fit well on the Country chart and also on the R&B and Pop charts. On the Country chart, it was a hit for Waylon Jennings and the Waylords on the RCA Victor label in 1967. Written by the prolific Harlan Howard, it's a song about a clingy type of love—"The Chokin' Kind."

Soul singer Joe Simon began making records in the late 1950s with a vocal group known as the Golden Tones on the Hush Records label. On the R&B chart, Simon had his say with a number 1 version of "The Chokin' Kind." It also just missed the Top 10 on the Pop charts and sold a million copies. It garnered him a Grammy for "Best R&B Male Vocal."

The song was remade by Joss Stone in 2003 on her *Soul Sessions* album (S-Curve #7243).

"CINDY, OH CINDY"

Composers: Robert Barron and Burt Long
Original Artist: Vince Martin and the Tarriers
Label: Glory Records; *Recording:* Glory #247 (45 and 78)
Release Year: 1956; *Chart:* #9 *Billboard* Hot 100
Cover Artist: Eddie Fisher
Label: RCA Victor Records; *Recording:* RCA Victor #6677 (45 and 78)
Release Year: 1956; *Chart:* #10 *Billboard* Hot 100

Set to a calypso beat, this was the song of a sailor longing for a letter from Cindy, his love. It was a hit first by Vince Martin and the Tarriers. In the group was a future Academy Award winner named Alan Arkin. It made Top 10 on the Glory Records label—a subsidiary of Derby Records.

Later that same year, the star of TV's *Coke Time*, Eddie Fisher, covered this maritime number with more of a Latin beat than the original. It reached number 10 on the Pop charts and was Fisher's final Top 10 hit.

In 1959, a doo-wop version by Billy Storm and the Valiants on the Shar-Dee record label (#703) changed the song's title to "Dear Cindy."

"THE CINNAMON CINDER"

Composer: Russ Regan
Original Artist: the Pastel Six
Label: Zen Records; *Recording:* Zen #102 (45)
Release Year: 1962; *Chart:* #25 *Billboard* Hot 100
Cover Artist: the Cinders
Label: Warner Brothers Records; *Recording:* Warner Brothers #5326 (45)
Release Year: 1962; *Chart:* did not chart

Named for a popular alcohol-free teenagers' nightclub in Southern California known as the Cinnamon Cinder, this was an attempt to mirror the success the Peppermint Lounge in New York City had enjoyed with Joey Dee and the Star-

The house band at the Cinnamon Cinder sings about their house.

liters' number 1 hit titled "Peppermint Twist." The Cinnamon Cinder's address was 11345 Ventura Boulevard in Studio City, California.

The first version was, appropriately, by the Pastel Six (the house band), who had the definitive hit version. It cracked the Top 30 on the Pop charts. A cover version by the Cinders on the Warner Brothers label failed to chart, even with the help of a major record company behind them. There was even a local West Coast TV program called *The Cinnamon Cinder Show* produced by Los Angeles disc jockey and future game show host Bob Eubanks. Other regulars on the show were local bands the Illusions, Jan and Dean, Dick and Dee Dee, and the Royal Monarchs. It aired every Saturday evening at 5 p.m. on KTTV, Metromedia Channel 11.

The hit song is famous for the line "C. C. Cinnamon Cinder—it's a very nice dance."

"CLOSE TO YOU"
Composers: Burt Bacharach and Hal David
Original Artist: Richard Chamberlain
Label: MGM Records; *Recording:* MGM #13170 (45)
Release Year: 1963; *Chart:* did not chart
Cover Artist: the Carpenters
Label: A & M Records; *Recording:* A & M #1183 (45)
Release Year: 1970; *Chart:* #1 *Billboard* Hot 100

Not only was Richard Chamberlain the star of TV's long-running *Dr. Kildare* and the star of so many TV miniseries, he was also a singer with numerous chart records. This original version of the Burt Bacharach and Hal David song "Close to You" was buried on the B-side of a marginal hit called "Blue Guitar" way back in 1963.

Seven years later, a yet unknown brother-and-sister duo called the Carpenters rerecorded the song, sometimes known as "(They Long to Be) Close to You" for Herb Alpert and Jerry Moss's A & M record label, and it became their first of four number 1 hits on the Pop charts. It was also the title cut of the duo's first platinum LP (A & M #4271).

"COME BACK, SILLY GIRL"
Composer: Barry Mann
Original Artist: Steve Lawrence
Label: ABC-Paramount Records; *Recording:* ABC-Paramount 10148 (45)
Release Year: 1960; *Chart:* did not chart
Cover Artist: the Lettermen
Label: Capitol Records; *Recording:* Capitol #4699 (45)
Release Year: 1962; *Chart:* #17 *Billboard* Hot 100

Written by Brill Building denizen Barry Mann, "Come Back, Silly Girl" was ignored the first time around. Steve Lawrence was the artist, and his rendition utilized a medium Latin tempo. It did not chart.

Two years later, this time as the follow-up to "When I Fall in Love" by the Lettermen on Capitol Records, it became a Top 20 hit. It was recorded considerably slower and without the Latin tempo.

In both versions the title is sung as "Come Back-a Silly Girl."

"COME BACK WHEN YOU GROW UP"
Composer: Martha Sharp
Original Artist: Shadden and the King Lears
Label: Arbet Records; *Recording:* Arbet #1016 (45)
Release Year: 1967; *Chart:* did not chart
Cover Artist: Bobby Vee
Label: Liberty Records; *Recording:* Liberty #55964 (45)
Release Year: 1967; *Chart:* #3 *Billboard* Hot 100

"Come Back When You Grow Up" is sometimes erroneously called "Paper Doll World." It was composed by Martha Sharp, who also penned "Single Girl" and "Born a Woman" for Sandy Posey. It was first recorded early in 1967, unsuccessfully, by a group known as Shadden and the King Lears on the tiny Arbet Records label (which was distributed by Dover Records).

Later that same year, this song with "Come Back" in the title became a huge comeback hit for Bobby Vee. This was his first time in the Top 10 since "The Night Has a Thousand Eyes" early in 1963 (Liberty #55521). "Come Back When You Grow Up" sold over a million copies. It also served as the title for Vee's 1967 Top 70 album (Liberty #7534).

"COME ON DOWN TO MY BOAT"
Composers: Wes Farrell and Gerald Goldstein
Original Artist: the Rare Breed
Label: Attack Records; *Recording:* Attack #1403 (45)
Release Year: 1966; *Chart:* did not chart
Cover Artist: Every Mother's Son
Label: MGM Records; *Recording:* MGM #13733 (45)
Release Year: 1967; *Chart:* #6 *Billboard* Hot 100

It came out first under the title "Come and Take a Ride in My Boat" as by the Rare Breed in 1966. It had a slightly harder edge—a more "garage rock" feel to it than the hit version that came one year later.

The hit version was by a New York group known as Every Mother's Son on the MGM label. It made Top 10 this time around, and the title was changed slightly to "Come on Down to My Boat." Truly a one-hit wonder, they never again cracked the Top 40. The group guest starred in a two-part episode of *The Man from U.N.C.L.E.*, on which they performed the song. The two episodes, originally titled "The Five Daughters Affair," were then edited together as a full-length feature and retitled *The Karate Killers*.

"COME SOFTLY TO ME"
Composers: Gretchen Christopher, Gary Troxel, and Barbara Ellis
Original Artist: the Fleetwoods
Label: Dolphin Records; *Recording:* Dolphin #1 (45)
Release Year: 1959; *Chart:* #1 *Billboard* Hot 100 and #5 R&B
Cover Artist: Ronnie Height
Label: Dore Records; *Recording:* Dore #516 (45)
Release Year: 1959; *Chart:* #48 *Billboard* Hot 100

Bob Reisdorf originally called his new Seattle, Washington, record label Dolphin Records in 1959. However, a little-known New York record company was already using the name (most notable for a doo-wop collectible titled "My Birthday Wish" by Faithe Robinson), and Reisdorf's label became Dolton Records.

Right off the bat, Dolphin/Dolton had a hit with a song by an area group known as the Fleetwoods. Gretchen Christopher of the group remembered,

> The original song I wrote at age 18 was called "Come Softly." Then I arranged my female melody and lyrics in counterpoint to the street corner humming of fellow Olympia High School classmate Gary Troxel, and Barbara Ellis harmonized to my lead. Performed a cappella, it was an immediate hit at our high school functions, and students asked us to record it so they could buy it. I then recorded us a cappella at home on my dad's tape recorder. In the Seattle studio, Dolphin President and producer Bob Reisdorf recognized that Gary's background part was so catchy, he should add lyrics to it; making his an alternating male/female lead with mine. It went to number 1 on the Pop charts and high on the R&B charts, despite there being a cover version by Ronnie Height on Dore Records.

It's interesting to note that Height's version of the song altered the onomatopoeia opening line to "Dum dum dumbidee doobie doobie doo," and he also performed the tune at a slightly faster tempo than the original. This version barely penetrated the Top 50 but did get considerable airplay in the Southern California area.

Christopher added, "Later that same year when 'Mr. Blue' went to number 1, we Fleetwoods became the first group in the rock and roll era to have multiple number 1 records top the *Billboard* Hot 100 in a single year."

About "Come Softly to Me" Christopher added, "A fan and collector recently sent me two CDs containing fifty-seven different commercially released versions of our song, including the Marty Kristian and the New Seekers' version from 1973 on MGM, and my own versions heard on the Gold Cup CD *Gretchen's Sweet Sixteen (Suite 16)*—a *Billboard* critic's pick for one of the Ten Best Albums of 2007."

"CONCRETE AND CLAY"

Composers: Tommy Moeller and Brian Parker
Original Artist: Unit 4 + 2
Label: London Records; *Recording:* London #9751 (45)
Release Year: 1965; *Chart:* #28 *Billboard* Hot 100
Cover Artist: Eddie Rambeau
Label: DynoVoice Records; *Recording:* DynoVoice #204 (45)
Release Year: 1965; *Chart:* #35 *Billboard* Hot 100

"Concrete and Clay" is a song about a very strong, durable love that, despite many obstacles, emerges unscathed. It was co-written by Tommy Moeller and Brian Parker—members of a British group who called themselves Unit 4 + 2.

This cover of the Unit 4 + 2 hit paved the way into the Top 40 for Eddie Rambeau.

Upon hearing the group's song in the United Kingdom, singer/songwriter/producer Bob Crewe hastily had the song covered by Eddie Rambeau on the DynoVoice Records label, attempting to beat the release of the original in the United States. Quick, but not quick enough—both versions were released in the States on the same day, May 1, 1965.

Unit 4 + 2's rendition was slightly bigger and reached number 28 on the Pop charts, while Rambeau's peaked at number 35.

"CRY"
Composer: Churchill Kohlman
Original Artist: Johnnie Ray

Label: Okeh Records; *Recording:* Okeh #6840 (45 and 78)
Release Year: 1951; *Chart:* #1 *Billboard* Hot 100 and R&B
Cover Artist: Ronnie Dove
Label: Diamond Records; *Recording:* Diamond #214 (45)
Release Year: 1966; *Chart:* #18 *Billboard* Hot 100

John Alvin Ray was already in his middle thirties when he recorded one of the biggest two-sided smashes in music history—"Cry" backed with "The Little White Cloud That Cried." Both sides made Top 10 on not only the Pop charts but also R&B. Ray penned the hit B-side, "The Little White Cloud That Cried," and his double-sided "crying" smash led to a string of successful and memorable hits including "You Don't Owe Me a Thing" (written by Marty Robbins) and "Just Walking in the Rain." Nicknamed "the cry guy," Ray influenced many up-and-coming rock and roll performers with his emotional stage performances.

Fifteen years later, prolific cover crooner Ronnie Dove released a remake of "Cry." Even though its sound was a bit out of place in the psychedelic sixties, it reached the Top 20 and became one of Dove's biggest hits.

Ray has a star on the Hollywood Walk of Fame at 6201 Hollywood Boulevard.

"CRY LIKE A BABY"

Composers: Dan Penn and Spooner Oldham
Original Artist: the Box Tops
Label: Mala Records; *Recording:* Mala #593 (45)
Release Year: 1968; *Chart:* #2 *Billboard* Hot 100
Cover Artist: Kim Carnes
Label: EMI America Records; *Recording:* EMI America #8058 (45)
Release Year: 1980; *Chart:* #44 *Billboard* Hot 100

Blue-eyed soul singer Alex Chilton, the front man for the Box Tops, had a very mature voice for an eighteen-year-old. He and the group had just come off a number 1 hit with "The Letter" the previous year, and just missed the top of the charts again with "Cry Like a Baby"—a song of regret over having treated a former love interest poorly. It was kept out of the number 1 spot by Bobby Goldsboro's "Honey" (United Artists #50283).

A dozen years later, the tune was a hit again when it was remade by Kim Carnes, who recalled, "I'd always loved the record by the Box Tops. If I cover a song, an outside song, I have to really love it as I record mostly songs that I write. It was exactly what was needed for the *Romance Dance* album [EMI America #17030]. I used to open each show with it. It's a great opener and has great energy." It should be noted that Carnes's next cover, "Bette Davis Eyes," became the biggest song of her career (see the entry for that song).

"CRY ME A RIVER"

Composer: Arthur Hamilton
Original Artist: Julie London
Label: Liberty Records; *Recording:* Liberty #55006 (45 and 78)
Release Year: 1955; *Chart:* #9 *Billboard* Hot 100
Cover Artist: Joe Cocker
Label: A & M Records; *Recording:* A & M #1200 (45)
Release Year: 1970; *Chart:* #11 *Billboard* Hot 100

Actress/singer/sex symbol Julie London had previously been married to Jack Webb of *Dragnet* fame. In 1956 she worked with future husband Bobby Troup on the rock and roll film *The Girl Can't Help It*. In the film, London performed her most famous song—the sultry and smoky "Cry Me a River." It was a Top 10 hit and a million-seller.

An edgy, up-tempo remake in 1970 from the million-selling *Mad Dogs and Englishmen* album (A & M #6002) by Joe Cocker (recorded live at the Fillmore East in New York) just missed the Top 10.

Justin Timberlake's "Cry Me a River" is a completely different song.

"CRYING"

Composers: Roy Orbison and Joe Melson
Original Artist: Roy Orbison
Label: Monument Records; *Recording:* Monument #447 (45)
Release Year: 1961; *Chart:* #2 *Billboard* Hot 100
Cover Artist: Don McLean
Label: Millennium Records; *Recording:* Millennium #11799 (45)
Release Year: 1981; *Chart:* #5 *Billboard* Hot 100

Roy Orbison is certainly among the most covered artists of the rock era. Most of his hits have also become hits for others. Among them is the song "Crying." Orbison's original version reached number 2 on the Pop charts and was kept out of the number 1 spot by "Hit the Road, Jack" by Ray Charles on the ABC-Paramount label.

A version by Jay and the Americans in 1966 (United Artists #50016) reached the Top 30, but a successful comeback by the "American Pie" guy, Don McLean, brought the song back into the Top 10. This updated rendition of "Crying" was included on McLean's *Chain Lightning* album (Millennium #7756). This LP contained numerous other cover songs, such as "It Doesn't Matter Anymore" (Buddy Holly), "Since I Don't Have You" (the Skyliners), and "Your Cheating Heart" (Hank Williams).

"CRYING IN THE CHAPEL"

Composer: Artie Glenn
Original Artist: Darrell Glenn

Label: Valley Records; *Recording:* Valley #105 (45 and 78)
Release Year: 1953; *Chart:* #6 *Billboard* Hot 100
Cover Artist: the Orioles
Label: Jubilee Records; *Recording:* Jubilee #5122 (45 and 78)
Release Year: 1953; *Chart:* #11 *Billboard* Hot 100 and #1 R&B

"Crying in the Chapel" was written by Artie Glenn and given to his son, Darrell, to record. It was released on the tiny Valley Records label from Knoxville, Tennessee, but eventually caught on and spawned numerous cover versions from the likes of Rex Allen, Ella Fitzgerald, and June Valli.

There were also a few cover versions on the R&B charts—one by the Four Dukes on the Duke Records label of Houston, Texas (Duke #116), and another by Sonny Til and the Orioles on the Jubilee label. The latter was a huge hit—number 1 on the R&B charts and number 11 on the Pop charts. This became the prolific, important, and seminal Orioles' biggest hit. It was included in the soundtrack for both *American Graffiti* in 1973 and *Revolutionary Road* in 2008.

Likely the most famous version of the song was recorded in 1960 by "the King of Rock and Roll," Elvis Presley, but it wasn't released until 1965. It became his only Top 10 hit of the middle 1960s and went platinum. It was later included on Presley's *How Great Thou Art* album (RCA Victor #3758) in 1967.

"CRYING TIME"

Composer: Buck Owens
Original Artist: Buck Owens
Label: Capitol Records; *Recording:* Capitol #5336 (45)
Release Year: 1965; *Chart:* did not chart
Cover Artist: Ray Charles
Label: ABC-Paramount Records; *Recording:* ABC-Paramount #10731 (45)
Release Year: 1965; *Chart:* #6 *Billboard* Hot 100 and #5 R&B

The prolific Buck Owens wrote and originally recorded "Crying Time" as the B-side of his biggest pop hit, "I've Got a Tiger by the Tail," in 1965.

That B-side didn't go unnoticed. It became the title cut for the *Crying Time* album (ABC-Paramount #544) from "the Genius of Soul," Ray Charles. "Crying Time" made Top 10 on the Pop and R&B charts, and garnered him a Grammy for Best R&B Song. Buck Owens's long-awaited biography, *Buck 'Em!*, was released in late 2013.

D

"DADDY, DON'T YOU WALK SO FAST"

Composers: Peter Callander and Geoff Stephens
Original Artist: Daniel Boone

Label: Epic Records; *Recording:* Epic #10787 (45)
Release Year: 1971; *Chart:* did not chart
Cover Artist: Wayne Newton
Label: Chelsea Records; *Recording:* Chelsea #0100 (45)
Release Year: 1972; *Chart:* #4 *Billboard* Hot 100

British singer/songwriter Daniel Boone recorded the first version of "Daddy, Don't You Walk So Fast." He didn't write the song, and even though it was a fair-sized hit in the United Kingdom, it did not leave an impression in the United States.

However, when this sad ballad about divorce as seen through the eyes of children was rerecorded by "Mr. Las Vegas," Wayne Newton, it caught on in a big way in the States. Released on songwriter/producer Wes Farrell's Chelsea Records label, the record reached number 4 on the Pop charts and sold well over a million copies. It became Newton's biggest single—even bigger than "Danke Schoen."

"DADDY-O"
Composers: Charlie Gore and Louis Innis
Original Artist: Bonnie Lou
Label: King Records; *Recording:* King #4835 (45 and 78)
Release Year: 1955; *Chart:* #14 *Billboard* Hot 100
Cover Artist: the Fontane Sisters
Label: Dot Records; *Recording:* Dot #15428 (45 and 78)
Release Year: 1955; *Chart:* #11 *Billboard* Hot 100

All the girls go batty over "Daddy-O." He always wore a T-shirt and a great big smile. He was smiling because there were two very similar versions of the song about him on the charts at the same time and each made Top 20.

Her real name was Mary Kath but she was known on her one and only hit on the King Records label as Bonnie Lou. Bonnie Lou gave us the original version of "Daddy-O," but a hastily released cover version by the Fontane Sisters became the bigger hit late in 1955. In fact, the version by the Fontanes was a two-sided hit with "Adorable" on the flip side—a cover of an R&B hit by the Colts and the Drifters.

"DANCING IN THE MOONLIGHT"
Composer: Sherman Kelly
Original Artist: Boffalongo
Label: United Artists Records; *Recording:* United Artists #50699 (45)
Release Year: 1970; *Chart:* did not chart
Cover Artist: King Harvest
Label: Perception Records; *Recording:* Perception #515 (45)
Release Year: 1973; *Chart:* #13 *Billboard* Hot 100

A little-known group named Boffalongo on the United Artists label recorded the little-known original version of "Dancing in the Moonlight" in 1969, and it was met with very little fanfare in 1970. This happy and positive medium-tempo song did get a second chance.

Just three years later, a remake of the Boffalongo tune was released on the Perception label by a group from New York known as King Harvest. Featuring Ron Altback on lead vocals, this time around the song caught on and just missed the Top 10 on the Pop charts in 1973. Truly a one-hit wonder, King Harvest never again reached the Top 50. The tune still receives a goodly amount of airplay, and it was used in a string of commercials for Hanes underwear in the 1990s.

"DANNY'S SONG"
Composer: Kenny Loggins
Original Artist: Gator Creek
Label: Mercury Records; *Recording:* Mercury #61311 (LP)
Release Year: 1970; *Chart:* did not chart
Cover Artist: Anne Murray
Label: Capitol Records; *Recording:* Capitol #3481 (45)
Release Year: 1973; *Chart:* #7 *Billboard* Hot 100

This song was written as a gift by Kenny Loggins for his brother, Danny. Loggins recorded the first version of the song with a group known as Gator Creek in 1970 on the Mercury Records label. The album and the song went absolutely nowhere.

Loggins rerecorded "Danny's Song" for the Loggins and Messina album titled *Sittin' In* (Columbia #31044) in 1972. This rendition of the tune received a lot of airplay, but was not a chart hit. It's what used to be known as a turntable hit.

The big hit single version came very early in 1973 when Canadian Anne Murray covered it for Capitol Records. "Danny's Song" is one of just a small number of hits in which the title of the song is never mentioned in the lyrics (along with "Unchained Melody," "For What It's Worth," "The 59th Street Bridge Song," and "Creeque Alley," to name a few).

"DARK MOON"
Composer: Ned Miller
Original Artist: Bonnie Guitar
Label: Fabor Records; *Recording:* Fabor #4018 (45 and 78)
Release Year: 1957; *Chart:* #6 *Billboard* Hot 100
Cover Artist: Gale Storm
Label: Dot Records; *Recording:* Dot #15558 (45 and 78)
Release Year: 1957; *Chart:* #4 *Billboard* Hot 100

This was a song of lost love that twice became a Top 10 entry. The original version of the song made both the Pop and Country charts. The artist on this version was

Bonnie Guitar, and it was first released on the small Fabor Records label. It was later leased to the same label for which Gale Storm recorded, Dot Records (#15550).

Storm had the distinct advantage of a TV series to promote her version in 1957. That sitcom known under two titles—*The Gale Storm Show* and *Oh, Susanna*—featured the song in an episode titled "Sing, Susanna, Sing" from the program's first season. Guest starring on that episode was Craig Stevens, later TV's *Peter Gunn*. Storm's version became the definitive hit.

The song's originator, Bonnie Guitar, later played on a few of the Fleet-woods' hit records. The composer of "Dark Moon," Ned Miller, later had a big hit of his own titled "From a Jack to a King" (Fabor #114) in 1962.

"DAYDREAM BELIEVER"
Composer: John Stewart
Original Artist: the Monkees
Label: Colgems Records; *Recording:* Colgems #1012 (45)
Release Year: 1967; *Chart:* #1 *Billboard* Hot 100
Cover Artist: Anne Murray
Label: Capitol Records; *Recording:* Capitol #4813 (45)
Release Year: 1979; *Chart:* #12 *Billboard* Hot 100

"Daydream Believer" was written by former Kingston Trio member John Stew-art and presented to the Monkees. Davy Jones was selected for lead vocals on this cut released late in 1967. Numerous takes and retakes of the song caused some dissension in the recording studio. The song hit number 1 and was included on *The Birds, the Bees and the Monkees* album (Colgems #109) in 1968.

A dozen years later, Anne Murray revived the song and made it a Top 20 hit all over again. There is a lyrical difference between the two renditions. In the Monkees' version, the line is "Without dollar one to spend," but in Murray's, the line is changed to or misinterpreted as "With a dollar one to spend."

In 1986 when the Monkees reunited, a remixed version of "Daydream Believer" was issued—this time on Arista Records (#9532)—and this time it peaked at number 79 on the Pop charts. Davy Jones died on leap day, February 29, 2012, at the age of sixty-six.

"DEEP PURPLE"
Composers: Peter DeRose and Mitchell Parish
Original Artist: Larry Clinton and His Orchestra
Label: RCA Victor Records; *Recording:* RCA Victor #0396 (78)
Release Year: 1938; *Chart:* #1 *Billboard* Music Hit Parade
Cover Artist: Nino Tempo and April Stevens
Label: Atco Records; *Recording:* Atco #6273 (45)
Release Year: 1963; *Chart:* #1 *Billboard* Hot 100

Not to be confused with the later rock group of the same name, the song titled "Deep Purple" has its origins in sheet music, where it became very popular. Once lyrics were added, many hit versions followed, including Larry Clinton and His Orchestra for RCA Victor in 1938, and Artie Shaw with Helen Forrest for Bluebird Records, also in 1938.

The song's popularity carried over into the rock and roll years. In 1957, Billy Ward and the Dominoes (featuring Eugene Mumford on lead vocals) on Liberty Records (#55099) brought a doo-wop version of the song into the Top 20 on the Pop charts.

Likely the biggest and most popular version of the song came about in 1963 by a brother-and-sister act known as Nino Tempo and April Stevens

This remake of "Deep Purple" hit number 1 only weeks before the Beatles hit it big in the United States.

(Atco #6273), featuring a harmonica as part of the musical accompaniment. It quickly scaled those sleepy garden walls and reached number 1 for one week in 1963.

Yet another brother-and-sister duo had a hit with the song—Donny and Marie Osmond on MGM Records in 1975. It reached number 14 on the Pop charts.

"DEVOTED TO YOU"
Composers: Felice and Boudleaux Bryant
Original Artist: the Everly Brothers
Label: Cadence Records; *Recording:* Cadence #1350 (45 and 78)
Release Year: 1958; *Chart:* #10 *Billboard* Hot 100
Cover Artist: Carly Simon and James Taylor
Label: Elektra Records; *Recording:* Elektra #45506 (45)
Release Year: 1978; *Chart:* #36 *Billboard* Hot 100

The husband-and-wife songwriting team of Felice and Boudleaux Bryant wrote both sides of Cadence Records number 1350 by Phil and Don Everly, and both sides reached the Top 10. It's interesting to note that the intended B-side, "Bird Dog" became the bigger hit—reaching number 1. The soft, gentle, romantic ballad on the A-side, "Devoted to You," peaked at number 10.

A very similar arrangement exactly twenty years later by Carly Simon and James Taylor from Simon's platinum *Boys in the Trees* album (Elektra #128) reached the Top 40. Despite the lyrics of "Devoted to You," Simon and Taylor divorced in 1983.

"DIFFERENT DRUM"
Composer: Mike Nesmith
Original Artist: the Greenbriar Boys
Label: Vanguard Records; *Recording:* Vanguard #79233 (LP)
Release Year: 1966; *Chart:* did not chart
Cover Artist: the Stone Poneys
Label: Capitol Records; *Recording:* Capitol #2004 (45)
Release Year: 1967; *Chart:* #13 *Billboard* Hot 100

Mike Nesmith wrote "Different Drum" before his involvement in the Monkees. It was recorded originally by a bluegrass band known as the Greenbriar Boys and included on their album titled *Better Late Than Never* on the Vanguard Records label. Even though opposites are supposed to attract, the singer tells of a reluctance to adhere to that. This original version was not a hit.

Almost two years later, a yet unknown Linda Ronstadt rerecorded the song with her band, Stone Poneys, for Capitol Records. It became not only her first

Top 20 hit but also her first of many cover records. It was included on the Stone Poneys' *Evergreen, Volume 2* album (Capitol #2763).

"DO YOU BELIEVE IN MAGIC?"
Composer: John Sebastian
Original Artist: the Lovin' Spoonful
Label: Kama Sutra Records; *Recording:* Kama Sutra #201 (45)
Release Year: 1965; *Chart:* #9 *Billboard* Hot 100
Cover Artist: Shaun Cassidy
Label: Warner Brothers/Curb Records; *Recording:* Warner Brothers/Curb #8533 (45)
Release Year: 1978; *Chart:* #31 *Billboard* Hot 100

"Do You Believe in Magic?"—a song about the magic of music and love—became the first Top 10 record by the Lovin' Spoonful in 1965. It was also the title cut of their first album (Kama Sutra #8050) and it made Top 40.

It became popular again in 1978 when it was covered by Shaun Cassidy. He previously had success covering the Crystals' "Da Doo Ron Ron," and "Do You Believe in Magic?" became a Top 40 hit, too.

The song still had another life. The next time around, "Do You Believe in Magic?" was a hit by a female duet known as Aly and A. J. in 2005 (Hollywood #2061-64100). This version reached the highest chart position—number 2 on the Pop charts.

In recent years, the song has been used in TV commercials for Kohl's stores.

"DOCTOR'S ORDERS"
Composers: Roger Cook, Roger Greenaway, and Geoff Stephens
Original Artist: Sunny
Label: Epic Records; *Recording:* Epic #11112 (45)
Release Year: 1974; *Chart:* #7 U.K. charts
Cover Artist: Carol Douglas
Label: Midland International Records; *Recording:* Midland International #10113 (45)
Release Year: 1974; *Chart:* #11 *Billboard* Hot 100

We are led to believe that "Doctor's Orders" is a two-way phone conversation. The woman has gone to see her doctor because she has been under the weather. The diagnosis: nothing is wrong; she is merely missing her man. The original version by Sunny was recorded in 1973 and released early in 1974. It employed a quick tempo and became a hit in the United Kingdom. Although it was released in the United States, it did not chart.

The cover version by Carol Douglas of Brooklyn was recorded a bit slower but with a disco beat. It just missed the Top 10 and was hugely influential on the burgeoning disco scene.

"DONNA"

Composer: Ritchie Valens
Original Artist: Ritchie Valens
Label: Del-Fi Records; *Recording:* Del-Fi #4110 (45)
Release Year: 1958; *Chart:* #2 *Billboard* Hot 100
Cover Artist: Cliff Richard
Label: EMI America Records; *Recording:* EMI America #8193 (45)
Release Year: 1983; *Chart:* did not chart

"Donna" was a song by rising Latino rock and roll star Ritchie Valens. The Donna was a real person—Donna Ludwig, an acquaintance of Valens's. It was released late in 1958, and it was only the second release by Valens. It was in the Top 10 when Valens perished in that tragic plane crash on February 3, 1959, which also claimed the young lives of Buddy Holly and the Big Bopper.

"Donna" was remade in 1983 by British singer Cliff Richard. In comparison to his superstardom in the United Kingdom, Richard's success in the United States was somewhat modest. His take on the Ritchie Valens ballad failed to make the charts. It was included on the *Give a Little Bit More* album (EMI America #17105).

Valens was inducted into the Rock and Roll Hall of Fame in 2001. He has received a star on the Hollywood Walk of Fame and was commemorated on a U.S. postage stamp. The motion picture *La Bamba*, which was based on Valens's life and starred Lou Diamond Phillips, was a big box office hit in 1987.

"DON'T CRY OUT LOUD"

Composers: Carole Bayer Sager and Peter Allen
Original Artist: the Moments
Label: Stang Records; *Recording:* Stang #5071 (45)
Release Year: 1977; *Chart:* #79 *Billboard* R&B
Cover Artist: Melissa Manchester
Label: Arista Records; *Recording:* Arista #3073 (45)
Release Year: 1978; *Chart:* #10 *Billboard* Hot 100

Written by Carole Bayer Sager and Peter Allen, the song's original title was "We Don't Cry Out Loud," and the first recording of it came in 1977 as by the Moments, most famous for "Love on a Two-Way Street." This soulful rendition barely scraped the bottom of the R&B charts in that year and made very little impact.

Late the following year, however, the Bronx's Melissa Manchester covered the song, now known as simply "Don't Cry Out Loud." This time around, the ballad received much more of a torch song approach, and it worked very well—becoming Manchester's very first Top 10 hit.

The person named "Baby" referenced in the song's lyrics was Peter Allen's little sister.

"DON'T GIVE IN TO HIM"

Composer: Gary Usher
Original Artist: Finders Keepers
Label: Challenge Records; *Recording:* Challenge #59364 (45)
Release Year: 1967; *Chart:* did not chart
Cover Artist: Gary Puckett and the Union Gap
Label: Columbia Records; *Recording:* Columbia #44788 (45)
Release Year: 1969; *Chart:* #15 *Billboard* Hot 100

Gary Usher was a songwriter and producer whose most famous work was with the Beach Boys. He continued with many musical projects over many years, but never matched his collaborations with Brian Wilson. Among Usher's compositions was a song titled "Don't Give In to Him" by a group known as Finders Keepers on Gene Autry's Challenge Records label. This version of the song from 1967 was not a hit.

Two years later, the red-hot Gary Puckett and the Union Gap covered the song on the Columbia Records label. It was produced by the prolific Jerry Fuller, who had written songs for Ricky Nelson. It became Puckett's fifth of six consecutive Top 20 hits and was included on *The New Gary Puckett and the Union Gap* album (Columbia #9935).

"DON'T KNOW MUCH"

Composers: Barry Mann, Cynthia Weil, and Tom Snow
Original Artist: Barry Mann
Label: Casablanca Records; *Recording:* Casablanca #7228 (LP)
Release Year: 1980; *Chart:* did not chart
Cover Artist: Linda Ronstadt and Aaron Neville
Label: Elektra Records; *Recording:* Elektra #69261 (45)
Release Year: 1989; *Chart:* #2 *Billboard* Hot 100

By no means was this famous song an overnight success. Co-written by the prolific Barry Mann, it was first released on his *Barry Mann* album on the Casablanca Records label in 1980. It was not a success.

In 1981, Bill Medley of the Righteous Brothers recorded his 45 version (Liberty #1402), and it peaked near the very bottom of the Pop charts at number 88. In 1983, Bette Midler tried to make the song a hit on 45 under the title "All I Need to Know" (Atlantic #89789), and it reached number 77 on the charts.

Wine, cheese, and this song definitely improve with age. In 1989, once again under the original title "Don't Know Much," the ballad finally became a hit with the right combination and chemistry—a duet consisting of Linda Ronstadt and Aaron Neville. It reached number 2 on the charts and quickly sold over a million copies, leading to another hit for the pairing—"All My Life" early in 1990 (Elektra #64987).

"Don't Say You Don't Remember"
Composers: Helen Miller and Estelle Levitt
Original Artist: the Goggles
Label: Audio Fidelity Records; *Recording:* Audio Fidelity #168 (45)
Release Year: 1971; *Chart:* did not chart
Cover Artist: Beverly Bremers
Label: Scepter Records; *Recording:* Scepter #12315 (45)
Release Year: 1971; *Chart:* #15 *Billboard* Hot 100

Despite a big build-up and an appearance on a special episode of *NBC Children's Theater* titled "Looking through Super Elastic Plastic Goggles at Color" on January 30, 1971, a group called the Goggles never really did catch on. Their biggest claim to fame was recording the first version of "Don't Say You Don't Remember" on the album simply titled *The Goggles* (Audio Fidelity #6244) and also released as a 45. If you say you don't remember their rendition, you're not alone.

The version that became the hit was released later in 1971, and the recording artist, Beverly Bremers, was unaware that the song had been previously recorded. Bremers said,

> I actually had no knowledge of the Goggles' recording. The composers, Helen and Estelle led me to believe that they wrote it fresh. Estelle even gave me a last-minute lyric change, and then changed it back. In retrospect, it really doesn't matter, but it is very interesting. At the recording session, Helen Miller continually told me to "sing dumber." I think she meant innocent and vulnerable. She was quite a character. I don't recall how many, but there were a lot of takes that day because I triple-voiced the lead (no fancy electronics in those days). I was also one of the background singers along with Miss Patti Austin. You'll see her name on the album jacket. She was just getting her career started.

David Spinoza of the Goggles later went on to do some work with James Taylor, as well as John Lennon, Paul McCartney, and Ringo Starr during their solo years.

"Don't Think Twice, It's All Right"
Composer: Bob Dylan
Original Artist: Bob Dylan
Label: Columbia Records; *Recording:* Columbia #42856 (45)
Release Year: 1963; *Chart:* did not chart
Cover Artist: Peter, Paul and Mary
Label: Warner Brothers Records; *Recording:* Warner Brothers #5385 (45)
Release Year: 1963; *Chart:* #9 *Billboard* Hot 100

"Don't Think Twice, It's All Right" was included on *The Freewheelin' Bob Dylan* album recorded in 1962 and released in 1963 (Columbia #1986). It was also the B-side of "Blowin' in the Wind" on an early and rare Dylan Columbia 45. It's a song about a breakup. The guy in the song is leaving, can't be talked out of that decision, but is not bitter about being treated badly by the girl in the relationship. The "it's alright" part of the title evokes forgiveness.

Peter, Paul and Mary covered both sides of that Columbia 45 ("Blowin' in the Wind" and "Don't Think Twice, It's All Right") and had Top 10 smashes with each one. Released on Warner Brothers Records, these versions by this trio were done in typical folk fashion.

"Don't Think Twice, It's All Right" also became a hit for a famous quartet, though the title was simply "Don't Think Twice." Released by the Four Seasons (Philips #40324) under the alias the Wonder Who (to have multiple hits on the chart simultaneously), this rendition was almost a parody of the original song and yet was endearing in its own right. Frankie Valli displays his trademark falsetto from beginning to end with the Seasons chiming in with "why babe, why babe?" It just missed the Top 10 in 1965. The group's distinctive sound didn't let us "wonder who" for very long.

"DON'T WORRY BABY"
Composers: Brian Wilson and Roger Christian
Original Artist: the Beach Boys
Label: Capitol Records; *Recording:* Capitol #5174 (45)
Release Year: 1964; *Chart:* #24 *Billboard* Hot 100
Cover Artist: B. J. Thomas
Label: MCA Records; *Recording:* MCA #40735 (45)
Release Year: 1977; *Chart:* #17 *Billboard* Hot 100

Even with all of the British Invasion music and all of the Motown of 1964, somehow the Beach Boys were able to sneak a number 1 hit in there with "I Get Around." As with most of their early releases, both sides became hits, and this 45 was no exception. The B-side was a wonderful ballad of reassurance titled "Don't Worry Baby."

A lucky thirteen years later, the song was remade by B. J. Thomas, who was now with MCA Records, and actually attained a higher position on the Pop charts than the original. Thomas said, "I have always loved the Beach Boys—all of their records. They could do no wrong in my book. Brian Wilson was amazing. It wasn't my biggest hit, but it did sell about 800,000 copies and I still perform it live in concert." It was included on the *B. J. Thomas* album (MCA #2286) in 1977.

"DREAM A LITTLE DREAM OF ME"
Composers: Fabian Andree, Wilbur Schwandt, and Gus Kahn
Original Artist: Ozzie Nelson

Label: Brunswick Records; *Recording:* Brunswick #6060 (78)
Release Year: 1931; *Chart:* did not chart
Cover Artist: Mama Cass Elliott
Label: Dunhill Records; *Recording:* Dunhill #4145 (45)
Release Year: 1968; *Chart:* #12 *Billboard* Hot 100

Long before he was the patriarch on *The Adventures of Ozzie and Harriet* on both radio and TV, Ozzie Nelson was a bandleader and singer. He released the first version of "Dream a Little Dream of Me" in 1931.

Cover versions abound. The song was rerecorded by the likes of Ella Fitzgerald, Wayne King, Frankie Laine, the Nat King Cole Trio, Dinah Shore, Dean Martin, and Doris Day with mixed results.

It may have sounded a wee bit out of place in 1968, but Mama Cass Elliott released a version as her first solo effort after leaving the Mamas and the Papas. It was so retro sounding and so different from everything else on the radio. It became a Top 20 hit. In fact, it just missed the Top 10. *Dream a Little Dream of Me* was also the title of her first solo album (Dunhill #50040).

"DREAM BABY (HOW LONG MUST I DREAM?)"
Composer: Cindy Walker
Original Artist: Roy Orbison
Label: Monument Records; *Recording:* Monument #456 (45)
Release Year: 1962; *Chart:* #4 *Billboard* Hot 100
Cover Artist: Glen Campbell
Label: Capitol Records; *Recording:* Capitol #3062 (45)
Release Year: 1971; *Chart:* #31 *Billboard* Hot 100

Not to be confused with "In Dreams," this Roy Orbison tune with a similar title came a year earlier. It's a song about a guy who meets his dream girl and awaits that dream coming to fruition. It's one of the few hits Orbison didn't write.

Almost a decade later, the host of *The Glen Campbell Goodtime Hour* on CBS recorded a remake, and again the song made Top 40. It's most interesting that Campbell sang "Sweet Dreams Baby" (with an *s*) in his version, although the Orbison original and the title on Campbell's record label was "Dream Baby."

"DRIFT AWAY"
Composer: Mentor Williams
Original Artist: John Kurtz
Label: ABC Records; *Recording:* ABC #11341 (45)
Release Year: 1972; *Chart:* did not chart
Cover Artist: Dobie Gray
Label: Decca Records; *Recording:* Decca #33057 (45)
Release Year: 1973; *Chart:* #5 *Billboard* Hot 100

Few people know that "Drift Away" was released first on ABC Records by an artist named John Kurtz, on both 45 rpm and his *Reunion* album (ABC #742) in 1972. Neither the 45 nor the LP charted.

One year later, however, a cover version by Dobie Gray soared into the Top 5 on the Pop charts and quickly sold well over a million copies.

Gray had another crack at the song as a featured artist on a remake in 2003 by Uncle Kracker. Once again, "Drift Away" became a Top 10 hit. Gray died just a few years later on December 6, 2011, at the age of seventy-one. The song's composer, Mentor Williams, is the brother of Paul Williams—songwriting talent was in the genes.

E

"EARLY IN THE MORNING"
Composers: Bobby Darin and Woody Harris
Original Artist: the Ding Dongs
Label: Brunswick Records; *Recording:* Brunswick #55073 (45 and 78)
Release Year: 1958; *Chart:* #24 *Billboard* Hot 100
Cover Artist: Buddy Holly
Label: Coral Records; *Recording:* Coral #62006 (45 and 78)
Release Year: 1958; *Chart:* #32 *Billboard* Hot 100

Here's a pop song with attitude and cockiness. The lyrics aver "You're gonna miss me, early in the morning, one of these days." It was co-written and originally recorded by Bobby Darin in his Decca recording days. Darin was released from his Decca contract when none of his releases on the label caught on. Once Darin had his first hit, "Splish Splash" on the Atco label, Decca tried to ride on his coattails and put out a previously unreleased song titled "Early in the Morning" on its Brunswick subsidiary as by the Ding Dongs, to mask the identity of Bobby Darin (because he was under contract at Atco). It was then rereleased (the same exact recording) on Atco (#6121) as by the Rinky-Dinks. The song made Top 30, but that was not the end of the story.

Decca had another subsidiary label—Coral Records—and a version of the song by Buddy Holly was quickly released; it, too, made the Top 40 in the summer of 1958.

This "Early in the Morning" is not to be confused with the songs of the same name by Vanity Fare, the Gap Band, and Robert Palmer.

"EBB TIDE"
Composers: Carl Sigman and Robert Maxwell
Original Artist: Frank Chacksfield

The original Bobby Darin release of "Early in the Morning" by the Ding Dongs.

Label: Decca Records; *Recording:* Decca #10122 (45 and 78)
Release Year: 1954; *Chart:* #2 *Billboard* Hot 100
Cover Artist: the Righteous Brothers
Label: Philles Records; *Recording:* Philles #130 (45)
Release Year: 1965; *Chart:* #5 *Billboard* Hot 100

Robert Maxwell composed the song and Carl Sigman wrote the lyrics. However, the first version of the song by Frank Chacksfield in 1954 was an instrumental. It began with ocean and bird sounds, not unlike "Harbor Lights" by the Platters and "So Much in Love" by the Tymes. It reached number 2 on the Pop charts.

A bevy of cover versions were released from the likes of Vic Damone, Roy Hamilton, the Avalons, Frank Sinatra, and Lenny Welch, to name a few. However, the best-known vocal version came from Phil Spector's Philles label and the Righteous Brothers—Bill Medley and Bobby Hatfield. This rendition was released late in 1965, and it peaked at number 5 on the Pop charts in 1966.

"ELVIRA"
Composer: Dallas Frazier
Original Artist: Dallas Frazier
Label: Capitol Records; *Recording:* Capitol #5560 (45)
Release Year: 1966; *Chart:* #72 *Billboard* Hot 100
Cover Artist: the Oak Ridge Boys
Label: MCA Records; *Recording:* MCA #51084 (45)
Release Year: 1981; *Chart:* #5 *Billboard* Hot 100

Long before the Oak Ridge Boys' version, the composer of "Elvira," Dallas Frazier, had recorded it first.

"Elvira" was both written and originally recorded by Dallas Frazier. The song is somewhat of a cross between country and doo-wop, and professes great love for a young lady named Elvira in lines such as, "My heart's on fire for Elvira."

Almost fifteen years after Frazier's original, a remake version from the *Fancy Free* album (MCA #5209) became the biggest hit for the Oak Ridge Boys (Duane Allen, Joe Bonsall, William Lee Golden, and Richard Sterban). The single sold well over a million copies, and the *Fancy Free* album went multiplatinum.

"Everlovin'"

Composer: Dave Burgess
Original Artist: Dave Burgess and the Chimes
Label: Challenge Records; *Recording:* Challenge #59045 (45)
Release Year: 1959; *Chart:* did not chart
Cover Artist: Rick Nelson
Label: Imperial Records; *Recording:* Imperial #5770 (45)
Release Year: 1961; *Chart:* #16 *Billboard* Hot 100

The original version of "Everlovin'" was recorded by the same gentleman who wrote the song, Dave Burgess, on Gene Autry's Challenge Records label. Burgess enjoyed a lot of success playing rhythm guitar for the Champs, but the magic did not translate to his attempt at a solo career.

However, his song did become a fair-sized hit two years later when it was recorded by Ricky Nelson. Actually, "Everlovin'" backed with "A Wonder Like You" was the very first 45 rpm release on which the *y* was gone from his name. Beginning with this release, he was grown up, and from here on, he was *Rick* Nelson. "A Wonder Like You" hit number 11, and "Everlovin'" reached number 16.

"Everybody Loves a Lover"

Composers: Robert Allen and Richard Adler
Original Artist: Doris Day
Label: Columbia Records; *Recording:* Columbia #41195 (45 and 78)
Release Year: 1958; *Chart:* #6 *Billboard* Hot 100
Cover Artist: the Shirelles
Label: Scepter Records; *Recording:* Scepter #1243 (45)
Release Year: 1962; *Chart:* #19 *Billboard* Hot 100

This finger snapper was Doris Day's final Top 10 hit. Like Peggy Lee's "Fever," the recording has very spare instrumentation. Then the record builds to a nice crescendo in the final minute with Day performing the song in the manner of an old-fashioned round—she is in a counterpoint harmony with herself, singing different lyrics.

The choice by the Shirelles to cover this song was an odd one—they had been recording original material from Carole King and Gerry Goffin, and also Burt Bacharach, so successfully. This cover mimicked the sound emanating from New Orleans in the early 1960s. It's akin to Doris Day meeting Barbara George of "I Know (You Don't Want Me No More)" fame (in fact, the instrumental break in the song is almost note-for-note identical to the Barbara George tune). This rendition did get quite a bit of airplay, and managed to crack the Top 20 early in 1963.

Doris Day's recording career may have slumped after this recording, but her movie career was in full swing with *Pillow Talk, Lover Come Back, Please Don't Eat the Daisies, The Thrill of It All, Send Me No Flowers,* and *With Six You Get Egg Roll.* She also got five seasons out of a sitcom on CBS—*The Doris Day Show.*

"EVERYBODY'S TALKIN'"
Composer: Fred Neil
Original Artist: Fred Neil
Label: Capitol Records; *Recording:* Capitol #2665 (LP)
Release Year: 1967; *Chart:* did not chart
Cover Artist: Harry Nilsson
Label: RCA Victor Records; *Recording:* RCA Victor #0161 (45)
Release Year: 1969; *Chart:* #6 *Billboard* Hot 100

"Everybody's Talkin'" was written by Fred Neil, and first issued on his *Fred Neil* album in 1966 for Capitol. The album was not a hit, but that song soon would be.

The cover version by Harry Nilsson was first issued as a single in 1968, but it went nowhere fast. It was also included on his 1968 album titled *Aerial Ballet* (RCA Victor #3956). However, when the song was selected as the theme for the 1969 United Artists motion picture *Midnight Cowboy* starring Jon Voight and Dustin Hoffman, it became a Top 10 smash. The film has the distinction of being the only X-rated film to win an Oscar.

"EVERYDAY"
Composers: Buddy Holly and Norman Petty
Original Artist: Buddy Holly
Label: Coral Records; *Recording:* Coral #61885 (45 and 78)
Release Year: 1957; *Chart:* did not chart
Cover Artist: James Taylor
Label: Columbia Records; *Recording:* Columbia #05681 (45)
Release Year: 1985; *Chart:* #61 *Billboard* Hot 100

"Everyday" by Buddy Holly is definitely a turntable hit. It was placed on the B-side of the monster-hit single "Peggy Sue" in 1957. "Everyday" did not chart, but its popularity belies that fact. Even though the artist on the label is listed solely as Buddy Holly, the Crickets were indeed there. In fact, it's interesting to note that there were no drums used on this recording—Cricket Jerry Allison was merely tapping out the beat on his Levi's (on his leg), making that percussive patting sound.

Many have covered "Everyday" over the years, but only John Denver (RCA Victor #0647) and James Taylor have charted with the song in the United States. It has been used in TV commercials for AT&T, Activia, and Macy's.

"EVERYTIME YOU GO AWAY"
Composer: Daryl Hall
Original Artist: Daryl Hall and John Oates
Label: RCA Victor Records; *Recording:* RCA Victor #3646 (LP)
Release Year: 1980; *Chart:* did not chart
Cover Artist: Paul Young
Label: Columbia Records; *Recording:* Columbia #04867 (45)
Release Year: 1985; *Chart:* #1 *Billboard* Hot 100

"Everytime You Go Away" by Daryl Hall and John Oates was included on their *Voices* album in 1980. The album spawned numerous hits—"You've Lost That Lovin' Feeling," "Kiss on My List," and "You Make My Dreams"—but for whatever reason, "Everytime You Go Away" was never released as a single.

The Hall and Oates rendition of "Everytime You Go Away" was quite well done, and it impressed British blue-eyed soul singer Paul Young enough to remake the song. It proved to be a good decision, and Young's version soared to number 1 on the Pop charts. It was included on his *The Secret of Association* album (Columbia #39957) in 1985, and it went gold.

F

"FALLIN' IN LOVE"
Composers: Ann and Dan Hamilton
Original Artist: Hamilton, Joe Frank and Reynolds
Label: Playboy Records; *Recording:* Playboy #6024 (45)
Release Year: 1975; *Chart:* #1 *Billboard* Hot 100
Cover Artist: La Bouche
Label: Logic Records; *Recording:* Logic #59018 (CD)
Release Year: 1996; *Chart:* #35 *Billboard* Hot 100

Hamilton, Joe Frank and Reynolds—a trio from California—had a Top 5 million-selling single in 1971 titled "Don't Pull Your Love" (Dunhill #4276).

Finding a follow-up hit proved tougher than expected, and a short while later, Tommy Reynolds left the group—but the name remained the same, even after adding new member Alan Dennison.

After signing with Playboy Records in 1975, the new version of Hamilton, Joe Frank and Reynolds struck gold again with a song about the unpredictability of romance. The song peaked at number 1 on both the Pop and Easy Listening charts and led to the *Fallin' in Love* album (Playboy #407) late in 1975.

The song was repopularized in 1996 when covered by an R&B duet known as La Bouche. This Top 40 hit opened with a spoken part not heard on the Hamilton, Joe Frank and Reynolds original. "Fallin' in Love" was also sampled on Drake's rap hit "The Best I Ever Had" in 2009 (Cash Money #DBESTCD-P1).

"THE 59TH STREET BRIDGE SONG"
Composer: Paul Simon
Original Artist: Simon and Garfunkel
Label: Columbia Records; *Recording:* Columbia #9363 (LP)
Release Year: 1966; *Chart:* did not chart
Cover Artist: Harper's Bizarre
Label: Warner Brothers Records; *Recording:* Warner Brothers #5890 (45)
Release Year: 1967; *Chart:* #13 *Billboard* Hot 100

The title of this breezy song is never mentioned in the lyrics. It is often mistakenly called "Feeling Groovy." Written by Paul Simon, the original Simon and Garfunkel version is included on the multiplatinum *Parsley, Sage, Rosemary and Thyme* album from 1966. It was the B-side of "At the Zoo" (Columbia #44046) on a 45 and never charted.

It was the 45 version by Harper's Bizarre that became the definitive hit—reaching number 13 on the Pop charts. It became the only Top 20 hit for this California group.

A few years later, Paul Simon filed a lawsuit against kids' show creators Sid and Marty Krofft because the theme song from *H.R. Pufnstuf* sounded very much like "59th Street Bridge Song." Simon's name was then added to the theme's composer credits.

The Fifty-ninth Street Bridge's official name is the Ed Koch Queensboro Bridge.

"THE FOOL ON THE HILL"
Composers: John Lennon and Paul McCartney
Original Artist: the Beatles
Label: Capitol Records; *Recording:* Capitol #2835 (LP)
Release Year: 1967; *Chart:* did not chart
Cover Artist: Sergio Mendes and Brasil '66

Label: A & M Records; *Recording:* A & M #961 (45)
Release Year: 1968; *Chart:* #6 *Billboard* Hot 100

"The Fool on the Hill" is a song about isolation—a song about a loner who is misunderstood and not taken seriously by others—with Paul McCartney providing the vocals. The song was included on *The Magical Mystery Tour* album, which hit number 1 and went multiplatinum.

"The Fool on the Hill" was remade the following year for the easy listening audience. The 45 by Sergio Mendes and Brasil '66 used a lot of brass and introduced the tune to a very large, new audience. The single hit number 6 on the Pop charts, and it was the title cut (A & M #4160) of a gold album released late in 1968.

"A Fool Such as I"

Composer: Bill Trader
Original Artist: Hank Snow
Label: RCA Victor Records; *Recording:* RCA Victor #5034 (45 and 78)
Release Year: 1952; *Chart:* #4 *Billboard* Country
Cover Artist: Elvis Presley
Label: RCA Victor Records; *Recording:* RCA Victor #7506 (45)
Release Year: 1959; *Chart:* #2 *Billboard* Hot 100

Often called "(Now and Then There's) A Fool Such as I," this original version by Hank Snow, "the Singing Ranger," and the Rainbow Ranch Boys was performed in typical country-and-western fashion in 1952. It's interesting to note that this rendition was on RCA Victor Records, and so were two other versions from the 1950s.

In 1953, an R&B vocal group known as the Robins recorded a haunting ballad version of the song on RCA Victor (#5175). It wasn't a hit but has become a treasured collector's item on 45 rpm.

While Elvis Presley was completing his army stint, his upbeat rendition of the song—yet again on RCA Victor—became a Top 5 two-sided smash ("I Need Your Love Tonight" was on the B-side).

Bob Dylan broke the chain of RCA releases with his Columbia 45 version (#45982) from late in 1973. It peaked at number 55 on the Pop charts.

"Fools Rush In"

Composers: Johnny Mercer and Rube Bloom
Original Artist: Glenn Miller and His Orchestra
Label: Bluebird Records; *Recording:* Bluebird #10728 (78)
Release Year: 1940; *Chart:* #3 *Billboard* Music Hit Parade
Cover Artist: Rick Nelson
Label: Decca Records; *Recording:* Decca #31533 (45)
Release Year: 1963; *Chart:* #12 *Billboard* Hot 100

The lyrics to "Fools Rush In" were written by the prolific Johnny Mercer. The full title on the original Glenn Miller release was "Fools Rush In (Where Angels Fear to Tread)." It featured vocals by Ray Eberle. The payoff line in the song is, "So open up your heart and let this fool rush in."

The tune was covered dozens of times, by the likes of the Four Freshmen, Jo Stafford, and Tommy Dorsey featuring Frank Sinatra. There was even a doo-wop rendition by the Cadets (Modern #1006). There were two Top 30 versions in the early 1960s. Brook Benton recorded his with a very rapid tempo for Mercury Records (#71722), and it peaked at number 24 on the Pop charts.

Likely the best-known rendition of the song came just as Rick Nelson signed with Decca Records in 1963. His reached number 12 on the Pop charts, and the guitar break by the brilliant James Burton was to have profound impact upon a young John Fogerty.

Fools Rush In was also the title of a 1997 motion picture starring Matthew Perry and Salma Hayek from Sony Pictures.

"FOR ONCE IN MY LIFE"
Composers: Ron Miller and Orlando Murden
Original Artist: Barbara McNair
Label: Motown Records; *Recording:* Motown #1123 (45)
Release Year: 1965; *Chart:* did not chart
Cover Artist: Stevie Wonder
Label: Tamla Records; *Recording:* Tamla #54174 (45)
Release Year: 1968; *Chart:* #2 *Billboard* Hot 100 and #2 R&B

Many people mistakenly believe that Stevie Wonder wrote and first recorded this song. It was written for the Motown Record Company in 1965 by Ron Miller and Orlando Murden, expressly for Barbara McNair, and was to be included on her Motown album titled *Here I Am* (Motown #644). For whatever reason, the release of her version was delayed. McNair may have recorded it first, but Jean DuShon released it first as a single (Cadet #5545). DuShon had a style similar to that of Gladys Knight.

Tony Bennett had a version (Columbia #44258) in 1967—performed as a ballad. Even though he has long been associated with popularizing the song, his rendition only reached number 91 on the Pop charts.

The following year, Stevie Wonder recorded a rendition that was amazingly similar to McNair's original—the instrumental track and the tempo were almost identical. The difference—Wonder's version made it all the way to number 2 on both the Pop and R&B charts. It was included on his *For Once in My Life* album (Tamla #291), released early in 1969.

Jackie Wilson had a very minor hit with the song very late in 1968 (Brunswick #55392). His version was recorded as a very emotional ballad, and it only scraped the very bottom of the Hot 100.

McNair briefly had her own syndicated talk/music show—*The Barbara McNair Show*—in 1969. Sadly, she died of a rare nasal cancer on February 4, 2007.

"FOR YOU"

Composers: Johnny Burke and Al Dubin
Original Artist: Glen Gray and His Orchestra
Label: Brunswick Records; *Recording:* Brunswick #6606 (78)
Release Year: 1933; *Chart:* did not chart
Cover Artist: Rick Nelson
Label: Decca Records; *Recording:* Decca #31574 (45)
Release Year: 1963; *Chart:* #6 *Billboard* Hot 100

"For You" was written for the Warner Brothers motion picture, *42nd Street*. The song tells the story of a man who would do anything for his girl, including "gathering stars out of the blue." Glen Gray recorded it first on the Brunswick label in 1933, with Kenny Sargent providing the vocals. For some reason, Gray's version was rereleased in 1957 on Decca Records (#30238). It has been covered by Perry Como, Dean Martin, and even the Ravens, for whom it translated well into R&B for National Records (#9034) in 1947.

Very late in 1963, Rick Nelson was having success remaking old standards such as "Fools Rush In" and "The Very Thought of You." His medium-tempo rock and roll interpretation of "For You" became the biggest of all versions—peaking at number 6 on the Pop charts early in 1964. It might have been even bigger, but coincidentally, Nelson's "For You" reached the Top 10 the same week the Beatles hit number 1 with "I Want to Hold Your Hand."

"FUNNY HOW TIME SLIPS AWAY"

Composer: Willie Nelson
Original Artist: Billy Walker
Label: Columbia Records; *Recording:* Columbia #42050 (45)
Release Year: 1961; *Chart:* #23 *Billboard* Country
Cover Artist: Joe Hinton
Label: Back Beat Records; *Recording:* Back Beat #541 (45)
Release Year: 1964; *Chart:* #13 *Billboard* Hot 100

The year 1961 was good for Willie Nelson. Two songs he wrote became crossover hits in that year—"Crazy" by Patsy Cline (Decca #31317) and "Funny How Time Slips Away" by Jimmy Elledge (RCA Victor #7946). The original version of the latter, however, was a country hit a few months earlier by the tall Texan Billy Walker. Many more versions of this song about running into an old love followed.

Native Floridian Johnny Tillotson had a Top 50 hit on the Pop charts with his version in 1963 on Archie Bleyer's Cadence Records label (#1441)—his final release for Cadence before signing with MGM.

However, the biggest version came about in 1964 on Houston, Texas's, Back Beat Records label by R&B vocalist Joe Hinton. It reached number 13 on the Pop charts and would likely have made Top 10 had the upper regions of the charts not been clogged with a bevy of Beatles singles. The amazing vocal range of Hinton is proven in a final note that can still bring chills to the listener. He also mentions his own name in the line, "You never can tell when Joe Hinton will come back in town."

In the 1970s, Dorothy Moore had a minor hit with a remake of the song, and the Spinners did, too, in the 1980s.

G

"THE GAMBLER"
Composer: Don Schlitz
Original Artist: Don Schlitz
Label: Capitol Records; *Recording:* Capitol #4576 (45)
Release Year: 1978; *Chart:* #65 *Billboard* Country
Cover Artist: Kenny Rogers
Label: United Artists Records; *Recording:* United Artists #1250 (45)
Release Year: 1978; *Chart:* #16 *Billboard* Hot 100

This country crossover hit was written by Don Schlitz, who recorded the first version for Capitol Records. This original rendition was a minor hit on the Country chart. Country legend Bobby Bare also recorded a rendition on his *Bare* album for Columbia Records (#35314) in 1978.

However, a version of the song on the United Artists label by Kenny Rogers was released very late in 1978 and peaked at number 16 on the Pop charts in 1979. The cards were definitely in Rogers's favor as "The Gambler" kicked off ten consecutive Top 20 hits.

"GEE WHIZ"
Composers: Jeanne Vikki and Jimmie Thomas
Original Artist: Bob and Earl
Label: Class Records; *Recording:* Class #231 (45 and 78)
Release Year: 1958; *Chart:* did not chart
Cover Artist: the Innocents
Label: Indigo Records; *Recording:* Indigo #111 (45)
Release Year: 1960; *Chart:* #28 *Billboard* Hot 100

The Bob and Earl who charted in the 1960s were different from the Bob and Earl who recorded in the 1950s. Well, actually, they were 50 percent different—in the sixties the Bob was Bobby Relf, and in the fifties the Bob was Bobby Day. The

Earl, Earl Nelson, was the same in both incarnations. While still having the original Bob, they recorded a ballad for Leon René's Class Records label titled "Gee Whiz," but it was not a hit. One of the co-writers of the song, however—Jimmie Thomas—was in reality the Class label owner, Leon René, under an alias.

This "Gee Whiz" was covered late in 1960 by the Innocents—the group that had backed up Kathy Young on "A Thousand Stars." This time "Gee Whiz" became a Top 30 hit, early in 1961. Coincidentally, "Gee Whiz" by Carla Thomas (Atlantic #2086), a totally different song, was on the chart at the same time.

"Georgia on My Mind"

Composer: Hoagy Carmichael
Original Artist: Hoagy Carmichael
Label: RCA Victor Records; *Recording:* RCA Victor #23013 (78)
Release Year: 1930; *Chart:* did not chart
Cover Artist: Ray Charles
Label: ABC-Paramount Records; *Recording:* ABC-Paramount #10135 (45)
Release Year: 1960; *Chart:* #1 *Billboard* Hot 100 and #3 R&B

This song from the Grammy Hall of Fame was likely written with some ambiguity so that it could interchangeably be about the state or a woman. The great Hoagy Carmichael wrote it and recorded the original version (he performed the vocals). It wasn't a big hit for Carmichael, but many cover versions did well, including one by Paul Whiteman on RCA Victor (#22880) in 1931.

The biggest hit came in 1960 when a native of Georgia named Ray Charles recorded it flawlessly, and it reached number 1 on the Pop charts. This rendition won two Grammy Awards—Best Vocal Performance Single or Track, Male and Best Performance by a Pop Single Artist. It was included on the Top 10 album titled *The Genius Hits the Road* (ABC-Paramount #335).

Willie Nelson added his own inimitable touch to "Georgia on My Mind" in 1978 (Columbia #10704), and it became a number 1 hit on the Country chart and even cracked the bottom of the Pop charts.

Charles's rendition was later used as the opening theme for CBS's sitcom titled *Designing Women*. It is also Georgia's state song.

"Get Together"

Composer: Chet Powers
Original Artist: We Five
Label: A & M Records; *Recording:* A & M #784 (45)
Release Year: 1965; *Chart:* #31 *Billboard* Hot 100
Cover Artist: the Youngbloods
Label: RCA Victor Records; *Recording:* RCA Victor #9752 (45)
Release Year: 1969; *Chart:* #5 *Billboard* Hot 100

"Get Together" is a song that was not, by any means, an overnight success. It was written by Dino Valenti, whose alias was Chet Powers. Jerry Burgan of We Five remembered, "Just like our first hit, 'You Were on My Mind,' this song was produced by Frank Werber for Trident Productions. The Kingston Trio released it first on their 1964 album, *Back in Town* [Capitol #2081], but it was never released as a single. Our original 45 version was titled 'Let's Get Together,' and it made Top 40 late in 1965, but it took until 1967 for it to appear on our *Make Someone Happy* album [A & M #4138]."

Jesse Colin Young and the Youngbloods recorded the song for RCA Victor in 1967 (#9264). Now known simply as "Get Together," the record did not even make the Top 50 this first time around. However, because of its use as the theme for a Public Service Announcement for the National Conference of Christians and Jews, interest in the song mounted, the 45 was rereleased (now as RCA #9752), and in the summer of 1969 it finally became a Top 5 hit and sold over a million copies.

"GINA"

Composers: Paul Vance and Leon Carr
Original Artist: Johnny Janis
Label: Columbia Records; *Recording:* Columbia #41797 (45)
Release Year: 1960; *Chart:* did not chart
Cover Artist: Johnny Mathis
Label: Columbia Records; *Recording:* Columbia #42582 (45)
Release Year: 1962; *Chart:* #6 *Billboard* Hot 100

There are connections between the two artists who recorded a song about a young lady named "Gina"—both were released on the Columbia Records label, and both singers were named Johnny. The original by the Johnny with the last name of Janis, however, was performed much slower and did not make the charts.

The 1962 cover version by the other Johnny was a bit of a comeback hit—Mathis had been out of the Top 20 for over two years. His rendition of "Gina" was recorded a bit faster than the Janis original, and it became his first of two consecutive Top 10 hits (the second was "What Will My Mary Say?" on Columbia #42666).

"GIRL WATCHER"

Composers: Buck Trail and Wayne Pittman
Original Artist: Ginger Thompson
Label: 123 Records; *Recording:* 123 Records #1702 (45)
Release Year: 1968; *Chart:* did not chart
Cover Artist: the O'Kaysions
Label: North State Records; *Recording:* North State #1001 (45)
Release Year: 1968; *Chart:* #5 *Billboard* Hot 100

This song changed genders before becoming a hit. If was first seen from the female perspective by Ginger Thompson, who recorded "Boy Watcher." It was not a hit, but it did inspire a million-selling cover.

Seeing the lyrics from the male point of view proved to be the right way to go. A blue-eyed soul group known as the O'Kaysions first released their take on the song for the tiny North State label from North Carolina. It was now called "Girl Watcher" and employed a very similar arrangement to the original. When the record started to catch on, it was leased to ABC Records (#11094). It became a Top 5 smash. The group's success was short-lived, however, and they never again made Top 50. The tune was included on the *Girl Watcher* album released late in 1968 (ABC #664).

"Girls, Girls, Girls (Made to Love)"
Composer: Phil Everly
Original Artist: the Everly Brothers
Label: Warner Brothers Records; *Recording:* Warner Brothers #1395 (LP)
Release Year: 1960; *Chart:* did not chart
Cover Artist: Eddie Hodges
Label: Cadence Records; *Recording:* Cadence #1421 (45)
Release Year: 1962; *Chart:* #14 *Billboard* Hot 100

Child star Eddie Hodges had quite a résumé, having been on Broadway in *The Music Man* and in the film *A Hole in the Head* with Frank Sinatra. Hodges also had a big Top 20 hit with "I'm Gonna Knock on Your Door" one year earlier. He cracked that very same Top 20 one more time with another cover song on Archie Bleyer's Cadence Record Label, "Girls, Girls, Girls (Made to Love)." Hodges said,

> Archie played Phil Everly's original demo version of "Made to Love." Phil had also written the song. The Everlys were my favorite artists at the time and I was eager to record it. Archie didn't tell me, however, that the Everlys had also recorded a studio version of the song with the intention of releasing it. If I had known, I would've been too intimidated to record it at all. In retrospect, it's probably better that I was in the dark about their cut. So, I recorded it, and Archie didn't like how the first session sounded in New York City, so we flew to Nashville and recorded it again at Owen Bradley Studios there with Charlie McCoy and his band. Archie was right, it did sound better. It was the first of my records for which I learned to play on the guitar and accompany myself. Much later, in Los Angeles, I saw Phil Everly and got to play it for him on his guitar. That was a treat! However, The Everly Brothers studio version remains my favorite version of the song to this day.

Eddie Hodges in the recording studio, guided by the great Lincoln Chase.
Courtesy of Eddie Hodges

It's interesting to note that the Everly Brothers' version was released, not on Cadence, but rather on the Warner Brothers label on the album titled *A Date with the Everly Brothers*. Eddie Hodges, a native of Mississippi, was recently inducted into the Mississippi Musicians Hall of Fame.

"Give Us Your Blessing"
Composers: Jeff Barry and Ellie Greenwich
Original Artist: Ray Peterson
Label: Dunes Records; *Recording:* Dunes #2025 (45)
Release Year: 1963; *Chart:* #70 *Billboard* Hot 100
Cover Artist: the Shangrilas
Label: Red Bird Records; *Recording:* Red Bird #030 (45)
Release Year: 1965; *Chart:* #29 *Billboard* Hot 100

This song, written by Jeff Barry and Ellie Greenwich, was perfect fodder for Ray Peterson. Previously, he had success with a tragedy song called "Tell Laura I Love Her" (RCA Victor #7745), and "Give Us Your Blessing" was definitely in the same mold. It told the tale of two young people very much in love who ask for their parents' blessing to be wed. When that blessing doesn't come, they take their own lives—heavy stuff for 1963.

Ray Peterson's original rendition, produced by Jerry Leiber and Mike Stoller, was not a big hit. However, the Shangrilas recorded the definitive version in 1965 on Leiber and Stoller's Red Bird Records label. Much like Ray Peterson, the Shangrilas had success in the past with a tragedy song—"Leader of the Pack" (Red Bird #014). Their version of "Give Us Your Blessing" made Top 30.

"Gloria"
Composer: Leon René
Original Artist: Buddy Baker and His Orchestra
Label: Exclusive Records; *Recording:* Exclusive #218 (78)
Release Year: 1946; *Chart:* did not chart
Cover Artist: the Mills Brothers
Label: Decca Records; *Recording:* Decca #24509 (78)
Release Year: 1948; *Chart:* #17 *Billboard* Hot 100

Not to be confused with the hit by Shadows of Knight nor the hit by Laura Branigan of the same name, this song titled "Gloria" was to become a doo-wop standard in the 1950s. The very first version, however, by Buddy Baker and His Orchestra with Bob Hayward on vocals, was pure pop. Cover versions were plentiful from the likes of Ray Anthony and Johnny Moore's Three Blazers (with Charles Brown). The Mills Brothers made it a hit on the Decca label in 1948.

There was then a gap until the next version was released by the Cadillacs (Josie #765) in 1954. It was the group's first release and became legendary in later years, but initially it was a poor seller. It's interesting to note that many of the original lyrics had changed. Intact was the "Gloria, it's not Marie, it's Gloria" line. Leon René was not credited on the record—in fact, no one was credited

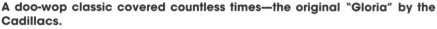

A doo-wop classic covered countless times—the original "Gloria" by the Cadillacs.

(there was no writer's name under the song's title). Sadly, the Cadillacs' affable and beloved lead singer, Earl "Speedo" Carroll, died on November 25, 2012, only a couple of weeks after his seventy-fifth birthday.

Inspired by the Cadillacs' rendition (and lyrics), several artists in the doo-wop realm covered this song, including Vito and the Salutations (Rayna #5009) and the Passions (Audicon #106). It has long been a favorite choice of a cappella vocal groups. The "Gloria" recorded by the doo-wop group called the Chariots on Time Records (#1006) is a wholly different tune.

"THE GLORY OF LOVE"
Composer: Billy Hill
Original Artist: Benny Goodman
Label: RCA Victor Records; *Recording:* RCA Victor #25316 (78)

The number 1 R&B rendition of Billy Hill's composition "The Glory of Love" by the legendary Five Keys.

Release Year: 1936; *Chart:* #1 *Billboard* Music Hit Parade
Cover Artist: the Five Keys
Label: Aladdin Records; *Recording:* Aladdin #3099 (45 and 78)
Release Year: 1951; *Chart:* #1 *Billboard* R&B

Not to be confused with the Peter Cetera song of the same name, "The Glory of Love" was written by Billy Hill and first became a hit for Benny Goodman and His Orchestra in 1936. The song's lyrics list the good and the bad, the ups and downs, the yin and yang of romance, all under the umbrella of "the story of, the glory of love."

This standard became quite popular among the African American community during the 1950s and early 1960s—especially among doo-wop singers. It was covered by the Skylarks (Decca #48241), the Hollywood Four Flames (recorded in Hollywood #165), the Velvetones (Aladdin #3372), and the Angels (Gee #1024) to name a few, but the biggest one came in 1951 from a group called the Five Keys from Newport News, Virginia. It became a number 1 hit on the R&B charts and it stayed there for four weeks.

"The Glory of Love" also became a minor hit for Otis Redding, the Dells, and Don Gardner and Dee Dee Ford. A version by Jacqueline Fontaine was included in the soundtrack for the hit 1967 motion picture *Guess Who's Coming to Dinner*.

"Go Away, Little Girl"
Composers: Carole King and Gerry Goffin
Original Artist: Steve Lawrence
Label: Columbia Records; *Recording:* Columbia #42601 (45)
Release Year: 1962; *Chart:* #1 *Billboard* Hot 100

A rare answer to Steve Lawrence's "Go Away, Little Girl" is "(I Won't) Go Way, Little Girl" by Jennie Smith.

Cover Artist: Donny Osmond
Label: MGM Records; *Recording:* MGM #14285 (45)
Release Year: 1971; *Chart:* #1 *Billboard* Hot 100

"Go Away, Little Girl" tells the tale of a guy who is making every attempt to remain faithful to his girlfriend by resisting the advances of a beautiful younger woman. It was composed by Brill Building legends Carole King and Gerry Goffin, and early in 1963 it became Steve Lawrence's only number 1 hit. A singer named Jennie Smith quickly released an answer song titled "(I Won't) Go Way, Little Girl" (Canadian American #150), but it wasn't a hit.

A few months later, the song was covered by Bobby Vee on his *The Night Has a Thousand Eyes* album (Liberty #7285), but it was never released as a single.

A group from New Jersey called the Happenings released a version, produced by the Tokens on their B. T. Puppy Records label (#522). Bob Miranda of the Happenings said,

> It was one of those great Carole King compositions. She used to come into the Tokens' office quite often to play songs she thought would be ideal for the Happenings. I was a bit reluctant at first, because it had been a number 1 hit for Steve Lawrence only four years earlier, and this was to be our follow-up to "See You in September." With follow-ups, you need to be very careful or you become a one-hit wonder. My fears were in vain, because it came out really good and established "the Happenings' sound." It wasn't as big as "See You in September," but it was a big hit in its own right.

"Go Away, Little Girl" joined a very elite grouping in 1971 when it was remade by Donny Osmond. Just like the Steve Lawrence original, it hit number 1. Both number 1 renditions sold well over a million copies each.

"Go Where You Wanna Go"

Composer: John Phillips
Original Artist: the Mamas and the Papas
Label: Dunhill Records; *Recording:* Dunhill #50006 (LP)
Release Year: 1966; *Chart:* did not chart
Cover Artist: the Fifth Dimension
Label: Soul City Records; *Recording:* Soul City #753 (45)
Release Year: 1967; *Chart:* #16 *Billboard* Hot 100

"Go Where You Wanna Go" is a song about breaking up. The singer is attempting to be supportive in the line, "Go where you wanna go, do what you wanna do." The singer is also attempting to be strong with a stiff upper lip, but is sorely missing the significant other after only a week apart. It was composed by John Phillips of the Mamas and the Papas and was included on the group's *If You Can Believe Your Eyes and Ears* album from 1966.

Just a year later, a very similar version released on 45 became the first hit for the Fifth Dimension on Johnny Rivers's Soul City Records label. The members of this group had been around for a while, many getting their start in unsuccessful groups called the Intervals and the Versatiles. Eleven more Top 20 hits followed for the Fifth Dimension. "Go Where You Wanna Go" was included on their *Up, Up and Away* album (Soul City #92000).

The song was used in the 2011 TV commercials for the Medicare advantage plan called Elderplan.

"GONE"

Composer: Smokey Rogers
Original Artist: Terry Preston
Label: Capitol Records; *Recording:* Capitol #2298 (45 and 78)
Release Year: 1953; *Chart:* did not chart
Cover Artist: Ferlin Husky and His Hush Puppies
Label: Capitol Records; *Recording:* Capitol #3628 (45 and 78)
Release Year: 1957; *Chart:* #4 *Billboard* Hot 100

Ferlin Husky recorded under a couple of aliases, and in fact, he released the original version of "Gone" as Terry Preston in 1953 on Capitol Records. It was not a hit that time around, but he covered his own song four years later using his real name and the second time was the charm. "Gone" became a Top 5 smash. The song tells the tale of how empty life has become "since you've gone."

Husky's rendition had a country feel, but another version some fifteen years later had more of a big Broadway flair. That updated Top 30 version came from actress/singer Joey Heatherton on MGM Records (#14387). She became quite famous for her sultry Serta Mattress TV commercials of the 1970s.

"GREENBACK DOLLAR"

Composer: Hoyt Axton
Original Artist: Hoyt Axton
Label: Horizon Records; *Recording:* Horizon #1601 (LP)
Release Year: 1962; *Chart:* did not chart
Cover Artist: the Kingston Trio
Label: Capitol Records; *Recording:* Capitol #4898 (45)
Release Year: 1963; *Chart:* #21 *Billboard* Hot 100

"Greenback Dollar" was written and originally recorded by Hoyt Axton on his *The Balladeer: Recorded Live at the Troubador* album. It's a song about a man with a gypsy soul who loves to travel and has little concern about money.

Axton's version wasn't a hit, but the cover version by the Kingston Trio was. In fact, it just missed the Top 20 in 1963. This version was included on the Trio's *The New Frontier* album (Capitol #1809) on which it is cut one on side one.

Axton also wrote a few other even more famous songs—"The No No Song" by Ringo Starr and "Joy to the World" and "Never Been to Spain," both by Three Dog Night.

"GREETINGS, THIS IS UNCLE SAM"
Composer: Peter Bennett
Original Artist: the Valadiers
Label: Miracle Records; *Recording:* Miracle #6 (45)
Release Year: 1961; *Chart:* #89 *Billboard* Hot 100

The first of two Motown-related versions of "Greetings, This Is Uncle Sam"— here by the Valadiers.

Cover Artist: the Monitors
Label: VIP Records; *Recording:* VIP #25032 (45)
Release Year: 1966; *Chart:* #100 *Billboard* Hot 100 and #21 R&B

Both versions of this ballad were released on Motown-related record labels. The rendition by the Valadiers is interesting—this was one of the first white groups to record for Motown. The composer on early copies of this version is listed as simply P. Bennett, while later copies list Robert Bateman, Brian Holland, the Valadiers, and Ronald Dunbar.

The second version of the song is by an African American group called the Monitors on Motown's VIP Records label. Both renditions are very similar. The song opens as a typical doo-wop ballad. The singer has received a draft notice and bemoans leaving his girl, family, and way of life behind to go off to fight in a foreign war. Near the end, a drill sergeant disrupts the smooth ballad and gives the tune a very rough edge. The unpopular Vietnam War rendered the 1966 version a much bigger hit.

Richard Street, who sang lead on this version, passed away suddenly on February 27, 2013.

"A GROOVY KIND OF LOVE"
Composers: Toni Wine and Carole Bayer Sager
Original Artist: Patti LaBelle and the Bluebelles
Label: Atlantic Records; *Recording:* Atlantic #8119 (LP)
Release Year: 1966; *Chart:* did not chart
Cover Artist: the Mindbenders
Label: Fontana Records; *Recording:* Fontana #1541 (45)
Release Year: 1966; *Chart:* #2 *Billboard* Hot 100

This groovy love song was written on a whim very quickly by Toni Wine and Carole Bayer Sager. If you were "in with the in-crowd" in 1965, you used the word *groovy* to describe good things, positive things. Of course, love is a very good and positive thing. The original rendition of the song by Diane and Annita on Wand Records was released in the United Kingdom, but the first release in the United States was by Patti LaBelle and the Bluebelles on the Atlantic label. LaBelle made some great music while with Atlantic, but had no big hits with them.

The rendition by the Mindbenders was released three months after LaBelle's. Previously known as Wayne Fontana and the Mindbenders, Fontana left the band shortly after "The Game of Love" (Fontana #1509) became a number 1 hit in 1965, and the group from then on was known as simply the Mindbenders. "A Groovy Kind of Love" in 1966 hit number 2 on the Pop charts, kept out of number 1 by Percy Sledge's "When a Man Loves a Woman" (Atlantic #2326).

The song did indeed hit number 1, however, in a remake by Phil Collins (Atlantic #89017) in 1988 (even though the word *groovy* had long ago become passé). This rendition was included in the soundtrack for the MGM motion picture *Buster*, which starred Phil Collins. Collins portrayed Buster Edwards, and his "A Groovy Kind of Love" sold well over a million copies.

H

"HARBOR LIGHTS"
Composers: Hugh Williams and Jimmy Kennedy
Original Artist: Frances Langford
Label: Decca Records; *Recording:* Decca #1441 (78)
Release Year: 1937; *Chart:* did not chart
Cover Artist: the Platters
Label: Mercury Records; *Recording:* Mercury #71563 (45)
Release Year: 1960; *Chart:* #8 *Billboard* Hot 100

"Harbor Lights" goes back a long way. It was first recorded by Frances Langford, who later found success in TV and radio as the world's most unhappy bride, Blanche Bickerson of *The Bickersons*. Her original rendition of "Harbor Lights" led to dozens more by the likes of Sammy Kaye, Bing Crosby, Guy Lombardo, and Ray Anthony.

The tune transitioned into R&B/rock and roll in 1951 when it was recorded by Clyde McPhatter and the Dominoes (Federal #12010). This version was not a hit, but one by another R&B vocal group named the Platters reached number 8 on the Pop charts in 1960. It opened with the sounds of the sea—splashing water, seagulls, and a ship's horn. It became the final Top 10 hit for the group.

Elvis Presley recorded a version in his days at Sun Records in the 1950s, but it wasn't released until years later.

"HAVE YOU HEARD?"
Composers: Lew Douglas, Charles LaVere, and Roy Rodde
Original Artist: Joni James
Label: MGM Records; *Recording:* MGM #11390 (45 and 78)
Release Year: 1953; *Chart:* #4 *Billboard* Hot 100
Cover Artist: the Duprees
Label: Coed Records; *Recording:* Coed #585 (45)
Release Year: 1963; *Chart:* #18 *Billboard* Hot 100

"Have You Heard?" is a song that became a hit twice—a decade apart. The first hit version was by balladeer Joni James, who had a long string of successes on the

MGM label in the 1950s. The song, here performed from the female perspective, tells of an old girlfriend who is still interested in what her ex-boyfriend is doing. She obviously still has feelings for the guy, and asks her friends if they've heard anything about him.

A vocal group from Jersey City, New Jersey, known as the Duprees recorded the song in 1963 from the male perspective, asking about an ex-girlfriend this time around. The beautiful ballad became a hit again—making Top 20 only a few weeks before the Beatles hit it big in the United States. It was the title cut from their second album (Coed #906). Prior to "Have You Heard?" the Duprees remade another Joni James song, "Why Don't You Believe Me?" (Coed #584) with slightly less success (see the entry for that song).

"HE AIN'T HEAVY, HE'S MY BROTHER"
Composers: Bobby Scott and Bob Russell
Original Artist: Kelly Gordon
Label: Capitol Records; *Recording:* Capitol #2442 (45)
Release Year: 1969; *Chart:* did not chart
Cover Artist: the Hollies
Label: Epic Records; *Recording:* Epic #10532 (45)
Release Year: 1969; *Chart:* #7 *Billboard* Hot 100

Written by two guys named Bob (Scott and Russell), "He Ain't Heavy, He's My Brother" is a heavy and powerful song about unconditional love. The first version by Kelly Gordon in 1969 was released as both a single, and on an album (*That's Life*). It was not a hit.

Later that same year, however, a much better recording became the definitive hit version. The Hollies made it a Top 10 smash and used it as the title cut of a Top 40 album in 1970 (Epic #26538).

Neil Diamond released his rendition on a 45 in 1970 (Uni #55264) and it reached the Top 20.

"HEART AND SOUL"
Composers: Hoagy Carmichael and Frank Loesser
Original Artist: Larry Clinton and His Orchestra
Label: RCA Victor Records; *Recording:* RCA Victor #26046 (78)
Release Year: 1938; *Chart:* #1 *Billboard* Music Hit Parade
Cover Artist: the Cleftones
Label: Gee Records; *Recording:* Gee #1064 (45)
Release Year: 1961; *Chart:* #18 *Billboard* Hot 100

Much like Hoagy Carmichael's "Georgia on My Mind," this composition of his also led a long and varied life. The first rendition by Larry Clinton and His

Orchestra (and vocalist Bea Wain) reached number 1. Other hit versions by the Four Aces and Eddy Duchin kept the song alive and popular.

"Heart and Soul" was a perfect fit for the doo-wop and rock and roll era, and many versions were recorded—the Spaniels (Vee Jay #301), the Four Buddies (Savoy #817), and Jan and Dean (Challenge #9111). The biggest doo-wop version, however, came from Herbie Cox and the Cleftones. The melody on this version was a bit different from the others, but the lyrics were identical.

"Heart and Soul" was the song Tom Hanks played while dancing on the piano on the floor of the toy store scene of the classic 1988 20th Century Fox motion picture *Big*.

"HE'LL HAVE TO GO"
Composers: Audrey and Joe Allison
Original Artist: Billy Brown
Label: Columbia Records; *Recording:* Columbia #41380 (45)
Release Year: 1959; *Chart:* did not chart
Cover Artist: Jim Reeves
Label: RCA Victor Records; *Recording:* RCA Victor #7643 (45)
Release Year: 1959; *Chart:* #2 *Billboard* Hot 100

"He'll Have to Go" is a telephone conversation in song. The singer is trying to reclaim his ex-girlfriend on the other end. He insists that she "tell that friend there with you, he'll have to go."

Billy Brown recorded the little-known original version in early 1959 for Columbia Records. It went unnoticed.

However, the cover version by Jim Reeves for RCA Victor became a monster hit early in 1960 and sold over a million copies. "He'll Have to Go" was so big, there was even a Top 5 answer record. Jeanne Black (Capitol #4368) released "He'll Have to Stay" very quickly and it, too, sold over a million copies. In this rebuttal she rebuffs the ex-boyfriend's attempts at reconciliation.

"He'll Have to Go" was also later covered by Elvis Presley on RCA on his *Moody Blue* album (RCA #2428) from 1977.

"HELLO, MARY LOU"
Composer: Gene Pitney
Original Artist: Johnny Duncan
Label: Leader Records; *Recording:* Leader #812 (45)
Release Year: 1960; *Chart:* did not chart
Cover Artist: Ricky Nelson
Label: Imperial Records; *Recording:* Imperial #5741 (45)
Release Year: 1961; *Chart:* #9 *Billboard* Hot 100

The hit version of "Hello, Mary Lou," by Ricky Nelson—a cover of Johnny Duncan's original.

"Hello, Mary Lou" was written by Gene Pitney and was originally recorded by Johnny Duncan on the small Leader label in 1960. The title on this release was "Hello, Mary Lou, Goodbye Heart." It was not a very inspired recording and was not a hit.

One year later, the title was shortened to merely "Hello, Mary Lou" and it was placed on the B-side of "Travelin' Man" by Ricky Nelson. The A-side was so big, even the B-side caught on, and this Gene Pitney composition entered the Top 10 as well. This was the final 45 released as by Ricky Nelson. After this one, Ricky dropped the *y* from his first name.

"HERE COMES THE SUN"
Composer: George Harrison
Original Artist: the Beatles

Label: Apple Records; *Recording:* Apple #383 (LP)
Release Year: 1969; *Chart:* did not chart
Cover Artist: Richie Havens
Label: Stormy Forest Records; *Recording:* Stormy Forest #656 (45)
Release Year: 1971; *Chart:* #16 *Billboard* Hot 100

"Here Comes the Sun" is one of the few songs on which "the Quiet Beatle" got to shine. George Harrison wrote it and sang lead, and it was included on the *Abbey Road* album in 1969. It wasn't released as a single, but became one of the most famous cuts on that Apple LP. It's a song about a long, cold winter finally coming to an end—the ice is melting, the sun is out, temperatures are rising, and people are smiling. It's definitely a "glass half full" song.

In 1971, Harrison performed the song live at the Concert for Bangladesh. In that same year, Richie Havens released his version on a 45, and it made Top 20. This version features a very long (over a minute) instrumental open. It was included on Havens's *Alarm Clock* album (Stormy Forest #6005). Havens had the distinction of opening the Woodstock Music and Art Fair in 1969. Havens died at the age of seventy-two on April 22, 2013.

"HERE YOU COME, AGAIN"
Composers: Barry Mann and Cynthia Weil
Original Artist: B. J. Thomas
Label: MCA Records; *Recording:* MCA #2286 (LP)
Release Year: 1977; *Chart:* did not chart
Cover Artist: Dolly Parton
Label: RCA Victor Records; *Recording:* RCA #11123 (45)
Release Year: 1977; *Chart:* #3 *Billboard* Hot 100

Much like "I Just Can't Help Believing," for another Barry Mann and Cynthia Weil composition, the first version released was not the hit version. "Here You Come, Again" debuted on the eponymous *B. J. Thomas* album on MCA Records (#2286) during the late summer of 1977. It's a tune about an involuntarily rekindled romance. Thomas said, "I recorded that song in Memphis. Both versions were note-for-note almost identical."

Very late in 1977, a million-selling cover version brought Dolly Parton to the forefront. She had previously had success on the Country charts, but early in 1978 this became her first big crossover hit. She remained at RCA Records until the middle 1980s.

"HE'S A REBEL"
Composer: Gene Pitney
Original Artist: Vikki Carr
Label: Liberty Records; *Recording:* Liberty #55493 (45)

Vikki Carr recorded it first, but the Crystals made "He's a Rebel" famous.

Release Year: 1962; *Chart:* did not chart
Cover Artist: the Crystals
Label: Philles Records; *Recording:* Philles #106 (45)
Release Year: 1962; *Chart:* #1 *Billboard* Hot 100

Produced by Snuff Garrett, "He's a Rebel" was originally recorded by Vikki Carr—indeed the same Vikki Carr who had a major hit five years later with "It Must Be Him." Her rendition of "He's a Rebel," however, did not make the charts for her in 1962. Phil Spector was A&R (artist and repertoire) man at Liberty Records and quickly brought the song, written by Gene Pitney, over to his own Philles Records label (where it became a number 1 hit by the Crystals). However, the real Crystals were on tour at the time of the recording session, and because Spector wanted to release it in a hurry, he used Darlene Love and the Blossoms, under the guise of the Crystals. By proxy, it became Darlene Love's only number

1 hit. She was inducted into the Rock and Roll Hall of Fame in 2011 and has appeared on *The Late Show with David Letterman*'s Christmas show for decades.

"HOLD ME, THRILL ME, KISS ME"
Composer: Harry Noble
Original Artist: Karen Chandler
Label: Coral Records; *Recording:* Coral #60831 (45 and 78)
Release Year: 1953; *Chart:* #5 *Billboard* Hot 100
Cover Artist: Mel Carter
Label: Imperial Records; *Recording:* Imperial #66113 (45)
Release Year: 1965; *Chart:* #8 *Billboard* Hot 100

This tender ballad became a Top 10 hit twice. The first version of "Hold Me, Thrill Me, Kiss Me," sold over a million copies on the Coral label for Karen Chandler, who, for the most part, was a one-hit wonder and never again hit the Top 10.

A marginally successful R&B vocal group rendition of the song by Sonny Til and the Orioles (Jubilee #5108) in that same year garnered some airplay on the R&B stations. The Orioles were just months away from scoring their biggest hit, "Crying in the Chapel" (see the entry for that song).

Actor/singer Mel Carter released his powerful take on the tune in 1965 for the Imperial Records label. Carter had previously recorded for Sam Cooke's Derby label, and he became the second artist to have a major hit with "Hold Me, Thrill Me, Kiss Me." About the song, Mel Carter said, "I never met Karen Chandler and hadn't listened to her recording of the song. The song was selected for me by Bob Skaff, A&R man for Imperial/Liberty Records. It was his choice to record it, not mine. I remember that I had to be directed to sing on the beat with the chorus and only had the freedom to stray in the bridge of the song. In those days, I considered myself a jazz singer [smile]. Nick DeCaro was the arranger on the song and it was his first writing assignment." It became Carter's biggest single, and his *Hold Me, Thrill Me, Kiss Me* album (Imperial #12289) sold well late in 1965. Carter added, "In later years when I auditioned for acting roles, I often got better and bigger parts if I mentioned I was the singer of 'Hold Me, Thrill Me, Kiss Me.'"

"HOOKED ON A FEELING"
Composer: Mark James
Original Artist: B. J. Thomas
Label: Scepter Records; *Recording:* Scepter #12230 (45)
Release Year: 1968; *Chart:* #5 *Billboard* Hot 100
Cover Artist: Blue Swede
Label: EMI Records; *Recording:* EMI #3627 (45)
Release Year: 1974; *Chart:* #1 *Billboard* Hot 100

Released late in 1968 and peaking at number 5 on the Pop charts in 1969, "Hooked on a Feeling" by B. J. Thomas was a million-selling smash. It featured a very distinctive electric sitar opening and closing.

Five years later, a unique rendition of "Hooked on a Feeling" by a Swedish group named Blue Swede consisted of an unforgettable "hook"—an "Oogah chocka oogah oogah" a cappella opening chant. This new version of the classic soared to number 1 on the Pop charts, and it, too, sold over a million copies.

So how did B. J. Thomas feel about this version? Thomas said, "It didn't bother me. I didn't write the song. Maybe if I had written it I might have felt differently. In the technical sense, it wasn't a cover record—it came about five years after mine and that was plenty of time. I don't like it when someone covers a song while it's on the charts—I think that's wrong. I was very happy for the composer of the song, Mark James. In the long run, it probably even created new interest in my original version."

"HOUSE AT POOH CORNER"
Composer: Kenny Loggins
Original Artist: the Nitty Gritty Dirt Band
Label: United Artists Records; *Recording:* United Artists #50769 (45)
Release Year: 1970; *Chart:* #53 *Billboard* Hot 100
Cover Artist: Loggins and Messina
Label: Columbia Records; *Recording:* Columbia #45664 (45)
Release Year: 1972; *Chart:* did not chart

The classic Winnie the Pooh stories from A. A. Milne inspired this song, written by Kenny Loggins. There are references to Pooh's famous adventures (such as getting a honey jar stuck on his nose) and Pooh's friends Eeyore, Owl, and Christopher Robin. The first version of the song was not by the composer, but rather the Nitty Gritty Dirt Band. It was included on their album titled *Uncle Charlie and His Dog Teddy* (Liberty #7642).

Kenny Loggins did finally record his own version of the song in 1972 in a duet with Jim Messina. It was included on their *Sittin' In* album (Columbia #31044). In 1994, Loggins recorded a sequel titled "Return to Pooh Corner" on a kid's album of the same name (Sony Wonder #57674).

"HOW AM I SUPPOSED TO LIVE WITHOUT YOU?"
Composer: Michael Bolton
Original Artist: Laura Branigan
Label: Atlantic Records; *Recording:* Atlantic #89805 (45)
Release Year: 1983; *Chart:* #12 *Billboard* Hot 100
Cover Artist: Michael Bolton
Label: Columbia Records; *Recording:* Columbia #73017 (45)
Release Year: 1989; *Chart:* #1 *Billboard* Hot 100

"How Am I Supposed to Live without You?" is a sad ballad about finding out and coping with the fact that one's significant other has found another and is leaving. In 1983, Michael Bolton had not yet had a solo hit. He was a struggling songwriter and placed this song with the red-hot Laura Branigan as a follow-up to "Gloria" and "Solitaire." It did very well and reached number 12 on the Pop charts.

Bolton had the opportunity to record his own version six years later when his solo career was in full swing. It became the Connecticut blue-eyed soul man's first number 1 hit and also his biggest hit. It was included on the gold album *Soul Provider* (Columbia #45012).

"HURTING EACH OTHER"
Composers: Gary Geld and Peter Udell
Original Artist: Jimmy Clanton
Label: Mala Records; *Recording:* Mala #500 (45)
Release Year: 1965; *Chart:* did not chart
Cover Artist: the Carpenters
Label: A & M Records; *Recording:* A & M #1322 (45)
Release Year: 1972; *Chart:* #2 *Billboard* Hot 100

The story of "Hurting Each Other" began in 1965. Singer Jimmy Clanton had recently signed with the Mala Records label and he remembered, "Brian Hyland brought me the song and I liked it a lot. I recorded it, it was released, and quickly forgotten. C'est la vie."

There were a few more unsuccessful cover versions by the Walker Brothers, Ruby and the Romantics, and even Rosemary Clooney. It took until very early in 1972 for the song to become a hit when it was recorded by the red-hot Carpenters on Herb Alpert and Jerry Moss's A & M label. It climbed all the way to number 2 on the Pop charts—kept out of number 1 by Harry Nilsson's "Without You" (RCA Victor #0604). It was included on the Carpenters' *A Song for You* album (A & M #3511).

"HUSHABYE"
Composers: Doc Pomus and Mort Shuman
Original Artist: the Mystics
Label: Laurie Records; *Recording:* Laurie #3028 (45)
Release Year: 1959; *Chart:* #20 *Billboard* Hot 100
Cover Artist: the Beach Boys
Label: Capitol Records; *Recording:* Capitol #5267 (EP)
Release Year: 1964; *Chart:* did not chart

"Hushabye" was composed by the prolific songwriting team of Doc Pomus and Mort Shuman, who also wrote numerous songs for the Drifters and Elvis Presley. George Galfo of the original Mystics recalled, "They wrote two monster hits within one week. The other song, 'A Teenager in Love,' was originally written for us, but was given to Dion and the Belmonts. What a great job they did with it." The Mystics, a quintet of Italian American guys from Brooklyn, got to record the other monster hit titled "Hushabye." Like "A Teenager in Love," it was released on Laurie Records. Nationally, the record peaked at number 20 on the Pop charts, but it fared even better in the bigger U.S. cities (and especially on the East Coast).

Five years later, a quintet known as the Beach Boys from three thousand miles away remade the song and repopularized the tune. It was included on their *4 by the Beach Boys* EP (extended play 45), from which came "Wendy" and "Little Honda."

Other covers of the song from Jay and the Americans (United Artists #50535) and Robert John (Atlantic #2884) kept the song top of mind for several years.

George Galfo offered his opinion of those cover versions: "The Beach Boys rendition of 'Hushabye' is terrific, as is the Jay and the Americans rendition. I feel very honored that these two groups recorded cover versions of our song. Never in my wildest dreams did I think I would be in a group with charted hits, and then get to meet and work with all the great recording artists I watched on TV and listened to on the radio. What a blast!"

I

"I Can't Stop Loving You"

Composer: Don Gibson
Original Artist: Don Gibson
Label: RCA Victor Records; *Recording:* RCA Victor #7133 (45)
Release Year: 1958; *Chart:* #81 *Billboard* Hot 100
Cover Artist: Ray Charles
Label: ABC-Paramount Records; *Recording:* ABC-Paramount #10330 (45)
Release Year: 1962; *Chart:* #1 *Billboard* Hot 100

"I Can't Stop Loving You" was a B-side for two different artists before it became a hit. It was composed by Don Gibson, and its first appearance was as the B-side of a Top 10 country crossover hit titled "Oh, Lonesome Me" from 1958. That time around, that B-side peaked at number 81.

Roy Orbison was next in line. He released "I Can't Stop Loving You" as the B-side of a moderate hit called "I'm Hurtin'" late in 1960. Orbison's take on the song was indeed different, beginning with the "those happy hours that we once knew" line instead of the title. This version did not chart.

Both the song's composer, Don Gibson, and Roy Orbison recorded "I Can't Stop Loving You" before Ray Charles.

The next time the song was released, however, it became legendary. "The Genius of Soul," Ray Charles, recorded that truly inspired rendition in 1962, and it soared to number 1 on the Pop charts and stayed there for five consecutive weeks. On the R&B charts, it was on top for ten weeks. It was the biggest single of the year, and the album from whence it came, *Modern Sounds in Country and Western Music* (ABC-Paramount #410), spent an amazing fourteen weeks atop the chart. Despite the album's country and western title, "I Can't Stop Loving You" won a Grammy for Best Rhythm and Blues Recording. It was inducted into the Grammy Hall of Fame in 2001. Both the single and the album garnered gold records for Brother Ray.

"I CAN'T STOP TALKING ABOUT YOU"
Composers: Carole King and Gerry Goffin
Original Artist: Tobin Matthews
Label: Warner Brothers Records; *Recording:* Warner Brothers #5398 (45)
Release Year: 1963; *Chart:* did not chart
Cover Artist: Steve Lawrence and Eydie Gorme
Label: Columbia Records; *Recording:* Columbia #42932 (45)
Release Year: 1963; *Chart:* #35 *Billboard* Hot 100

Pop singer Tobin Matthews recorded for a bevy of record labels (Chief, Columbia, USA), but not with a lot of success. Even on a major label like Warner Brothers with a song written by Carole King and Gerry Goffin, it just wasn't meant to be.

However, when that perky King and Goffin song titled "I Can't Stop Talking about You" was recorded by Steve Lawrence and Eydie Gorme, it became a Top 40 entry. Lawrence previously had success with King and Goffin's "Go Away, Little Girl," and Gorme struck gold with their "Blame It on the Bossa Nova." Gorme died at the age of eighty-four on August 10, 2013.

"I FOUND SOMEONE"
Composer: Michael Bolton
Original Artist: Laura Branigan
Label: Atlantic Records; *Recording:* Atlantic #89451 (45)
Release Year: 1986; *Chart:* #90 *Billboard* Hot 100
Cover Artist: Cher
Label: Geffen Records; *Recording:* Geffen #28191 (45)
Release Year: 1987; *Chart:* #10 *Billboard* Hot 100

"I Found Someone" was the second of two Michael Bolton compositions recorded by Laura Branigan. The first one, "How Am I Supposed to Live without You?" was a much bigger hit (see the entry for that song).

The following year, Cher kicked off one of her many comebacks with a Top 10 remake of this ballad about starting anew after a rocky relationship. It was included as the first cut on her platinum album simply titled *Cher* (Geffen #24164) from 1987.

"I GOT RHYTHM"
Composers: George and Ira Gershwin
Original Artist: Loring "Red" Nichols
Label: Brunswick Records; *Recording:* Brunswick #6711 (78)
Release Year: 1930; *Chart:* #2 *Billboard*
Cover Artist: the Happenings
Label: B. T. Puppy Records; *Recording:* B. T. Puppy #527 (45)
Release Year: 1967; *Chart:* #3 *Billboard* Hot 100

This Gershwin tune, "I Got Rhythm," originated in the Ethel Merman and Ginger Rogers Broadway musical *Girl Crazy* in 1930. The show debuted at the Alvin Theatre, and in 1943 became a hit MGM musical motion picture starring Mickey Rooney and Judy Garland.

The first recording of "I Got Rhythm" was an instrumental interpretation by Loring "Red" Nichols on Brunswick Records in 1930. Louis Armstrong quickly released his rendition in 1931 on a Columbia 78. Many big names have recorded the song—Bing Crosby, Peggy Lee, Ella Fitzgerald, Glenn Miller, Ethel Waters, and Sarah Vaughan to name a few.

"I Got Rhythm" enjoyed renewed popularity in 1951 when it was included in the soundtrack for Gene Kelly's classic MGM motion picture *An American in Paris*.

One of the biggest chart versions, and certainly one of the most unique and creative, came to be in 1967 when a New Jersey vocal group known as the Happenings put their stamp on it. It became their biggest hit—a Top 3 smash—and Bob Miranda of the Happenings remembered,

> I loved the title of the song. We were searching for an old song which, lyrically, would stand up in 1967. We went to the 1930s for this one, and we did change a couple of lyrics in the second verse. I wrote the intro to the song, and I was nervous about that. I mean, this was a Gershwin tune, and I was adding to it, but the publishers never said a word about that. It's the only record we did which, when it was played back in the studio, I was 100 percent certain was going to be a giant hit. It sounded perfect. My instincts were right on. It became our biggest hit.

"I JUST CAN'T HELP BELIEVING"
Composers: Barry Mann and Cynthia Weil
Original Artist: Bobby Vee
Label: Liberty Records; *Recording:* Liberty #7612 (LP)
Release Year: 1969; *Chart:* did not chart
Cover Artist: B. J. Thomas
Label: Scepter Records; *Recording:* Scepter #12283 (45)
Release Year: 1970; *Chart:* #9 *Billboard* Hot 100

Before this catchy Barry Mann and Cynthia Weil composition became a hit single, it was included on a couple of unsuccessful 1969 LPs—Bobby Vee's *Gates, Grills and Railings* and Leonard Nimoy's *The Touch of Leonard Nimoy* (Dot #25910).

Finally, in 1970, the first 45 and the definitive version of "I Just Can't Help Believing" was released. The artist, B. J. Thomas, remembered, "It was produced in Memphis by the great Chips Moman. What I remember most was that it took a couple of days to get it right. We did a lot of takes, but it was all worth it when the record caught on. A short time after my version, Elvis Presley recorded it and his rendition was very, very good." Presley's version was included on the *That's the Way It Is* album (RCA Victor #4445).

The year 1970 was a great one for B. J. Thomas. Earlier that year, his "Raindrops Keep Fallin' on My Head" (Scepter #12265) hit number 1.

"I KNEW YOU WHEN"

Composer: Joe South
Original Artist: Wade Flemons
Label: Vee Jay Records; *Recording:* Vee Jay #614 (45)
Release Year: 1964; *Chart:* did not chart
Cover Artist: Billy Joe Royal
Label: Columbia Records; *Recording:* Columbia #43390 (45)
Release Year: 1965; *Chart:* #14 *Billboard* Hot 100

Joe South sang on a couple of his own hit records—"Games People Play" and "Walk a Mile in My Shoes" for Capitol Records. He also wrote many popular songs for others, such as "Hush" for Deep Purple (Tetragrammaton #1503) and "Down in the Boondocks" for Billy Joe Royal (Columbia #43305).

Another Joe South composition, "I Knew You When," eventually became a hit cover record for Billy Joe Royal, but the first version was quite good, too. It was performed by Wade Flemons on the Vee Jay label in 1964. Despite being a well-produced product, it failed to chart. Likely, it got very little promotion, as Vee Jay in 1964 was immersed in releasing product by the red-hot Beatles. Billy Joe Royal released his rendition one year later, and had the definitive and memorable Top 20 hit version.

Linda Ronstadt attempted to repopularize the song late in 1982 (Asylum #69853), but despite a lot of airplay, it barely cracked the Top 40. All three versions contain several strings of "Yeahs."

"I LOVE HOW YOU LOVE ME"

Composers: Barry Mann and Larry Kolber
Original Artist: the Paris Sisters
Label: Gregmark Records; *Recording:* Gregmark #6 (45)
Release Year: 1961; *Chart:* #5 *Billboard* Hot 100
Cover Artist: Bobby Vinton
Label: Epic Records; *Recording:* Epic #10397 (45)
Release Year: 1968; *Chart:* #9 *Billboard* Hot 100

Without question, "I Love How You Love Me" was one of the softest records of 1961. There were many big names associated with the record—Barry Mann co-wrote the song, Lester Sill and Lee Hazlewood owned the label, and Phil Spector was the supervisor and arranger. Albeth, Sherrell, and Priscilla Paris—

collectively the Paris Sisters—hailed from San Francisco and had this one big hit. Even though the group was a one-hit wonder, the song was not.

Seven years after the original Paris Sisters rendition, almost out of nowhere, a struggling Bobby Vinton successfully remade the song, had a Top 10 hit, and sold well over a million copies. It led to the *I Love How You Love Me* album early in 1969 (Epic #26437).

"I LOVE YOU, BECAUSE"

Composer: Leon Payne
Original Artist: Leon Payne
Label: Capitol Records; *Recording:* Capitol #40238 (78)
Release Year: 1949; *Chart:* #1 *Billboard* Country
Cover Artist: Al Martino
Label: Capitol Records; *Recording:* Capitol #4930 (45)
Release Year: 1963; *Chart:* #3 *Billboard* Hot 100

Leon Payne wrote and performed the first version of "I Love You, Because" for Capitol Records in 1949. The record was a number 1 country hit for Payne, who, despite recording for a half dozen other labels, never matched that success. His song, however, has been covered numerous times.

Elvis Presley recorded a rendition on his 1956 *Elvis Presley* album (RCA Victor #1254). The LP hit number 1 and garnered a gold record for Presley. It was also released on a 45 (RCA #6639). Presley's version began with whistling and really exemplified his southern, genuine country side.

Just like the Leon Payne version from 1949, Al Martino released his 1963 version on Capitol Records and had a Top 3 smash. Martino's popularity was cut short in 1964 when another act on Capitol Records usurped the Pop charts. Martino got to play Johnny Fontane in the original *Godfather* movie in 1972.

"I LOVE YOU MADLY"

Composer: Charles Jones
Original Artist: Charlie and Ray
Label: Herald Records; *Recording:* Herald #438 (45 and 78)
Release Year: 1954; *Chart:* did not chart
Cover Artist: the Four Coins
Label: Epic Records; *Recording:* Epic #9082 (45 and 78)
Release Year: 1955; *Chart:* #28 *Billboard* Hot 100

Charlie and Ray were way ahead of their time. Easily the first openly gay performers of the rock and roll era, in 1954 they caused quite a stir. Even though their original version of "I Love You Madly" didn't hit the charts, it got a lot of airplay and sold well in the big cities of the United States. Their stage performances were like no other.

"I Love You Madly" was covered by a pop vocal group from Canonsburg, Pennsylvania, known as the Four Coins very early in 1955, and briefly reached the Top 30 on the Pop charts. The group's chart success earned them a spot in the 1957 Warner Brothers rock and roll motion picture *Jamboree*.

"I MISS YOU SO"

Composers: Jimmie Henderson, John Scott, and Sid Robin
Original Artist: the Cats and the Fiddle
Label: RCA Victor Records; *Recording:* RCA Victor #4393 (45 and 78)
Release Year: 1940; *Chart:* #20 *Billboard* Music Popularity Chart
Cover Artist: Chris Connor
Label: Atlantic Records; *Recording:* Atlantic #1105 (45 and 78)
Release Year: 1956; *Chart:* #34 *Billboard* Hot 100

This beautiful ballad about reminiscing and pining for a former romantic interest has been recorded dozens of times. The first successful version came from the Cats and the Fiddle, an African American vocal group who, along with the Mills Brothers and Ink Spots, had immense influence upon the earliest doo-wop groups of rock and roll's infancy—among them, Sonny Til and the Orioles, who released their version twice in the 1950s with modest success (Jubilee #5051 and #5107).

However, perhaps the most popular version of the song came in 1956 from Chris Connor—among the first white artists to record for the Atlantic Records label. Connor's version made Top 40—a feat repeated in 1959 with Canadian Paul Anka (ABC-Paramount #10011) and again late in 1965 with Little Anthony and the Imperials (DCP #1149).

"I ONLY HAVE EYES FOR YOU"

Composers: Harry Warren and Al Dubin
Original Artist: Ben Selvin
Label: Columbia Records; *Recording:* Columbia #2936 (78)
Release Year: 1934; *Chart:* #2 *Billboard*
Cover Artist: the Flamingos
Label: End Records; *Recording:* End #1046 (45 and 78)
Release Year: 1959; *Chart:* #11 *Billboard* Hot 100 and #3 R&B

The musical *Dames* spawned some very famous songs—among them, "I Only Have Eyes for You." The Warner Brothers musical starred Dick Powell, Joan Blondell, and Ruby Keeler. The earliest known recording of the tune came from Ben Selvin and His Orchestra, with Howard Phillips on vocals in 1934.

The haunting ballad has been recorded many times, including an early R&B interpretation by a seminal doo-wop group known as the Swallows (King

#4533). It's likely this is the version that inspired the Flamingos to record theirs in 1959—the most famous version of all. Recorded for George Goldner's End Records label, it became a big hit on the Pop and R&B charts. This rendition was included in the soundtrack for motion pictures such as *American Graffiti* and *Something's Gotta Give*. It's interesting to note that the Flamingos recorded two other songs from the musical *Dames*—"Love Walked In" and "Goodnight Sweetheart."

Art Garfunkel's take on the song in 1975 (Columbia #10190) became a Top 20 hit—introducing it to a whole new generation.

"I ONLY WANT TO BE WITH YOU"
Composers: Mike Hawker and Ivor Raymonde
Original Artist: Dusty Springfield
Label: Philips Records; *Recording:* Philips #40162 (45)
Release Year: 1964; *Chart:* #12 *Billboard* Hot 100
Cover Artist: Bay City Rollers
Label: Arista Records; *Recording:* Arista #0205 (45)
Release Year: 1976; *Chart:* #12 *Billboard* Hot 100

"I Only Want to Be with You" is all about meeting the ideal person and wanting to spend a lot of time with him or her. In 1964, it became the first of a string of hits for Dusty Springfield.

No version of "I Only Want to Be with You" made Top 10, but it was a hit three times around. The second hit version came from a Scottish group who were supposed to rival the success of the Beatles. They didn't quite live up to expectations, but they did manage to have four Top 20 hits, and their remake of Springfield's song was one of them. Coincidentally, both versions peaked at number 12 on the Pop charts.

"I Only Want to Be with You" was a hit in the 1960s and the 1970s, so it was attempted again in the 1980s. Nicolette Larson, famous for "Lotta Love," released a rendition in 1982 (Warner Brothers #29948). It got a lot of airplay, but only peaked at number 53. Samantha Fox tried yet again in 1989 (Jive #1192) with similar results.

"I REALLY DON'T WANT TO KNOW"
Composers: Don Robertson and Howard Barnes
Original Artist: Les Paul and Mary Ford
Label: Capitol Records; *Recording:* Capitol #2735 (45 and 78)
Release Year: 1954; *Chart:* #11 *Billboard* Hot 100
Cover Artist: Elvis Presley
Label: RCA Victor Records; *Recording:* RCA Victor #9960 (45)
Release Year: 1970; *Chart:* #21 *Billboard* Hot 100

"I Really Don't Want to Know" is a song of curiosity. The singer wonders how many times his lover has been in love. The singer is curious but really doesn't want to know. Les Paul and Mary Ford recorded it first and hit number 11 on the Pop charts.

Others who have covered the song include the Flamingos, Eddy Arnold, Tommy Edwards, Solomon Burke, Esther Phillips, and Ronnie Dove. Even Elvis Presley covered the song, and in 1971 his version just missed the Top 20. It sold a million copies and was included on the *Elvis Country (I'm 10,000 Years Old)* album (RCA Victor #4460).

"I WILL ALWAYS LOVE YOU"
Composer: Dolly Parton
Original Artist: Dolly Parton
Label: RCA Victor Records; *Recording:* RCA Victor #0234 (45)
Release Year: 1974; *Chart:* #1 *Billboard* Country
Cover Artist: Whitney Houston
Label: Arista Records; *Recording:* Arista #12490 (CD)
Release Year: 1992; *Chart:* #1 *Billboard* Hot 100

"I Will Always Love You" took a while to become a Pop hit. It was originally released on Dolly Parton's *Jolene* album (RCA Victor #0473) and became a number 1 hit single on the Country chart, but it did not cross over. In 1982, Parton rereleased the song for the Universal motion picture *The Best Little Whorehouse in Texas*. The movie starred Parton and Burt Reynolds, and when released as a single this time, "I Will Always Love You" made the Pop charts, but only got as high as number 53.

A decade later, the emotional ballad was recorded by the red hot Whitney Houston. It became her tenth number 1 single, her biggest hit, and her signature song. It was number 1 for fourteen weeks and went multiplatinum. It was included in the soundtrack for the Kevin Costner Warner Brothers motion picture *The Bodyguard*. Houston portrayed Rachel Marron in the film.

"I WILL FOLLOW HIM"
Composers: Paul Mauriat, Franck Pourcel, Norman Gimbel, Jacques Plante, and Arthur Altman
Original Artist: Petula Clark
Label: Laurie Records; *Recording:* Laurie #3156 (45)
Release Year: 1963; *Chart:* did not chart
Cover Artist: Little Peggy March
Label: RCA Victor Records; *Recording:* RCA Victor #8139 (45)
Release Year: 1963; *Chart:* #1 *Billboard* Hot 100 and #1 R&B

Originally an instrumental called "Chariot," this song brought Petula Clark a lot of success in the vocal version—and she performed it in several different languages. Strangely, her later 1963 English version on Pye Records in the United Kingdom and on Laurie Records in the United States was not a hit.

When rerecorded by Little Peggy March (real name: Margaret Battavio), the song caught on quickly. It was produced by Hugo Peretti and Luigi Creatore and hit number 1 on both the Pop and R&B charts. March became the youngest female artist to have a number 1 hit—at the tender age of fifteen. It became her only Top 10 hit. In 1989, she portrayed herself in the TV movie titled *My Boyfriend's Back*.

The song was made popular again by its inclusion in the soundtrack for the popular 1992 Whoopi Goldberg Touchstone motion picture titled *Sister Act*.

"I Write the Songs"
Composer: Bruce Johnston
Original Artist: the Captain and Tennille
Label: A & M Records; *Recording:* A & M #4552 (LP)
Release Year: 1975; *Chart:* did not chart
Cover Artist: Barry Manilow
Label: Arista Records; *Recording:* Arista #0157 (45)
Release Year: 1975; *Chart:* #1 *Billboard* Hot 100

Bruce Johnston was not only a member of the Rip Chords of "Hey, Little Cobra" fame (Columbia #42921); he was also a longtime Beach Boy. Oh, and he also wrote a very famous song called "I Write the Songs."

The tune first appeared on the *Love Will Keep Us Together* album by the Captain and Tennille in the spring of 1975. It was the final cut on the album and was never released as a single.

Then, shortly thereafter, the song appeared on a David Cassidy album produced by Bruce Johnston titled *The Harder They Climb* (RCA Victor #1066), but "I Write the Songs" still wasn't a hit.

Finally, late in 1975, Barry Manilow released his version and it became a number 1 hit, his biggest hit, a million-seller, and a Grammy winner for Song of the Year in 1976. "I Write the Songs" was included on the *Trying to Get the Feeling Again* album (Arista #4060). Because of the song's title, many mistakenly believe that Barry Manilow wrote it.

"If I Had a Hammer"
Composers: Pete Seeger and Lee Hays
Original Artist: the Weavers
Label: People's Artists Hootenanny Records; *Recording:* Hootenanny #101 (78)
Release Year: 1950; *Chart:* did not chart

Cover Artist: Peter, Paul and Mary
Label: Warner Brothers Records; *Recording:* Warner Brothers #5296 (45)
Release Year: 1962; *Chart:* #10 *Billboard* Hot 100

Pete Seeger and Lee Hays wrote "If I Had a Hammer" and even sang on the first version of it with the Weavers in 1950 on the tiny People's Artists Hootenanny Records label. The song was not a hit—yet.

Over a dozen years later when the folk music craze began to mushroom, Peter, Paul and Mary turned the Weavers' modest protest song into a Top 10 hit—their first of six. Suddenly, they had a song to sing all over this land.

It was "hammer time" again a year later when Latino singer Trini Lopez covered the song (Reprise #198) and had the biggest hit version. Lopez's rendition reached number 3 on the Pop charts. Two years later, Lopez covered another Peter, Paul and Mary song, "Lemon Tree" (Reprise #0336), and had another Top 20 smash.

"IF I WERE A CARPENTER"

Composer: Tim Hardin
Original Artist: Bobby Darin
Label: Atlantic Records; *Recording:* Atlantic #2350 (45)
Release Year: 1966; *Chart:* #8 *Billboard* Hot 100
Cover Artist: the Four Tops
Label: Motown Records; *Recording:* Motown #1124 (45)
Release Year: 1968; *Chart:* #20 *Billboard* Hot 100 and #17 R&B

Written by Tim Hardin, "If I Were a Carpenter" created numerous scenarios in the lyrics—a lot of "what ifs" about a relationship. Recorded by Bobby Darin (occasionally at this time calling himself Bob Darin), it became a comeback hit in 1966 (and Darin's tenth and final Top 10 hit). It sold extremely well, despite the fact that it wasn't the sound one came to expect from Darin.

"If I Were a Carpenter" made Top 20 again two years later when covered by Motown's Four Tops. There was one more trip into the Top 40 for the song in 1970 in a country crossover rendition by Johnny Cash and June Carter (Columbia #45064).

To attempt to repay the favor, Darin wrote a song for Tim Hardin, "Simple Song of Freedom" in 1970 (Columbia #44920). It reached the Top 50.

"IF NOT FOR YOU"

Composer: Bob Dylan
Original Artist: Bob Dylan
Label: Columbia Records; *Recording:* Columbia #30290 (LP)
Release Year: 1970; *Chart:* did not chart
Cover Artist: Olivia Newton-John
Label: Uni Records; *Recording:* Uni #55281 (45)
Release Year: 1971; *Chart:* #25 *Billboard* Hot 100

Written by Bob Dylan, "If Not for You" made its first appearance on his *New Morning* album in 1970. It was a Top 10 gold album, but the song was not released as a single in the United States.

The song's next appearance was on a 1970 George Harrison album titled *All Things Must Pass* (Apple #639). Once again, the song was not released as a single in the United States.

Finally, in 1971, an Australian singer named Olivia Newton-John released her take on the song on a 45. It became her first chart record, peaking at number 25. More importantly, it kicked off a career that spawned fifteen Top 10 hits.

"I'LL BE THERE"
Composer: Bobby Darin
Original Artist: Bobby Darin
Label: Atco Records; *Recording:* Atco #6167 (45)

In between Bobby Darin's original and the hit version by Gerry and the Pacemakers, the Uptones released their rendition of "I'll Be There."

Release Year: 1960; *Chart:* #79 *Billboard* Hot 100
Cover Artist: Gerry and the Pacemakers
Label: Laurie Records; *Recording:* Laurie #3279 (45)
Release Year: 1964; *Chart:* #14 *Billboard* Hot 100

Not to be confused with the Jackson Five classic of the same name, this "I'll Be There" was written and originally performed by Bobby Darin in 1960. It was a minor hit on the flip side of "Won't You Come Home, Bill Bailey."

On its second go-round, the song was recorded by a California doo-wop group known as the Uptones (Lute #6225) in 1962 on the B-side of their regional hit called "No More." This group also made several records as the Senders.

The third time around was the charm. Very late in 1964, Gerry and the Pacemakers released their take on "I'll Be There" and had the definitive hit version, which just missed the Top 10 early in 1965.

"I'M A FOOL TO CARE"
Composer: Ted Daffan
Original Artist: Ted Daffan's Texans
Label: Okeh Records; *Recording:* Okeh #05573 (78)
Release Year: 1940; *Chart:* did not chart
Cover Artist: Joe Barry
Label: Jin Records; *Recording:* Jin #144 (45)
Release Year: 1961; *Chart:* #24 *Billboard* Hot 100

"I'm a Fool to Care" is a song about unrequited love, originally written and performed by Ted Daffan in 1940. A flurry of cover versions followed from Les Paul and Mary Ford, Jim Reeves, Connie Francis, Ray Charles, Oscar Black, and even a Philadelphia R&B vocal group called the Castelles.

Besides the Top 10 version by Les Paul and Mary Ford, the rendition most often remembered is by Louisiana native Joe Barry on the tiny Jin Records label. He was a white recording artist who sounded a lot like Fats Domino on his version of "I'm a Fool to Care." The record caught on, and the Jin label leased the record to Smash Records (#1702). It became Barry's biggest hit—and he never again reached the Top 30. In 2013, the song was used in TV commercials for Southern Comfort.

"I'M GONNA BE STRONG"
Composers: Barry Mann and Cynthia Weil
Original Artist: Frankie Laine
Label: Columbia Records; *Recording:* Columbia #42884 (45)
Release Year: 1963; *Chart:* did not chart
Cover Artist: Gene Pitney
Label: Musicor Records; *Recording:* Musicor #1045 (45)
Release Year: 1964; *Chart:* #9 *Billboard* Hot 100

Sounding similar to Fats Domino, New Orleans' Joe Barry covered the old standard "I'm a Fool to Care."

Even having a major label, a major recording star, and a song written by a very consistent and prolific team does not guarantee a hit record. Such was the case when Frankie Laine recorded a powerful ballad written by Barry Mann and Cynthia Weil on the Columbia Records label. The combination looked good on paper, but this original version of the song didn't make the charts.

However, a year later as the follow-up to "It Hurts to Be in Love" (see the entry for that song), Gene Pitney covered "I'm Gonna Be Strong" and truly made it his own. It was his fourth and final Top 10 record.

"I'M NOT IN LOVE"
Composers: Eric Stewart and Graham Gouldman
Original Artist: 10cc
Label: Mercury Records; *Recording:* Mercury #73678 (45)

Release Year: 1975; *Chart:* #2 *Billboard* Hot 100
Cover Artist: Will to Power
Label: Epic Records; *Recording:* Epic #73636 (45)
Release Year: 1990; *Chart:* #7 *Billboard* Hot 100

Likely inspired by Phil Spector's "wall of sound," "I'm Not in Love" by 10cc employed layer upon layer upon layer of overdubbed voices to produce a chorus-like effect. The song tells the tale of a man trying to convince himself that he's not in love. Obviously, that love is not reciprocated, as the almost psychedelic midsection of the song repeats the words "big boys don't cry" in a whisper. This was 10cc's biggest chart hit, although they did make Top 10 again with the catchy "The Things We Do for Love" in 1977.

"I'm Not in Love" reached the Top 10 again in 1990—this time by a racially mixed R&B group known as Will to Power. They remade the song in rather a smooth jazz fashion. It should be noted that this rendition did not contain the "big boys don't cry" part of the song. Previously, this group from Florida had chart success making a medley out of "Baby, I Love Your Way" by Peter Frampton and "Freebird" by Lynyrd Skynyrd.

"I'M SO LONESOME I COULD CRY"

Composer: Hank Williams
Original Artist: Hank Williams
Label: MGM Records; *Recording:* MGM #10560 (78)
Release Year: 1949; *Chart:* did not chart
Cover Artist: B. J. Thomas
Label: Pacemaker Records; *Recording:* Pacemaker #227 (45)
Release Year: 1964; *Chart:* #8 *Billboard* Hot 100

"I'm So Lonesome I Could Cry" by Hank Williams was on the B-side of the smash hit "My Bucket's Got a Hole in It." Even though it wasn't technically a hit in its own right, it is extremely famous and has been covered by countless artists.

Among those who remade this Hank Williams classic is Texan B. J. Thomas who recalled,

> The song was covered about seventy-two times by the time I did it. My dad loved Hank Williams's music and he requested that I record the song. At the time, I was recording with a group known as the Triumphs and I wanted to sing R&B songs. However, being a good son, I recorded the song in three takes and it was placed on the B-side of a 45. Wouldn't you know it, disc jockeys in Houston started playing that B-side and the record caught on and became a number 1 hit in Houston. At that point Scepter Records [#12129] picked up the record from the tiny Pacemaker label and—thanks to my dad—I had my first national Top 10 record. Father really does know best.

"I'M YOUR PUPPET"

Composers: Dan Penn and Spooner Oldham
Original Artist: Dan Penn
Label: MGM Records; *Recording:* MGM #13415 (45)
Release Year: 1965; *Chart:* did not chart
Cover Artist: James and Bobby Purify
Label: Bell Records; *Recording:* Bell #648 (45)
Release Year: 1966; *Chart:* #6 *Billboard* Hot 100 and #5 R&B

The co-writer of "I'm Your Puppet" recorded the first version, a nice blue-eyed soul take on the tune on the MGM label in 1965. It's a song about a man who is so much in love, he doesn't mind being totally controlled by the woman in his life. This original rendition of the song was not a hit; that would occur one year later.

A duo known as James and Bobby Purify—a pair of cousins from Florida—covered the song in 1966 on the Bell Records label, and it became a Top 10 hit on both the Pop and R&B charts. Their fame was short-lived, as they were unable to have a "string" of hits.

"I'm Your Puppet" was recently used in TV commercials for Nike.

"IN THE MOOD"

Composer: Joe Garland
Original Artist: Glenn Miller and His Orchestra
Label: Bluebird Records; *Recording:* Bluebird #10416 (78)
Release Year: 1939; *Chart:* #1 *Billboard* Music Hit Parade
Cover Artist: Ernie Fields
Label: Rendezvous Records; *Recording:* Rendezvous #110 (45)
Release Year: 1959; *Chart:* #4 *Billboard* Hot 100

Truly one of the most famous instrumentals of all time, "In the Mood" by Glenn Miller was released in 1939 and became a number 1 hit in 1940. It was written by Joe Garland and consisted of a series of musical triplets and arpeggios. Miller's version was inducted into the Grammy Hall of Fame in 1983.

Just about twenty years after the original, the public was "in the mood" to hear the song again, so it was reworked for the burgeoning rock and roll market. Recorded by the Ernie Fields Orchestra on Southern California's tiny Rendezvous Records label, "In the Mood" was once again a Top 5 hit.

"INDIAN RESERVATION"

Composer: John D. Loudermilk
Original Artist: Marvin Rainwater
Label: MGM Records; *Recording:* MGM #12865 (45)
Release Year: 1959; *Chart:* did not chart

Cover Artist: the Raiders
Label: Columbia Records; *Recording:* Columbia #45332 (45)
Release Year: 1971; *Chart:* #1 *Billboard* Hot 100

Composed by the prolific John D. Loudermilk, "Indian Reservation" began in 1959 as "Pale-Faced Indian" by Marvin Rainwater, who was one-quarter Cherokee. Not politically correct today, the song bemoaned the treatment of Native Americans who were placed on reservations while being stripped of all their customs. This first version of the song also included Native American chants and a few lyrics that were removed in later recordings.

The second time around, the tune was retuned and recorded by British artist Don Fardon as "(The Lament of the Cherokee) Indian Reservation" (GNP Crescendo #405). This seldom-heard rendition made Top 20 in 1968.

However, bigger things were still ahead for this Loudermilk lament. In 1971, Paul Revere and the Raiders, listed solely as the Raiders on the label, recorded the definitive rendition of "Indian Reservation." Much more like Don Fardon's version than Marvin Rainwater's, it became the group's only number 1 hit and went multiplatinum.

"Is That All There Is?"

Composers: Jerry Leiber and Mike Stoller
Original Artist: Dan Daniels
Label: Epic Records; *Recording:* Epic #10297 (45)
Release Year: 1968; *Chart:* did not chart
Cover Artist: Peggy Lee
Label: Capitol Records; *Recording:* Capitol #2602 (45)
Release Year: 1969; *Chart:* #11 *Billboard* Hot 100

This was quite a departure from the compositions we were used to hearing from Jerry Leiber and Mike Stoller. It tells the tale of life's disappointments and was first recorded in the spring of 1968 by radio personality Dan Daniels. Most of the song is spoken—only the chorus is sung. This version was not a hit.

The song was instantly covered by Leslie Uggams and Tony Bennett, but when Peggy Lee recorded it in 1969, magic happened. The song's co-writer, Mike Stoller, said that, of all of his compositions, "Hound Dog" by Willie Mae Thornton and "Is That All There Is?" by Peggy Lee are his proudest moments. The latter, at over four minutes in length, was one of the longest songs on the radio at that time. It just missed the Top 10 and garnered Lee a Grammy for Best Female Pop Vocal Performance. The song was inducted into the Grammy Hall of Fame in 1999. And that's all there is.

"IT DOESN'T MATTER ANYMORE"
Composer: Paul Anka
Original Artist: Buddy Holly
Label: Coral Records; *Recording:* Coral #62074 (45)
Release Year: 1959; *Chart:* #13 *Billboard* Hot 100
Cover Artist: Linda Ronstadt
Label: Asylum Records; *Recording:* Asylum #4050 (45)
Release Year: 1975; *Chart:* #47 *Billboard* Hot 100

Written by Paul Anka, this historic song was recorded by Buddy Holly in 1958. Unlike earlier Holly releases, this and the flip side, "Raining in My Heart," were recorded with a full orchestra conducted by Dick Jacobs. The two-sided hit was released posthumously—in fact, less than three weeks after Holly's death in that tragic plane crash that also claimed the young lives of Ritchie Valens and the Big Bopper. If you think about it, both sides of the record had rather prophetic titles.

Years later, Linda Ronstadt had a great deal of success covering songs by both Smokey Robinson and Buddy Holly. Her "It's So Easy" (Asylum #45438) reached number 5, her "That'll Be the Day" (Asylum #45340) peaked at number 11, and her take on "It Doesn't Matter Anymore" as a ballad reached number 47 in 1975. Don McLean also covered the song on his *Chain Lightning* album (Millennium #7756) in 1981.

Buddy Holly was in the first group of inductees into the Rock and Roll Hall of Fame in Cleveland in 1986. His induction was presented by John Fogerty.

"IT HURTS TO BE IN LOVE"
Composers: Howard Greenfield and Helen Miller
Original Artist: Neil Sedaka
Label: RCA Victor Records; *Recording:* RCA Victor Demo (45)
Release Year: Unreleased; *Chart:* did not chart
Cover Artist: Gene Pitney
Label: Musicor Records; *Recording:* Musicor #1040 (45)
Release Year: 1964; *Chart:* #7 *Billboard* Hot 100

This was supposed to be a Neil Sedaka 45 on RCA Victor Records. It was even co-written by Sedaka's usual songwriting partner, Howard Greenfield. However, Sedaka recalled a fly in the ointment:

> I heard the song and I flipped out. I went in and made a finished demo that sounded like a master. I then went to my label, RCA Victor, and I told them I wanted to put it out. However, they said that I would have to rerecord it because my contract plainly stated that I

must record everything in their studios. I tried that, but those takes of "It Hurts to Be in Love" never did compare to that original demo I did. A couple of weeks later, Gene Pitney heard the song, wiped my voice off as lead singer, and put his own voice on it.

The "it hurts" in the song's title definitely rings true. Gene Pitney had the Top 10 hit with the song and even an *It Hurts to Be in Love* album (Musicor #3019) in 1964. Sedaka added, "It became a Top 10 hit for Pitney but with my piano and my 'Oohs' and 'Ahhs' in the background."

"IT'S ALL IN THE GAME"
Composers: Charles Dawes and Carl Sigman
Original Artist: Tommy Edwards
Label: MGM Records; *Recording:* MGM #11035 (78)
Release Year: 1951; *Chart:* #18 *Billboard* Hot 100
Cover Artist: Tommy Edwards
Label: MGM Records; *Recording:* MGM #12688 (45 and 78)
Release Year: 1958; *Chart:* #1 *Billboard* Hot 100 and #1 R&B

Tommy Edwards joins Neil Sedaka ("Breaking Up Is Hard to Do") and the Dells ("Oh, What a Night") as one of a very elite group of artists who had a hit with different versions of the same song years apart. Edwards's original 1951 rendition of "It's All in the Game" was slower and backed by violins. The first time around, the song peaked at number 18 on the charts.

Seven years later, the tune was updated, but again recorded by Tommy Edwards and again released on MGM Records. It was an even bigger hit, reaching number 1 on both the Pop and R&B charts the second time around. This version has been included in several motion pictures, including MGM's *Diner* in 1982 and Universal's *October Sky* in 1999. The song was a hit yet again when covered by British superstar Cliff Richard in 1963 (Epic #9633)—reaching number 25 on the Pop charts. Charles Dawes, who cowrote the song as "Melody in A-Major," was Calvin Coolidge's vice president.

"IT'S MY PARTY"
Composers: John Gluck, Wally Gold, and Herb Weiner
Original Artist: Helen Shapiro
Label: Epic Records; *Recording:* Epic #24075 (LP)
Release Year: 1963; *Chart:* did not chart
Cover Artist: Lesley Gore
Label: Mercury Records; *Recording:* Mercury #72119 (45)
Release Year: 1963; *Chart:* #1 *Billboard* Hot 100

Helen Shapiro was a singer and actress from the United Kingdom. Before Lesley Gore arrived at the party, Shapiro recorded her take on "It's My Party" very early in 1963. Even though she was a teenager, she had a very mature voice and didn't appropriately convey the feelings of teen heartbreak in the song's lyrics. It was not released as a single in the United States, but rather only issued on an Epic LP titled *Introducing Helen Shapiro: A Teenager in Love.*

Shortly thereafter, Lesley Gore heard the song on a pile of demo records and opted to record it. Gore's sessions were produced by Quincy Jones for Mercury Records, and her much more youthful-sounding rendition caught on quickly and soared to number 1 on the Pop charts. Gore hastily released an answer record titled "Judy's Turn to Cry" (Mercury #72143), and it became almost as big as its predecessor.

Years later, Amy Winehouse remade "It's My Party" in her own inimitable fashion for the Quincy Jones tribute album titled *Q: Soul Bossa Nostra* (Qwest/Interscope #1429402).

"It's No Sin"

Composers: George Hoven and Chester Shull
Original Artist: the Four Aces
Label: Victoria Records; *Recording:* Victoria #101 (45 and 78)
Release Year: 1951; *Chart:* #4 *Billboard* Hot 100
Cover Artist: the Duprees
Label: Coed Records; *Recording:* Coed #587 (45)
Release Year: 1964; *Chart:* #74 *Billboard* Hot 100

Two versions of this ballad were duking it out in the Top 10 in the fall of 1951. The Four Aces version beat the Eddy Howard rendition (Mercury #5711) onto the *Billboard* charts by one week, but at the time they were with a smaller record label, Victoria Records, and eventually the Eddy Howard Mercury release (called "It's No Sin" on some copies and simply "Sin" on others) surpassed the Four Aces and reached number 1. After this Top 10 triumph for the Four Aces, they were signed to the much larger Decca Records label and continued having hit singles.

Very early in 1964, a vocal group from Jersey City, New Jersey, called the Duprees had been having success with old standards such as "You Belong to Me" and "Have You Heard?" and tried their luck with a remake of "It's No Sin." However, the ballad might have fared much better had it not been for a group of four Liverpudlians who were garnering all of the attention of America's youth at that same time. The Duprees' fine version of "It's No Sin" only reached number 74 on the charts.

"It's Now or Never"

Composers: Aaron Schroeder and Wally Gold
Original Artist: Elvis Presley
Label: RCA Victor Records; *Recording:* RCA Victor #7777 (45)
Release Year: 1960; *Chart:* #1 *Billboard* Hot 100

Cover Artist: John Schneider
Label: Scotti Brothers Records; *Recording:* Scotti Brothers #02105 (45)
Release Year: 1981; *Chart:* #14 *Billboard* Hot 100

This song went through numerous transitions before it became "It's Now or Never." It began as "O Sole Mio," which was written by Eduardo DiCapua in the late 1800s. Utilizing the same melody but different lyrics, the tune was later titled "There's No Tomorrow," and it became a hit in 1949 for Tony Martin (RCA Victor #3078). The songwriting credits now went to Hoffman, Corday, and Carr. However, there's still more to the story.

From "There's No Tomorrow," the song morphed into "It's Now or Never," which credited Aaron Schroeder and Wally Gold as the writers. Elvis Presley released a version of this new interpretation of the song shortly after returning from the army. It went to number 1 and stayed there for five consecutive weeks. Eventually, it became his biggest worldwide hit.

Riding the crest of his popularity from *The Dukes of Hazzard* on CBS, John Schneider, who portrayed Bo Duke on the show, remade Presley's "It's Now or Never" in 1981 and just missed the Top 10.

"IT'S ONLY MAKE BELIEVE"

Composers: Jack Nance and Conway Twitty
Original Artist: Conway Twitty
Label: MGM Records; *Recording:* MGM #12677 (45 and 78)
Release Year: 1958; *Chart:* #1 *Billboard* Hot 100
Cover Artist: Glen Campbell
Label: Capitol Records; *Recording:* Capitol #2905 (45)
Release Year: 1970; *Chart:* #10 *Billboard* Hot 100

He was born Harold Lloyd Jenkins but opted for a much flashier moniker derived from the names of two towns, Conway and Twitty. In 1958, a song he co-wrote titled "It's Only Make Believe" zoomed to number 1 on the Pop charts. The song is a fantasy—the singer is envisioning the woman he loves reciprocating that love, but for now, "It's Only Make Believe." This MGM single replaced another MGM single at the top of the charts—"It's All in the Game" by Tommy Edwards (see the entry for that song).

A dozen years later, the song was ready to be heard again. Glen Campbell brought it back into the Top 10 in 1970 and, honestly, having a hit variety series on CBS titled *The Glen Campbell Goodtime Hour* certainly didn't hurt any. In fact, it was the first cut on *The Glen Campbell Goodtime Album* (Capitol #493).

"I'VE BEEN HURT"

Composer: Ray Whitley
Original Artist: Ray Whitley

The rare original version of "I've Been Hurt" by its composer, Ray Whitley.

Label: Dunhill Records; *Recording:* Dunhill #201 (45)
Release Year: 1965; *Chart:* did not chart
Cover Artist: Bill Deal and the Rhondels
Label: Heritage Records; *Recording:* Heritage #812 (45)
Release Year: 1969; *Chart:* #35 *Billboard* Hot 100

"I've Been Hurt" is an up-tempo song that nowadays is categorized as northern soul or, in the Carolinas, as beach music. It was written by singer/songwriter Ray Whitley, and Whitley also released the first version in 1965 on the new Dunhill Records label. The record was not a hit, but Whitley was friendly with the Tams and got them to cover the song for ABC-Paramount Records (#10741) late in 1965. This version also failed to chart.

It took until 1969 for "I've Been Hurt" to finally become a hit. Bill Deal and the Rhondels had success with a remake of another Tams record, "What

Kind of Fool Do You Think I Am?" and "I've Been Hurt" was no exception. The record peaked at number 35 nationally, but was much bigger in the Carolinas and Virginia. Both songs were included on *The Best of Bill Deal and the Rhondels* album (Heritage #35006) in 1970.

"I'VE GOT YOU UNDER MY SKIN"
Composer: Cole Porter
Original Artist: Ray Noble
Label: RCA Victor Records; *Recording:* RCA Victor #25422 (78)
Release Year: 1936; *Chart:* did not chart
Cover Artist: the Four Seasons
Label: Philips Records; *Recording:* Philips #40393 (45)
Release Year: 1966; *Chart:* #9 *Billboard* Hot 100

"I've Got You under My Skin" is a legendary Cole Porter composition that made its first appearance in the MGM musical titled *Born to Dance* in 1936. In that year, Ray Noble released his rendition with Al Bowlly on vocals. It was recorded with a Latin beat for RCA Victor on a 78.

One of the best-known renditions of the song came from "Old Blue Eyes," Frank Sinatra, on his *Songs for Swingin' Lovers* album (Capitol #653). The album was inducted into the Grammy Hall of Fame in 2000, and "I've Got You under My Skin" became one of his signature songs.

In 1966, the song was popularized yet again and made Top 10 when released by the Four Seasons. Produced brilliantly by Bob Crewe, Porter's song was introduced to a whole new generation.

"I'VE TOLD EV'RY LITTLE STAR"
Composers: Jerome Kern and Oscar Hammerstein II
Original Artist: the Jack Denny Orchestra
Label: RCA Victor Records; *Recording:* RCA Victor #24183 (78)
Release Year: 1932; *Chart:* #10 *Billboard*
Cover Artist: Linda Scott
Label: Canadian American Records; *Recording:* Canadian American #123 (45)
Release Year: 1961; *Chart:* #3 *Billboard* Hot 100

"I've Told Ev'ry Little Star" was written by Jerome Kern and Oscar Hammerstein II for the musical *Music in the Air* in 1932. It also became a 1934 20th Century Fox motion picture starring Gloria Swanson, but the first hit single version of "I've Told Ev'ry Little Star" came in 1932 by Jack Denny and his Waldorf Astoria Orchestra featuring the vocals of Paul Small. It became a Top 10 hit.

The song has been covered by the likes of Bing Crosby and Margaret Whiting, but no version was bigger than the 1961 version by young Linda Scott for

Canadian American Records. This memorable version began with a long series of "Dum, da dum, da da da da da da da da das," and became a Top 3 smash. This rendition was later used in the soundtrack for the bizarre 2001 Universal motion picture titled *Mulholland Drive*. Scott attempted to revive several other old standards ("I Don't Know Why" and "Count Every Star"), but they were only marginally successful.

"IVORY TOWER"
Composers: Jack Fulton and Lois Steele
Original Artist: Cathy Carr
Label: Fraternity Records; *Recording:* Fraternity #734 (45 and 78)
Release Year: 1956; *Chart:* #2 *Billboard* Hot 100
Cover Artist: the Charms
Label: Deluxe Records; *Recording:* Deluxe #6093 (45 and 78)
Release Year: 1956; *Chart:* #11 *Billboard* Hot 100 and #5 R&B

This is a song of elitism and condescension. The singer in "Ivory Tower" is madly in love and fears that the object of affection is "too far above to see" and, thus, keeps asking, "Come down from your Ivory Tower." This song was thrice a hit in 1956. New York City's Cathy Carr recorded it first (for Cincinnati's Fraternity Records label) and had the biggest hit. However, there were two other popular versions on her coattails.

For the R&B market, Otis Williams and his Charms added their rendition of "Ivory Tower" to the fray next (only a couple of weeks after Carr's), and it was a hit on both the Pop and R&B charts.

In between hit TV sitcoms *My Little Margie* and *Oh, Susanna*, Gale Storm had a slew of hit cover songs, and "Ivory Tower" was one of the biggest—peaking at number 6 (Dot #15458). This rendition of "Ivory Tower" was released several weeks after the first two.

J

"JOHNNY ANGEL"
Composers: Lyn Duddy and Lee Pockriss
Original Artist: Laurie Loman
Label: ABC-Paramount Records; *Recording:* ABC-Paramount #10108 (45)
Release Year: 1960; *Chart:* did not chart
Cover Artist: Shelley Fabares
Label: Colpix Records; *Recording:* Colpix #621 (45)
Release Year: 1962; *Chart:* #1 *Billboard* Hot 100

You may be amazed to know that several artists recorded "Johnny Angel" before Shelley Fabares. The first version came from Laurie Loman on ABC-Paramount Records in April of 1960. It was not a hit. Only weeks later, a rendition by Georgia Lee on Decca Records (#31075) also failed to make the charts. The singers just sounded too mature to successfully "put over" the song's lyrics about unrequited teenager love.

In 1962, Screen Gems (a division of Columbia Pictures) had the brilliant idea of involving the young members of the cast of *The Donna Reed Show* with their record label known as Colpix, which was short for Columbia Pictures. Paul Petersen had two Top 20 hits ("My Dad" and "She Can't Find Her Keys"), and a reluctant Shelley Fabares, upon rerecording "Johnny Angel," had a number 1 hit. Fabares, as Mary Stone, performed the song in the fourth season episode titled "Donna's Prima Donna" on February 1, 1962. Singing background on the record is Rock and Roll Hall of Fame inductee Darlene Love with the Blossoms. A follow-up hit titled "Johnny Loves Me" (Colpix #636) did not make the Top 20. Fabares never had another hit record, but she did have a long run on TV in shows such as *The Brian Keith Show*, *The Practice*, *One Day at a Time*, *Highcliffe Manor*, and *Coach*.

"JUST A GIGOLO/I AIN'T GOT NOBODY"

Composers: Roger Graham, Spencer Williams, Irving Caesar, and Leonello Casucci
Original Artist: Louis Prima
Label: Capitol Records; *Recording:* Capitol #755 (LP)
Release Year: 1956; *Chart:* did not chart
Cover Artist: David Lee Roth
Label: Warner Brothers Records; *Recording:* Warner Brothers #29040 (45)
Release Year: 1985; *Chart:* #12 *Billboard* Hot 100

Both of the songs in this medley had previously been recorded by several artists. "Just a Gigolo" was recorded by Ted Lewis and Leo Reisman. The "I Ain't Got Nobody" part of the song was initially performed by Marion Harris, Bing Crosby, the Mills Brothers, and Louis Armstrong, to name a few. But, like that old Reese's candy commercial about someone getting peanut butter on my chocolate and chocolate on my peanut butter, when combined, these two songs made for a very tasty medley. Louis Prima—Keely Smith's other half—popularized this elongated and clever version of the song as the first cut on his *The Wildest* album on Capitol Records from 1956. It became a signature song for him.

This medley was covered a few years later and performed a la disco on the *Macho Man* album by the very novel Village People (Casablanca #7096) in 1978.

However, a rendition by David Lee Roth of Van Halen in 1985 rivals Prima's original for popularity. It was a very unique sound for 1985, but very memorable and fun. It was included on Roth's platinum *Crazy from the Heat* EP (Warner #25222). *Crazy from the Heat* was also utilized as the title for Roth's autobiography in 1998.

"JUST A LITTLE BIT BETTER"
Composer: Kenny Young
Original Artist: Kenny Young
Label: Atco Records; *Recording:* Atco #6322 (45)
Release Year: 1964; *Chart:* did not chart
Cover Artist: Herman's Hermits
Label: MGM Records; *Recording:* MGM #13398 (45)
Release Year: 1965; *Chart:* #7 *Billboard* Hot 100

Written and originally recorded by Kenny Young (who co-wrote "Arizona" and "Under the Boardwalk"), "Just a Little Bit Better" is a song in which the singer attempts to convince a young lady that he is better than the rich guy she's been seeing. Even though the wealthy man can buy her fancy clothes from Paris, furs, and diamond rings, the singer is better for her because he can give her sweet, true love. While trying to convince the girl, he is also trying to convince himself.

Young's rendition of his own composition was not a hit, but the cover version by Peter Noone and Herman's Hermits a year later reached the Top 10. Noone also recorded another song written by Kenny Young—"Don't Go out in the Rain (You're Going to Melt)" on the MGM label (#13761) in 1967, and it became the group's final Top 20 hit.

K

"KILLING ME SOFTLY WITH HIS SONG"
Composers: Norman Gimbel and Charles Fox
Original Artist: Lori Lieberman
Label: Capitol Records; *Recording:* Capitol #11081 (LP)
Release Year: 1972; *Chart:* did not chart
Cover Artist: Roberta Flack
Label: Atlantic Records; *Recording:* Atlantic #2940 (45)
Release Year: 1973; *Chart:* #1 *Billboard* Hot 100 and #1 R&B

Singer/songwriter Lori Lieberman recorded the original version of "Killing Me Softly with His Song" in 1972 on her self-titled Capitol album. This version was not a hit. Lieberman had been inspired and moved by a performance of "Empty Chairs" by Don McLean at a live concert, and she told composers Norman Gimbel and Charles Fox about the experience. The song was written about that experience.

However, when the song was covered by Roberta Flack a year later, it caught on big time. It soared to number 1 on both the Pop and R&B charts. It garnered Flack two Grammys in 1973—Record of the Year and Best Pop Vocal Performance, Female. The song was included on Flack's *Killing Me Softly* album (Atlantic #7271). It was inducted into the Grammy Hall of Fame in 1999.

The song hit number 1 again on the R&B charts in 1996 (and number 2 on the Pop charts) when it was covered and updated by the Fugees (on the Ruffhouse label), who omitted "with His Song" from the title. This rendition also won a Grammy—Best R&B Performance by a Duo or Group with Vocal.

L

"LADY MARMALADE"
Composers: Bob Crewe and Kenny Nolan
Original Artist: Eleventh Hour
Label: 20th Century Records; *Recording:* 20th Century #435 (LP)
Release Year: 1974; *Chart:* did not chart
Cover Artist: Labelle
Label: Epic Records; *Recording:* Epic #50048 (45)
Release Year: 1974; *Chart:* #1 *Billboard* Hot 100 and #1 R&B

Before his own big hit, "I Like Dreaming" (20th Century #2287), singer/songwriter Kenny Nolan co-wrote tunes such as "My Eyes Adored You" and "Lady Marmalade." The first artist to record the latter was known as Eleventh Hour, and their Pop version failed to make the Pop charts in 1974.

Much later in that same year, Patti LaBelle's group, at this time known simply as Labelle, recorded an R&B rendition of "Lady Marmalade." It was the first single released from the group's *Nightbirds* album (Epic #33075), and it quickly soared to number 1 on both the Pop and R&B charts.

The song hit number 1 again in 2001 when it was covered by Christina Aguilera (Interscope #497066). Aguilera was awarded a Grammy for Best Pop Vocal Collaboration.

"THE LAST KISS"
Composer: Wayne Cochran
Original Artist: Wayne Cochran
Label: Gala Records; *Recording:* Gala #117 (45)
Release Year: 1961; *Chart:* did not chart
Cover Artist: J. Frank Wilson and the Cavaliers
Label: Le Cam Records; *Recording:* Le Cam #722 (45)
Release Year: 1964; *Chart:* #2 *Billboard* Hot 100

Famous for his white pompadour, Wayne Cochran was the composer and the originator of the teen tragedy tune "The Last Kiss." Released in 1961 on the small Gala Records label of Georgia, the original rendition was all but ignored.

Then, in 1964, the tear-jerking love song was covered by J. Frank Wilson and the Cavaliers—originally on the Le Cam Records label. When the song caught on, it was leased to Tamara Records (#761) and then to Josie Records (#923) to handle the distribution. This record, with off-key background singers, got all the way to number 2 on the Pop charts—kept out of number 1 by the Supremes' biggest hit, "Baby Love." Wilson went to the well again five years later with "Last Kiss '69" (Charay #13), but this updated version was not a hit.

A Canadian group known as Wednesday issued a remake of "The Last Kiss" (Sussex #507) in 1974. It reached the Top 40 on the Pop charts and incited new interest in the song, and thus the 1964 J. Frank Wilson rendition was rereleased and made the charts, this time on the Virgo label (#506).

The song became popular yet again when it was remade in 1999 by Seattle grunge band Pearl Jam. Coincidentally, this version, like J. Frank Wilson's, reached number 2 on the Pop charts.

"LEAVING ON A JET PLANE"

Composer: John Denver
Original Artist: the Mitchell Trio
Label: Reprise Records; *Recording:* Reprise #0588 (45)
Release Year: 1967; *Chart:* did not chart
Cover Artist: Peter, Paul and Mary
Label: Warner Brothers Records; *Recording:* Warner Brothers #7340 (45)
Release Year: 1969; *Chart:* #1 *Billboard* Hot 100

"Leaving on a Jet Plane" was written by a young and yet unknown John Denver. It was written as "Babe, I Hate to Go," and to shop the song around, Denver recorded his own version and pressed up a few copies as demos in 1966. Denver was with the Chad Mitchell Trio at this time. Chad left the group and Denver joined them—then known as simply the Mitchell Trio. The song was released on a 45 but was not a hit. At this time the song became known as "Leaving on a Jet Plane"—a song about a guy bidding adieu to his girlfriend, albeit briefly. He doesn't know when he'll be back again, but when he does return, he'll bring a wedding ring. The reason for his exit is never clearly given, but because of the time frame one can surmise he was going off to war.

Meanwhile, Peter, Paul and Mary included the song on 1967's *Album 1700* (Warner Brothers #1700). The LP was a hit and eventually went platinum, but "Leaving on a Jet Plane" wasn't released as a single until 1969. It became their biggest hit, their final hit, and their only number 1 on the Pop charts.

Denver released his own version on his *Rhymes and Reasons* album (RCA Victor #8348). After Denver died in a plane crash on October 12, 1997, the lyrics of this song turned eerily prophetic.

"LEMON TREE"
Composer: Will Holt
Original Artist: Peter, Paul and Mary
Label: Warner Brothers Records; *Recording:* Warner Brothers #5274 (45)
Release Year: 1962; *Chart:* #35 *Billboard* Hot 100
Cover Artist: Trini Lopez
Label: Reprise Records; *Recording:* Reprise #0336 (45)
Release Year: 1965; *Chart:* #20 *Billboard* Hot 100

"Lemon Tree" was written in the 1960s by Will Holt, but it was inspired by an old Spanish folk song from the 1930s. The lyrics state that the lemon tree is very much like "the fair sex"—what's on the outside may be sweet and beautiful, but what's on the inside tells the real tale. Peter, Paul and Mary had their very first chart entry with their version in 1962, and it peaked at number 35.

The song became even bigger the next time around when it was remade by Trini Lopez for Reprise Records. Lopez's rendition became the definitive version of the tune.

The song was adapted for a long-running furniture polish TV commercial as "Lemon Pledge, very pretty" in the 1970s.

An early *Seinfeld* episode titled "The Phone Message," which originally aired on February 13, 1991, utilized "Lemon Tree" as a signal between Jerry and George. When the song was first mentioned in the episode, George asked, "Peter, Paul and Mary?" Jerry's response was, "No, Trini Lopez."

"LET IT BE ME"
Composers: Gilbert Becaud and Mann Curtis
Original Artist: Jill Corey
Label: Columbia Records; *Recording:* Columbia #40878 (45 and 78)
Release Year: 1957; *Chart:* #57 *Billboard* Hot 100
Cover Artist: the Everly Brothers
Label: Cadence Records; *Recording:* Cadence #1376 (45)
Release Year: 1960; *Chart:* #7 *Billboard* Hot 100

Originally a French song from 1955, the Anglicized lyrics were written by Mann Curtis in 1957 for the almost forgotten original U.S. version of "Let It Be Me" by Jill Corey (who was better known for the song "Love Me to Pieces"). Corey performed the song on a 1957 episode of the anthology series *Climax* on CBS, and then released the song for CBS's record label, Columbia. It was a minor hit—peaking at number 57. Costars on that episode of *Climax* included Eddie Albert, Maureen O'Sullivan, Charlie Ruggles, and Steve Forrest, for which the subject matter was corruption within the recording industry.

In 1960, Phil and Don, the Everly Brothers, remade "Let It Be Me" in a big string-laden production (one of their last on Archie Bleyer's Cadence Records label), and had a Top 10 hit.

However, the best was yet to come for the tune. Jerry Butler and Betty Everett were both recording for Vee Jay Records in 1964, and they teamed up to record the song as a duet. This time around, "Let It Be Me" (Vee Jay #613) reached number 5 on the Pop charts and number 1 R&B.

"LET ME GO, LOVER"
Composers: Al Hill and Jenny Lou Carson
Original Artist: Joan Weber
Label: Columbia Records; *Recording:* Columbia #40366 (45 and 78)
Release Year: 1954; *Chart:* #1 *Billboard* Hot 100
Cover Artist: Patti Page
Label: Mercury Records; *Recording:* Mercury #70511 (45 and 78)
Release Year: 1954; *Chart:* #8 *Billboard* Hot 100

Much like "Let It Be Me," "Let Me Go, Lover" was also introduced on a TV anthology show—one titled *Studio One*—on November 15, 1954. Joan Weber performed the song on the "Let Me Go, Lover" episode, and Columbia was prepared for a barrage of requests for the single release. It quickly hit number 1 on the Pop charts and spawned numerous cover versions.

Both Patti Page and Teresa Brewer (Coral #61315) released cover versions on the same day—exactly two weeks after Joan Weber's original. All three renditions reached the Top 10. There was even a version for the R&B market by a vocal group from Indianapolis called the Counts (Dot #1235), but it didn't chart.

"LET'S HANG ON"
Composers: Bob Crewe, Sandy Linzer, and Denny Randell
Original Artist: the Four Seasons
Label: Philips Records; *Recording:* Philips #40317 (45)
Release Year: 1965; *Chart:* #3 *Billboard* Hot 100
Cover Artist: Barry Manilow
Label: Arista Records; *Recording:* Arista #0675 (45)
Release Year: 1982; *Chart:* #32 *Billboard* Hot 100

Several songs originated by the Four Seasons enjoyed an afterlife—"Working My Way Back to You" (by the Spinners); "Beggin'" (by Madcon); and "Let's Hang On." The latter was a song about hanging on through the bad times in a relationship. Written by the prolific team of Bob Crewe, Sandy Linzer, and Denny Randell, the Four Seasons made it a Top 3 hit.

The 1982 remake by fellow tristate area native Barry Manilow updated the song, but kept the slow "there ain't no good in our goodbying" intro intact. It wasn't as big as the original by the Four Seasons, but it reached the Top 40. It was included on the *If I Should Love Again* album (Arista #9573).

"LINDA"
Composer: Jack Lawrence
Original Artist: Ray Noble's Orchestra with Buddy Clark
Label: Columbia Records; *Recording:* Columbia #37215 (78)
Release Year: 1946; *Chart:* #1 *Billboard* Music Popularity Chart
Cover Artist: Jan and Dean
Label: Liberty Records; *Recording:* Liberty #55531 (45)
Release Year: 1963; *Chart:* #28 *Billboard* Hot 100

This tune was written by Jack Lawrence about a very young Linda Eastman. Yes, indeed, the same Linda Eastman who years later married Sir Paul McCartney. It was recorded by Ray Noble's Orchestra featuring Buddy Clark on vocals. It was released in 1946, but reached number 1 on the charts in 1947.

The song was remade many times over the years by the likes of Bing Crosby, Frank Sinatra, Jim Reeves, Perry Como, Jerry Vale, and Dennis Day. There was even a rock and roll version in 1963 by Jan and Dean. This hit came right before the duo really found their niche with songs relating to the "surfing craze." In fact, it was included on the album titled *Jan and Dean Take Linda Surfin'* (Liberty #7294) in the summer of 1963.

"THE LION SLEEPS TONIGHT"
Composers: George David Weiss, Hugo Peretti, and Luigi Creatore
Original Artist: Solomon Linda's Original Evening Birds
Label: Gallotone Records; *Recording:* Gallotone #1527 (78)
Release Year: 1939; *Chart:* did not chart
Cover Artist: the Tokens
Label: RCA Victor Records; *Recording:* RCA Victor #7954 (45)
Recording: 1961; *Chart:* #1 *Billboard* Hot 100

"The Lion Sleeps Tonight" had its origins in South Africa as a song titled "Mbube" by Solomon Linda's Original Evening Birds on the Gallotone Records label in the 1930s. It really had no lyrics, but the falsetto, the melody, and the "wimowehs" were all accounted for. As "Wimoweh," the song was a Top 20 hit for the Weavers on the Decca label (#27928) in 1951. The song, at this point still had no actual lyrics. That came a decade later. These early versions merely "wimo-whet" our appetite.

In 1961, with English lyrics and the song's credits now given to George Weiss, Hugo Peretti, and Luigi Creatore (Hugo and Luigi also produced it), the Tokens got the lion's share from the record-buying public; they hit number 1 and sold a million copies with what was now titled "The Lion Sleeps Tonight." The song was so popular, there was even an answer record—"The Tiger's Wide Awake" by the Romeos on the Amy Records label (#840), but it wasn't a hit.

Another million copies were sold a decade later when the famous falsetto of Robert John brought "The Lion Sleeps Tonight" back in a big way with a Top 3 remake for Atlantic Records (#2846).

The classic Tokens' version of the song was utilized in multiple episodes of the NBC sitcom *Friends* as the favorite song of Ross's pet monkey, Marcel. The song was introduced to a whole new group of youngsters when it was included in the soundtrack of the megahit animated Walt Disney motion picture *The Lion King* in 1994. It has also been utilized in TV commercials for Cosequin animal products and the 1993 Family Channel sitcom called *The Mighty Jungle*.

"LITTLE BIT OF SOUL"
Composers: John Carter and Ken Lewis
Original Artist: the Little Darlins
Label: Fontana Records; *Recording:* Fontana #539 (45)
Release Year: 1965; *Chart:* did not chart
Cover Artist: the Music Explosion
Label: Laurie Records; *Recording:* Laurie #3380 (45)
Release Year: 1967; *Chart:* #2 *Billboard* Hot 100

"Little Bit of Soul" was originally recorded by a British group known as the Little Darlins. The gist of the song is that no matter what's wrong with your life, a little bit of soul is the cure-all. It wasn't a hit in the United States, but it did spark a cover version by a group from the Buckeye State called the Music Explosion. Said group definitely lived up to their name and exploded upon the music scene. Their rendition of "Little Bit of Soul" sold a million copies and reached number 2 on the Pop charts, kept out of number 1 by the Association's "Windy" (Warner Brothers #7041). The Music Explosion never again cracked the Top 50.

An attempt at a remake of "Little Bit of Soul" by Iron Cross on the Spark label (#08) in 1972 fell flat.

"LONELY NIGHT (ANGEL FACE)"
Composer: Neil Sedaka
Original Artist: Neil Sedaka
Label: Rocket Records; *Recording:* Rocket #2157 (LP)
Release Year: 1975; *Chart:* did not chart

Cover Artist: the Captain and Tennille
Label: A & M Records; *Recording:* A & M #1782 (45)
Release Year: 1976; *Chart:* #3 *Billboard* Hot 100

Written by Neil Sedaka, "Lonely Night (Angel Face)" was included on the 1975 album *The Hungry Years* but not released as a single.

Just as they did with "Love Will Keep Us Together," the Captain and Tennille (Daryl Dragon and Toni Tennille) covered "Lonely Night (Angel Face)," and once again they were glad that Sedaka was back. It became a Top 3 hit and sold well over a million copies.

The magic happened a third time with "You Never Done It Like That" (see the entry for that song) in 1978 from Sedaka's *A Song* album (Elektra #102).

"Love Hurts"
Composers: Felice and Boudleaux Bryant
Original Artist: the Everly Brothers
Label: Warner Brothers Records; *Recording:* Warner Brothers Records #1395 (LP)
Release Year: 1960; *Chart:* did not chart
Cover Artist: Nazareth
Label: A & M Records; *Recording:* A & M #1671 (45)
Release Year: 1975; *Chart:* #8 *Billboard* Hot 100

The husband-and-wife songwriting team of Felice and Boudleaux Bryant composed many great songs for the Everly Brothers. One titled "Love Hurts" was buried on a 1960 Warner Brothers album titled *A Date with the Everly Brothers.* The album made the Top 10, but "Love Hurts" was not released as a single. "Love Hurts" is what one might call an anti–love song, as it warns others that "love is just a lie."

The following year, a cover of "Love Hurts" by Roy Orbison was hidden on the B-side of his number 1 smash "Running Scared" (Monument #438). That B-side did not chart.

Fourteen years later, "Love Hurts" morphed into an intense rock ballad as performed by a Scottish group called Nazareth. Because the song was not a hit for the Everly Brothers or Roy Orbison, for most people "Love Hurts" was a brand new song, and with this unique interpretation it truly was. It reached the Top 10 and was included on the gold album *Hair of the Dog* (A & M #4511).

"Love Is Blue"
Composers: Andre Popp, Pierre Cour, and Brian Blackburn
Original Artist: Paul Mauriat
Label: Philips Records; *Recording:* Philips #40495 (45)
Release Year: 1968; *Chart:* #1 *Billboard* Hot 100

Cover Artist: the Dells
Label: Cadet Records; *Recording:* Cadet #5641 (45)
Release Year: 1969; *Chart:* #22 *Billboard* Hot 100 and #5 R&B

Originally written as "L'amour Est Bleu," Paul Mauriat's version on the Philips Records label early in 1968 peaked at number 1 on the Pop charts for five weeks, and sold well over a million copies. Along with the Singing Nun who recorded "Dominique," Mauriat is among the first French or Belgian artists to reach number 1 on the Pop charts.

Mauriat's version of "Love Is Blue" is an instrumental, but the song did have lyrics, and they were translated to English by Brian Blackburn. Al Martino and Claudine Longet recorded vocal versions of the song, but they only dented the very bottom of the Hot 100.

A soulful medley version by Chicago's Dells on the Cadet label became a big hit—number 22 on the Pop charts and number 5 R&B. The full title of the medley was "I Can Sing a Rainbow/Love Is Blue." *Love Is Blue* was also the title of a hit 1969 album by the group (Cadet #829).

"LOVE LETTERS"
Composers: Victor Young and Eddie Heyman
Original Artist: Dick Haymes
Label: Brunswick Records; *Recording:* Brunswick #03638 (78)
Release Year: 1945; *Chart:* #11 *Billboard* Music Popularity Chart
Cover Artist: Ketty Lester
Label: Era Records; *Recording:* Era #3068 (45)
Release Year: 1962; *Chart:* #5 *Billboard* Hot 100 and #2 R&B

"Love Letters" the song first appeared in *Love Letters* the 1945 Paramount motion picture. It starred Joseph Cotten and Jennifer Jones, and the title song was nominated for an Oscar, but lost to "It Might as Well Be Spring" from *State Fair.* The Dick Haymes recording of that Oscar-nominated song in 1945 just missed the Top 10.

A 1962 remake by Ketty Lester, an actress and singer who hailed from Hope, Arkansas (the home of President Bill Clinton), became the only Top 10 version. It was released on Southern California's Era Records label and became Lester's only Top 40 hit.

Elvis Presley, during the lull in his career in 1966, recorded a rendition very similar to Ketty Lester's, and it became a Top 20 hit on RCA Victor (#8870).

"LOVE ME TENDER"
Composers: Elvis Presley and Vera Matson
Original Artist: Elvis Presley

Label: RCA Victor Records; *Recording:* RCA Victor #6643 (45 and 78)
Release Year: 1956; *Chart:* #1 *Billboard* Hot 100
Cover Artist: Percy Sledge
Label: Atlantic Records; *Recording:* Atlantic #2414 (45)
Release Year: 1967; *Chart:* #40 *Billboard* Hot 100

The melody of "Love Me Tender" began as a Civil War song known as "Aura Lee." Here, in its original form, the composers were listed as W. W. Fosdick and George Poulton. However, almost a century later, the tune was reworked and retitled "Love Me Tender." It's interesting that Elvis Presley got credit as co-writer on his number 1 single. *Love Me Tender* was also the title of his first motion picture, filmed in black and white for 20th Century Fox and released a short time after the single.

A doo-wop group known as the Fidels recorded an up-tempo rendition of the song in 1957 for the Music City Records label (#806). It wasn't a hit, but it was an interesting and notable interpretation of the classic song. Presley and Matson are credited as the composers on this version, too.

The man who gave us the original "When a Man Loves a Woman," Percy Sledge, brought "Love Me Tender" back into the Top 40 in 1967 with his soulful Atlantic remake. The song was once again a ballad.

"LOVE WILL KEEP US TOGETHER"
Composers: Neil Sedaka and Howard Greenfield
Original Artist: Neil Sedaka
Label: MGM Records; *Recording:* MGM #2315-248 (LP)
Release Year: 1973; *Chart:* did not chart
Cover Artist: the Captain and Tennille
Label: A & M Records; *Recording:* A & M #1672 (45)
Release Year: 1976; *Chart:* #1 *Billboard* Hot 100

"Love Will Keep Us Together" came about during Neil Sedaka's career lull in 1973, and he first released it on an LP titled *The Tra-La Days Are Over.* It then reappeared late in 1974 on *Sedaka's Back* (Rocket #463) during Neil's big comeback. For whatever reason, the catchy, hook-laden song was not released as a single.

Opportunity was indeed knocking for someone to cover the tune, and the Captain and Tennille jumped at the chance. Released in the spring of 1975, the song zoomed up the Pop chart to number 1 and sold well over a million copies. An homage to the song's originator can be heard at the very end when Toni Tennille sings, "Sedaka is back." Over the next few years, the duo reached Top 10 with two more Sedaka compositions "Lonely Night (Angel Face)" and "You Never Done It Like That." "Love Will Keep Us Together" was used as the theme song for *The Captain and Tennille* variety show on ABC.

M

"MacArthur Park"
Composer: Jimmy Webb
Original Artist: Richard Harris
Label: Dunhill Records; *Recording:* Dunhill #4134 (45)
Release Year: 1968; *Chart:* #2 *Billboard* Hot 100
Cover Artist: Donna Summer
Label: Casablanca Records; *Recording:* Casablanca #939 (45)
Release Year: 1978; *Chart:* #1 *Billboard* Hot 100 and #8 R&B

Richard Harris did it all—acting, producing, directing, writing, and singing. Regarding the latter, Harris had one huge hit record—a song written on singer/musician Buddy Greco's piano by the prolific Jimmy Webb. The song, laden with metaphoric lyrics, was based upon a relationship between Jimmy Webb and Susan Ronstadt, Linda's cousin. "MacArthur Park" is a real place on West Sixth Street in Los Angeles, and Jimmy and Susan often met there. Harris's unique recording of Webb's composition didn't sound like anything else being played on the radio. Plus, the song was over seven minutes in length—rivaled only by "Hey, Jude" in 1968. The record became a big hit and reached number 2 on the Pop charts—kept out of the number 1 spot by "This Guy's in Love with You" by Herb Alpert (A & M #929).

A decade later, the song was revived very differently by disco diva Donna Summer. This time around, the song did reach number 1. Summer's rendition timed out to three minutes, fifty-three seconds—about half the length of Harris's original. It was included on her *Live and More* album (Casablanca #7119).

"Mack the Knife"
Composers: Kurt Weill, Bertolt Brecht, and Marc Blitzstein
Original Artist: Louis Armstrong
Label: Columbia Records; *Recording:* Columbia #40587 (45 and 78)
Release Year: 1956; *Chart:* #20 *Billboard* Hot 100
Cover Artist: Bobby Darin
Label: Atco Records; *Recording:* Atco #6147 (45)
Release Year: 1959; *Chart:* #1 *Billboard* Hot 100 and #6 R&B

"Mack the Knife" was originally conceived as an afterthought for *The Three-penny Opera* in 1928 in Germany. The English translation of the opera from Marc Blitzstein played off-Broadway for many years in the 1950s. Satchmo's 1956 version of the show's signature song barely reached the Top 20.

Only a short three years later, Bobby Darin released his version. "Mack the Knife" was certainly an interesting choice for a guy who, up until then, was known as a rock and roll singer. Thus far, Darin had Top 10 hits with "Splish Splash," "Queen of the Hop," and "Dream Lover." Many, including Dick Clark, considered releasing the song to be a poor career decision. Those doubters couldn't have been more wrong. Mackie was back in town, and he stayed at number 1 for nine weeks. The record sold well over a million copies and set Darin up for similarly produced follow-ups such as "Beyond the Sea" (see the entry for that song), "Artificial Flowers," "Won't You Come Home, Bill Bailey," and "Clementine." The song won a Grammy for Record of the Year and was inducted into the Grammy Hall of Fame in 1999.

Kevin Spacey performed "Mack the Knife" in his 2004 Bobby Darin biopic *Beyond the Sea*.

"MAKE IT EASY ON YOURSELF"
Composers: Burt Bacharach and Hal David
Original Artist: Jerry Butler
Label: Vee Jay Records; *Recording:* Vee Jay #451 (45)
Release Year: 1962; *Chart:* #20 *Billboard* Hot 100 and #18 R&B
Cover Artist: the Walker Brothers
Label: Smash Records; *Recording:* Smash #2009 (45)
Release Year: 1965; *Chart:* #16 *Billboard* Hot 100

Dionne Warwick recorded the original demo of "Make It Easy on Yourself," but for whatever reason that version was not released. Instead, the Burt Bacharach/ Hal David song featuring Warwick's lead vocals was shopped around to entice other singers. "The Iceman," Jerry Butler, jumped at the chance to record this great song, and it became a big Top 20 hit on both the Pop and R&B charts. However, it might have been even bigger had it not been for another song on the charts at the exact same time by Neil Sedaka titled "Breaking Up Is Hard to Do." The final lyric of "Make It Easy on Yourself" is "because breaking up is so very hard to do," and it may have been overkill.

"Make It Easy on Yourself" was even bigger the second time around. A group from Los Angeles called the Walker Brothers, with a sound not unlike the Righteous Brothers, brought their version of the song to number 16 in 1965. Like the Righteous Brothers, they weren't really brothers. The Walker Brothers had three charts hits in the United States, but fared much better in the United Kingdom.

The song came full circle in 1970 when the artist who sang on the original demo, Dionne Warwick, released a new version (Scepter #12294) and reached the Top 40.

"MAKE THE WORLD GO AWAY"
Composer: Hank Cochran
Original Artist: Timi Yuro
Label: Liberty Records; *Recording:* Liberty #55587 (45)

Release Year: 1963; *Chart:* #24 *Billboard* Hot 100
Cover Artist: Eddy Arnold
Label: RCA Victor Records; *Recording:* RCA Victor #8679 (45)
Release Year: 1965; *Chart:* #6 *Billboard* Hot 100

In 1963, there were two versions of "Make the World Go Away" on the charts at the same time. On the Pop charts, the song was a hit for Chicago blue-eyed songstress Timi Yuro. On the country charts, it was a Top 10 hit for Ray Price (Columbia #42827). The song tells the story of a man who wants his sad, empty life to return to the way it was. If not, the whole world may just as well go away.

A couple of years later, the song became an even bigger hit when it was remade by "the Tennessee Plowboy," Eddy Arnold. It had been almost a decade since Arnold had penetrated the Top 40, so this smash hit caught many by surprise.

The song got one more go-round in the Top 50 in 1975 (MGM #14807) by Donny and Marie Osmond. *Make the World Go Away* was also the title of a 1975 album by the famous duo (MGM #4996).

Elvis Presley also took a stab at it on his *Elvis Country (I'm 10,000 Years Old)* album (RCA Victor #4460) in 1971.

"Mandy"
Composers: Scott English and Richard Kerr
Original Artist: Scott English
Label: Janus Records; *Recording:* Janus #171 (45)
Release Year: 1972; *Chart:* #91 *Billboard* Hot 100
Cover Artist: Barry Manilow
Label: Bell Records; *Recording:* Bell #613 (45)
Release Year: 1974; *Chart:* #1 *Billboard* Hot 100

Singer/songwriter/producer Scott English wrote and recorded the original version of "Mandy" as "Brandy" in 1972. It barely cracked the charts, peaking at number 91. Three months later, a totally different "Brandy" by a New Jersey band called Looking Glass (Epic #10874) reached number 1 on the Pop charts and sold well over a million copies. This "Brandy" was such a big hit that when the Scott English song was covered, the girl's name was changed to "Mandy."

"Mandy" not only reached number 1 on the Pop charts early in 1975, it also became the first hit in Barry Manilow's long and storied career. "Mandy" was included on the *Barry Manilow II* album (Arista #4016) and it went platinum.

"Marie"
Composer: Irving Berlin
Original Artist: Rudy Vallee and His Connecticut Yankees
Label: Velvet Tone Records; *Recording:* Velvet Tone #1834 (78)
Release Year: 1929; *Chart:* #2 *Billboard*

Cover Artist: the Four Tunes
Label: Jubilee Records; *Recording:* Jubilee #5128 (45 and 78)
Release Year: 1953; *Chart:* #11 *Billboard* Hot 100 and #2 R&B

Written by the legendary Irving Berlin, the first rendition of "Marie" was by an up-and-coming Rudy Vallee, who was just warming up his megaphone in 1929 when his version of the song got to number 2 on the charts. A few years later in 1937, Tommy Dorsey remade the song (RCA Victor #25523) and had a number 1 hit with it. However, the song found new life in rock and roll.

An R&B vocal group known as the Four Tunes recorded the most innovative rendition of the song in 1953 for Jubilee Records. This version employed some clever fills, trills, rolling *R*s, and falsetto vocals. It became a hit on both the Pop and R&B charts.

"Marie" was even part of the 1960s when the Irish group known as the Bachelors updated the song in 1965 (London #9762) and reached number 15 on the Pop charts.

Irving Berlin died on September 22, 1989, at the ripe old age of 101, leaving behind the legacy of having also composed "God Bless America," "Blue Skies," "Easter Parade," and "White Christmas."

"MEMORIES ARE MADE OF THIS"
Composers: Terry Gilkyson, Richard Dehr, and Frank Miller
Original Artist: Dean Martin
Label: Capitol Records; *Recording:* Capitol #3295 (45 and 78)
Release Year: 1955; *Chart:* #1 *Billboard* Hot 100
Cover Artist: the Drifters
Label: Atlantic Records; *Recording:* Atlantic #2325 (45)
Release Year: 1966; *Chart:* #48 *Billboard* Hot 100

"Memories Are Made of This" was written by the same trio who wrote and popularized the calypso tune "Marianne" (Columbia #40817). Dean Martin recorded the definitive rendition, with Gilkyson, Dehr, and Miller performing the "sweet sweet, the memories you gave to me" in the background. It reached number 1 and stayed there for six weeks early in 1956.

Very quickly, Gale Storm (Dot #15436) and Mindy Carson (Columbia #40573) jumped on the bandwagon with 1956 cover versions. Storm's version reached number 5 on the Pop charts.

A decade later, the Drifters made more memories and revived the song, with moderate success. This updated version peaked at number 48 on the Pop charts.

"MIDNIGHT CONFESSIONS"
Composer: Lou Josie
Original Artist: Evergreen Blues
Label: Mercury Records; *Recording:* Mercury #72756 (45)

Recording: 1968; *Chart:* did not chart
Cover Artist: the Grass Roots
Label: Dunhill Records; *Recording:* Dunhill #4144 (45)
Release Year: 1968; *Chart:* #5 *Billboard* Hot 100

"Midnight Confessions" was composed by Lou Josie—a singer/songwriter who got his start recording doo-wop records on the Argo, Baton, and Rendezvous labels. Writing "Midnight Confessions" was his big claim to fame, but the song's success didn't occur overnight. The original version by Evergreen Blues was released in the spring of 1968. It went nowhere.

During the summer of 1968, the Grass Roots released their rendition of the song. The arrangement was extremely similar to the original version by Evergreen Blues, only a wee bit slower. This rendition caught on, became a Top 5 hit, and sold well over a million copies. It was included on their *Golden Grass* album (Dunhill #50047) late in 1968. "Midnight Confessions" was also used as the title of a frequent sketch on *The Tonight Show with Jay Leno*, in which members of the studio audience shared embarrassing stories.

"MIDNIGHT TRAIN TO GEORGIA"
Composer: Jim Weatherly
Original Artist: Cissy Houston
Label: Janus Records; *Recording:* Janus #206 (45)
Release Year: 1972; *Chart:* did not chart
Cover Artist: Gladys Knight and the Pips
Label: Buddah Records; *Recording:* Buddah #383 (45)
Release Year: 1973; *Chart:* #1 *Billboard* Hot 100 and #1 R&B

This song was written by Jim Weatherly as "Midnight Plane to Houston," but as "Midnight Train to Georgia," it was first recorded by Cissy Houston—Whitney's mom—on the Janus Records label. It was a well-produced single, but it wasn't a hit. Houston was much more successful as a background singer—working with Elvis Presley, Aretha Franklin, and Otis Redding.

Just a year later, "Midnight Train to Georgia" by Gladys Knight and the Pips became the definitive hit version. At this time, the Pips were estranged from Motown Records, now contracted to Buddah Records. A native of Georgia, Gladys Knight had a natural fit with the song, and it soared to number 1 on both the Pop and R&B charts. This tune is about a guy who tried to make it as an actor, but after giving it his best shot, returned to the life and the girl he left behind. The group won a Grammy for Best R&B Vocal Performance by a Duo, Group or Chorus in 1974. It was inducted into the Grammy Hall of Fame in 1999.

"MISTER LONELY"
Composers: Bobby Vinton and Gene Allen
Original Artist: Bobby Vinton

Label: Epic Records; *Recording:* Epic #26020 (LP)
Release Year: 1962; *Chart:* did not chart
Cover Artist: Buddy Greco
Label: Epic Records; *Recording:* Epic #9536 (45)
Release Year: 1962; *Chart:* #64 *Billboard* Hot 100

This song about a lonely soldier, co-written by Bobby Vinton, had many lives on Epic Records. It first appeared on Vinton's *Roses Are Red* album in 1962, but was not released as a single.

The first version of the song to make the charts was by Buddy Greco—also on the Epic label. Greco had a long and successful association with Epic and recalled, "I loved recording 'Mr. Lonely.' In fact, Bobby Vinton and I used the same track, although I'm not sure why. I guess they wanted two different versions by two very different singers in very different styles." Greco's version reached number 64 on the Pop charts in 1962.

The Vinton version became a single for the first time in 1964, possibly because of the escalation of the war in Vietnam. It was very timely, and this time around, the song caught on in a big way and topped the charts. Buddy Greco added, "I'm so glad that Bobby Vinton had a hit with it. Wish I did, but I'm so happy for him."

"MISTER SANDMAN"
Composer: Pat Ballard
Original Artist: the Chordettes
Label: Cadence Records; *Recording:* Cadence #1247 (45 and 78)
Release Year: 1954; *Chart:* #1 *Billboard* Hot 100
Cover Artist: the Four Aces
Label: Decca Records; *Recording:* Decca #29344 (45 and 78)
Release Year: 1954; *Chart:* #5 *Billboard* Hot 100

Written by Pat Ballard, "Mister Sandman" is a musical fantasy—a bedtime prayer to meet the perfect guy. The Chordettes had the first and biggest version of the song on Archie Bleyer's Cadence Records label. Much like "Everyday" by Buddy Holly (see the entry for that song), there are no drums on the record—someone is merely tapping on his leg near a microphone. That someone was Bleyer, who is amusingly credited on the record label as "Knees Played by Archie Bleyer." The song hit number 1, but there was a big cover version.

The Four Aces covered the song late in 1954 for Decca Records, but changed the lyrics to reflect a guy trying to find the perfect girl. Gone in this version is the line, "Give him a lonely heart like Pagliacci, and lots of wavy hair like Liberace." This rendition reached number 5 on the Pop charts, and this is the version featured in the 1985 megahit motion picture *Back to the Future.*

Emmylou Harris recorded all three vocal parts for her 1981 45 rpm remake (Warner #49684), and her version reached the Top 40. The song was also reworked as a holiday song titled "Mister Santa."

"MISTY"
Composers: Errol Garner and Johnny Burke
Original Artist: Errol Garner
Label: EmArcy Records; *Recording:* EmArcy #36001 (LP)
Release Year: 1954; *Chart:* did not chart
Cover Artist: Johnny Mathis
Label: Columbia Records; *Recording:* Columbia #41483 (45)
Release Year: 1959; *Chart:* #12 *Billboard* Hot 100

This romantic ballad was co-written by piano virtuoso Errol Garner and first appeared on his 1954 EmArcy Album titled *Contrasts*. For what would become Johnny Mathis's legendary remake, lyrics were added by Johnny Burke. Even though "Misty" wasn't Mathis's biggest chart hit (it just missed the Top 10), it has undoubtedly become one of his signature songs.

In 1963, "Mr. Personality," Lloyd Price, totally reinvented the ballad with a swing feel that just missed the Top 20 on his own Double-L Records label (#722).

"Misty" took on a nefarious taint in 1971 when it became a pivotal element in the hit low-budget Clint Eastwood motion picture *Play Misty for Me*. The Errol Garner rendition is part of the soundtrack.

"MOODY RIVER"
Composer: Gary Bruce
Original Artist: Chase Webster
Label: Southern Sound Records; *Recording:* Southern Sound #101 (45)
Release Year: 1961; *Chart:* did not chart
Cover Artist: Pat Boone
Label: Dot Records; *Recording:* Dot #16209 (45)
Release Year: 1961; *Chart:* #1 *Billboard* Hot 100

"Moody River" was another of those teen tragedy songs (such as "Teen Angel" and "Tell Laura I Love Her") that were so popular in the late 1950s and early 1960s. In "Moody River," a young man goes to the river only to discover that his girl has committed suicide because of guilt she felt after cheating on him with a friend. The song was composed by Gary Bruce, the alter ego of the song's original performer, Chase Webster.

Webster's rendition was not a hit, but an almost identical cover version by Pat Boone was. In fact, it became Boone's sixth and final number 1 hit. Boone also had a *Moody River* album (Dot #3384), and it reached the Top 30.

"MOON RIVER"
Composers: Henry Mancini and Johnny Mercer
Original Artist: Henry Mancini
Label: RCA Victor Records; Recording: RCA Victor #7916 (45)
Release Year: 1961; Chart: #11 Billboard Hot 100
Cover Artist: Jerry Butler
Label: Vee Jay Records; Recording: Vee Jay #405 (45)
Release Year: 1961; Chart: #11 Billboard Hot 100

The motion picture Breakfast at Tiffany's starred Audrey Hepburn and George Peppard. The most important element of the film, however, was a song titled "Moon River." The first version was released by the song's co-writer, the immortal Henry Mancini. His rendition reached number 11 on the Pop charts and was an instrumental. It won Grammys for both Record of the Year and Song of the Year.

Up next, "the Butler did it." A cover version by Jerry Butler utilized Johnny Mercer's brilliant lyrics. Like Mancini, the Butler version also peaked at number 11 on the Pop charts.

Amazingly, "Moon River" is most associated with the late Andy Williams, but his version never entered the singles charts. It can, however, be found on the Moon River and Other Great Movie Themes album (Columbia #1809). Williams garnered a gold record for that LP.

A song called "Breakfast at Tiffany's" by Deep Blue Something from 1996 (Interscope #98138) stated that a love for the classic film was the only thing the singer and his estranged girlfriend had in common.

"MORE THAN I CAN SAY"
Composers: Jerry Allison and Sonny Curtis
Original Artist: the Crickets
Label: Coral Records; Recording: Coral #62198 (45)
Release Year: 1960; Chart: did not chart
Cover Artist: Leo Sayer
Label: Warner Brothers Records; Recording: Warner Brothers #49565 (45)
Release Year: 1980; Chart: #2 Billboard Hot 100

This song was written by and originally released by the Crickets after the untimely passing of Buddy Holly in the plane crash that also claimed the lives of the Big Bopper and Ritchie Valens.

The first rendition to make the charts came from Bobby Vee on the flip side of a John D. Loudermilk composition titled "Stayin' In." Vee's version of "More Than I Can Say" reached number 61 in 1961. Jerry Allison played drums and Howard Roberts was on guitar. It was a bigger hit in the United Kingdom than in the States. In fact, it was a huge international hit. Vee was in the airport in Hong Kong to return home after a performance, and a customs agent looked at

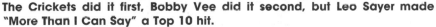

The Crickets did it first, Bobby Vee did it second, but Leo Sayer made "More Than I Can Say" a Top 10 hit.

his passport, which read Robert Thomas Velline (a.k.a. Bobby Vee). He leaned over and whispered to Vee, "Whoa whoa yay yay"—a line from the song. At that point, Vee realized that his music had gone global.

Indeed, the song had spoken to the world when a British singer named Leo Sayer rerecorded it in 1980 and had the biggest hit version. Sayer's rendition sold a million copies and was included on his *Living in a Fantasy* album (Warner Brothers #3483).

"THE MOST BEAUTIFUL GIRL"
Composers: Norro Wilson, Bill Sherrill, and Rory Bourke
Original Artist: Norro Wilson
Label: Smash Records; *Recording:* Smash #2192 (45)

Release Year: 1968; *Chart:* did not chart
Cover Artist: Charlie Rich
Label: Epic Records; *Recording:* Epic #11040 (45)
Release Year: 1973; *Chart:* #1 *Billboard* Hot 100

Norro Wilson co-wrote a song titled "Hey Mister" with Rita Welty in 1968. One of the lyrics was, "Hey, Mister, did you happen to see the most beautiful girl in the world? And if you did, was she crying?" That line, sans the "mister," surfaced again five years later in a similar, yet very different song.

The melody of and lyrics for that line can be heard in "The Most Beautiful Girl"—a number 1 hit by "the Silver Fox," Charlie Rich, in 1973. For the

The original version of "The Most Beautiful Girl," titled "Hey Mister," by Norro Wilson.

most part, however, the two songs share little else. There was enough similarity to warrant giving Norro Wilson credits as co-writer (but for some reason, Rita Welty wasn't included).

"The Most Beautiful Girl" was included on the *Behind Closed Doors* album (Epic #32247). The album went multiplatinum and won a Country Music Association Award for Album of the Year.

"THE MOTOWN SONG"
Composer: Larry John McNally
Original Artist: Larry John McNally
Label: Atlantic Records; *Recording:* Atlantic #81631 (LP)
Release Year: 1986; *Chart:* did not chart
Cover Artist: Rod Stewart and the Temptations
Label: Warner Brothers Records; *Recording:* Warner Brothers #19322 (CD)
Release Year: 1991; *Chart:* #10 *Billboard* Hot 100

"The Motown Song" pays homage to "those old Motown Records" and also mentions the Miracles in the lyrics. The song's composer, Larry John McNally, wrote and performed the song for the Columbia Pictures 1986 Kevin Bacon movie titled *Quicksilver*. McNally's original rendition can be found on the *Quicksilver* soundtrack album.

Rod Stewart's love of Motown has been proven over and over again with remakes such as "(I Know) I'm Losing You" and "This Old Heart of Mine." In 1991, with the assistance of the Temptations, Stewart rerecorded "The Motown Song" and had himself a Top 10 smash. On the B-side of the 45 was a remake of a soul classic—Arthur Conley's biggest hit, "Sweet Soul Music."

"MOUNTAIN OF LOVE"
Composer: Harold Dorman
Original Artist: Harold Dorman
Label: Rita Records; *Recording:* Rita #1003 (45)
Release Year: 1960; *Chart:* #21 *Billboard* Hot 100 and #7 R&B
Cover Artist: Johnny Rivers
Label: Imperial Records; *Recording:* Imperial #66075 (45)
Release Year: 1964; *Chart:* #9 *Billboard* Hot 100

Mississippi native Harold Dorman recorded for the legendary Sun Records label in the 1950s, but without much success. His big claim to fame came in 1960 with a song he wrote and originally recorded for a small Tennessee label called Rita Records. This tune, "Mountain of Love," tells the tale of a wedding in progress. The singer was supposed to be the groom, but things didn't work out and the girl in the song found someone else. It was a good-sized hit

Harold Dorman did it first, but Johnny Rivers's cover version of "Mountain of Love" made it a Top 10 number.

for Dorman; it just missed the Top 20 on the Pop charts and reached number 7 on the R&B charts.

Four years later, one of music's most prolific cover artists, Johnny Rivers, remade the song for Imperial Records and had the definitive hit version—reaching number 9 on the Pop charts in 1964.

Country Charley Pride released yet another remake of "Mountain of Love" in 1981 (RCA Victor #13014), and it hit number 1 on the Country chart—very high on a mountain of love, indeed.

"Mrs. Robinson"
Composer: Paul Simon
Original Artist: Simon and Garfunkel
Label: Columbia Records; *Recording:* Columbia #44511 (45)
Release Year: 1968; *Chart:* #1 *Billboard* Hot 100

Cover Artist: Booker T. and the MGs
Label: Stax Records; *Recording:* Stax #0037 (45)
Release Year: 1969; *Chart:* #37 *Billboard* Hot 100

The song was originally written by Paul Simon as "Mrs. Roosevelt" long before the duo was approached to supply music for a United Artists motion picture titled *The Graduate*. Director Mike Nichols selected "The Sounds of Silence" and "Scarborough Fair" for the soundtrack, but needed one more tune. Garfunkel then reminded Simon about that unfinished song called "Mrs. Roosevelt," which he thought could easily be adapted as "Mrs. Robinson," and the rest is history. Released as a single in 1968, the seductive song reached number 1 on the Pop charts. The "Coo-coo-katchoo" part of the song had previously been part of "I Am the Walrus" by the Beatles (Capitol #2056).

One year later, Booker T. and the MGs released an instrumental take on the same song on the legendary Stax Record label and had a Top 40 hit. It immediately followed two other songs from motion pictures—"Hang 'Em High" from the Clint Eastwood movie of the same name and "Time Is Tight" from the film *Up Tight*. "Mrs. Robinson," the 1993 version by the Lemonheads (Atlantic #87412), is part of the soundtrack for the 2013 hit film *The Wolf of Wall Street*.

"MUSIC, MUSIC, MUSIC"

Composers: Stephen Weiss and Bernie Baum
Original Artist: Teresa Brewer
Label: London Records; *Recording:* London #605 (78)
Release Year: 1950; *Chart:* #1 *Billboard* Hot 100
Cover Artist: the Happenings
Label: B. T. Puppy Records; *Recording:* B. T. Puppy #538 (45)
Release Year: 1968; *Chart:* #96 *Billboard* Hot 100

Sometimes called "The Nickel Song," this became Teresa Brewer's signature song, and she rerecorded it many times on many labels during her long career. "Music, Music, Music" is a song about a love for music and dancing close.

Inflation was taken into account when the song was covered by Philadelphia R&B group, the Sensations (Argo #5391). The nickel part became "put another dime in."

The Happenings remade the song in 1968 and slowed down the tempo considerably. This clever, well-produced version of the classic song begins with the group chanting, "Do it, do it, do it, do it." The arrangement and the harmony made for some very pleasing "Music, Music, Music." Bob Miranda of the Happenings said, "I saw Teresa Brewer on TV as a kid. I loved her—she was so cute and full of energy. When searching for the next song for the group to do, this one came up. We did a good job with it, but it wasn't exactly our sound. And it wasn't a big hit for us, either—but I like it."

"MUSKRAT LOVE"
Composer: Willis Alan Ramsey
Original Artist: Willis Alan Ramsey
Label: Shelter Records; *Recording:* Shelter #2124 (LP)
Release Year: 1972; *Chart:* did not chart
Cover Artist: America
Label: Warner Brothers Records; *Recording:* Warner #7725 (45)
Release Year: 1973; *Chart:* #67 *Billboard* Hot 100

Originally written and performed as "Muskrat Candlelight," the first version came from the song's composer Willis Alan Ramsey on his eponymously titled album in 1972. It was not a hit.

One year later the song evolved into "Muskrat Love," and under that title, was first recorded by America (one of very few songs not written by the group). This time around the song made the Pop charts, but only reached number 67.

For Muskrat Susie and Muskrat Sam, the third time was the charm as yet another remake, this one by the Captain and Tennille, became a Top 5 million-selling smash in 1976. The song is extremely polarizing, and music lovers have very strong opinions about the song—either you love it or you hate it.

"MY BOY LOLLIPOP"
Composers: Johnny Roberts and Robert Spencer
Original Artist: Barbie Gaye
Label: Darl Records; *Recording:* Darl #1002 (45 and 78)
Release Year: 1956; *Chart:* did not chart
Cover Artist: Millie Small
Label: Smash Records; *Recording:* Smash #1893 (45)
Release Year: 1964; *Chart:* #2 *Billboard* Hot 100

Written by Robert Spencer and Johnny Roberts, the original 1956 rendition of "My Boy Lollypop" was recorded by a fourteen-year-old Coney Island girl named Barbie Gaye. With a big push from disc jockey Alan Freed, the song became a fair-sized New York area hit, but it failed to catch on elsewhere. At this time, the word *lollypop* was spelled with a *y*. On the next version—the hit version—the *y* was changed to an *i*.

That next version was by a singer named Millie Small who was dubbed "The Blue Beat Girl." The record became a smash hit on the Smash Records label and reached number 2 on the Pop charts—kept out of the number 1 spot by the Beach Boys' classic "I Get Around" (Capitol #5174). Small never again hit the Top 30 on the "lolli-Pop" charts.

"MY HEART IS AN OPEN BOOK"
Composers: Hal David and Lee Pockriss
Original Artist: Jimmy Dean

Not as big as Millie Small, Barbie Gaye did "My Boy Lollypop" first.

Label: Columbia Records; *Recording:* Columbia #41265 (45 and 78)
Release Year: 1958; *Chart:* did not chart
Cover Artist: Carl Dobkins Jr.
Label: Decca Records; *Recording:* Decca #30803 (45)
Release Year: 1959; *Chart:* #3 *Billboard* Hot 100

In 1958, Jimmy Dean had his own daytime TV show on CBS. Written by the prolific Hal David and Lee Pockriss, Dean recorded the original version of "My Heart Is an Open Book," but it didn't chart.

The book was reopened a year later, and a singer from Cincinnati named Carl Dobkins Jr. remade Dean's "My Heart Is an Open Book." This time around the record clicked, and Dobkins had a Top 3 million-selling single. Following up that hit, however, proved difficult. The closest he came was with "Lucky Devil" (Decca #31020)—a Top 30 entry early in 1960.

"MY MAMMY"

Composers: Walter Donaldson, Joe Young, and Sam Lewis
Original Artist: Al Jolson
Label: Brunswick Records; *Recording:* Brunswick #3912 (78)
Release Year: 1928; *Chart:* #2 *Billboard*
Cover Artist: the Happenings
Label: B. T. Puppy Records; *Recording:* B. T. Puppy #530 (45)
Release Year: 1967; *Chart:* #13 *Billboard* Hot 100

This song originated in Vaudeville and had a long association with entertainer Al Jolson. Jolson's first recording of "My Mammy" was released in 1928 on a Brunswick 78. He had performed the song in *The Jazz Singer* one year earlier.

Al Jolson and Jerry Lewis's "My Mammy," with a 1960s' feel from the Happenings.

It's interesting to note that the description of the record on the label stated, "Comedian with Orchestra."

Speaking of "Comedian with Orchestra," the song is also associated, although less so, with Jerry Lewis. Lewis's version was released on 45 and 78 in 1957 (Decca #30345). Lewis occasionally performed the song on his yearly MDA (Muscular Dystrophy Association) Labor Day Telethon.

Bob Miranda and the Happenings of New Jersey updated "My Mammy" in 1967. This innovative rendition began a cappella and kept building. Produced by the Tokens, it just missed the Top 10, peaking at number 13. However the song has a stigma attached to it. Bob Miranda, lead singer of the Happenings explains,

> We stopped doing the song for a while in our live performances. Al Jolson and Jerry Lewis used to sing the song in blackface, and we omitted it from our show for quite a while. However, it was a legitimate hit for us—a very well-produced one, and on certain shows we brought it back because people were asking for it. We never performed "My Mammy" in blackface. We just thought it was a good song and we were very comfortable with it. We brought it back with mixed response—kind of a damned if you do and damned if you don't thing. Some people were pissed when we didn't do it, while others walked out when we did do it. You can't please everyone.

"My Maria"

Composers: B. W. Stevenson and Daniel Moore
Original Artist: B. W. Stevenson
Label: RCA Victor Records; *Recording:* RCA Victor #0030 (45)
Release Year: 1973; *Chart:* #9 *Billboard* Hot 100
Cover Artist: Brooks and Dunn
Label: Arista Records; *Recording:* Arista #12993 (CD)
Release Year: 1996; *Chart:* #79 *Billboard* Hot 100

"My Maria" is a song about a long-distance love affair. The singer is on a plane and very excited that he will soon get to see the woman who takes his blues away—Maria. The song was co-written and performed by the late B. W. Stevenson of Dallas, Texas.

The original version of the song made Top 10 on the Pop charts and fared even better on the Adult Contemporary chart—reaching number 1.

Over twenty years later, a very similar version of "My Maria" once again became a hit for the very consistent country duo Brooks and Dunn. It crossed over to number 79 on the Pop charts and introduced the catchy tune to a whole new generation.

"MY OWN TRUE LOVE"
Composers: Mack David and Max Steiner
Original Artist: Jimmy Clanton
Label: Ace Records; *Recording:* Ace #567 (45)
Release Year: 1959; *Chart:* #33 *Billboard* Hot 100
Cover Artist: the Duprees
Label: Coed Records; *Recording:* Coed #571 (45)
Release Year: 1962; *Chart:* #13 *Billboard* Hot 100

The melody of "My Own True Love" is based on "Tara's Theme" from the legendary 1939 motion picture *Gone with the Wind*. The lyrics were provided by songwriter Hal David's big brother, Mack. The original version of the song with lyrics was released by Jimmy Clanton in 1959, and it became a Top 40 hit. Clanton said, "Then and now, when we do this song live the girls go crazy."

Late in 1962, a vocal group from Jersey City, New Jersey, called the Duprees released their version as a follow-up to their biggest hit, "You Belong to Me." Clanton recalled, "This is a sore spot for me—a thorn in my side. I always felt it was my song."

The Duprees' version just missed the Top 10 and was included on the *You Belong to Me* album (Coed #905) late in 1962. For many years, the original "Tara's Theme" melody was used as the theme song for WOR-TV's popular *Million Dollar Movie* series.

"MY PRAYER"
Composers: Georges Boulanger and Jimmy Kennedy
Original Artist: Glenn Miller and His Orchestra
Label: Bluebird Records; *Recording:* Bluebird #10404 (78)
Release Year: 1939; *Chart:* #2 *Billboard* Music Hit Parade
Cover Artist: the Platters
Label: Mercury Records; *Recording:* Mercury #70893 (45 and 78)
Release Year: 1956; *Chart:* #1 *Billboard* Hot 100 and #1 R&B

Georges Boulanger wrote the music for this tune in the 1920s, but the famous lyrics were added by Jimmy Kennedy in the 1930s. Several hit versions followed—one from Glenn Miller and His Orchestra in 1939 and another Top 10 rendition by the Ink Spots (Decca #66608).

However, the best remembered rendition came from the R&B vocal group Tony Williams and the Platters in 1956. It was number 1 on the Pop charts for five consecutive weeks, and in 2008 it was included in the soundtrack for Brad Pitt's Paramount motion picture *The Curious Case of Benjamin Button*.

Ray, Goodman and Brown tried to revive the song in 1980 (Polydor #2016) and reached Top 50 on both the Pop and R&B charts.

"MY SPECIAL ANGEL"
Composer: Jimmy Duncan
Original Artist: Bobby Helms
Label: Decca Records; *Recording:* Decca #30423 (45 and 78)
Release Year: 1957; *Chart:* #7 *Billboard* Hot 100
Cover Artist: the Vogues
Label: Reprise Records; *Recording:* Reprise #0766 (45)
Release Year: 1968; *Chart:* #7 *Billboard* Hot 100

Houston, Texas, native Jimmy Duncan wrote a bunch of songs in his day, but none became as famous as "My Special Angel." In fact, the song became a big hit twice. First time around it reached the Top 10 for Bobby Helms, who also gave us the perennial holiday classic "Jingle Bell Rock" (Decca #30513). Both songs garnered gold records for Helms. In the 2007 motion picture *Crazy*, Helms was portrayed by actor Brad Hawkins.

Shortly after the Helms hit, a group called the Sonny Land Trio released a very echo-laden version, complete with an accordionist first on the Cue Records label (#7935) and then on Prep (#115). It wasn't a big hit for either label.

However, in 1968, the Vogues from Pittsburgh were having success with remakes at this time in their career, and their rendition of "My Special Angel" once again brought the dreamy slow dance back into the Top 10. In fact, co-incidentally, both the Vogues and Bobby Helms reached number 7 on the Pop charts. Special, indeed.

"MY WAY"
Composer: Paul Anka
Original Artist: Frank Sinatra
Label: Reprise Records; *Recording:* Reprise #0807 (45)
Release Year: 1969; *Chart:* #27 *Billboard* Hot 100
Cover Artist: Elvis Presley
Label: RCA Victor Records; *Recording:* RCA Victor #11165 (45)
Release Year: 1977; *Chart:* #22 *Billboard* Hot 100

Canadian American teen idol Paul Anka wrote and recorded a string of hits in the late 1950s and early 1960s, but even bigger things were ahead for him—including writing the theme song for *The Tonight Show with Johnny Carson* and "My Way." Well, to be honest, he based the melody of "My Way" on a French song titled "Comme d'habitude." The melody intrigued him and he tweaked it a bit and wrote new lyrics for the song. He wrote it expressly for Frank Sinatra. In fact, Anka's record label was rather perturbed that Anka didn't record the song himself. Sinatra made the song legendary and cracked the Top 30 in 1969—becoming one of his signature songs. Anka eventually recorded his own version of the song, but not until Sinatra's version had fallen off the charts.

In the 1970s, another big name became associated with "My Way." Elvis Presley performed the song on a regular basis in concert, and shortly after his death on August 16, 1977, RCA Victor released a live version of the song on a 45, and it became Presley's final million-selling single.

"My Way" has truly become one of the most covered songs of all time. There was even a bizarre punk rock version by Sex Pistols' member Sid Vicious that became a Top 10 hit in the United Kingdom in 1978.

Sinatra's version of "My Way" was inducted into the Grammy Hall of Fame in 2000.

N

"NA NA HEY HEY (KISS HIM GOODBYE)"
Composers: Paul Leka, Gary DeCarlo, and Dale Frashuer
Original Artist: Steam
Label: Fontana Records; *Recording:* Fontana #1667 (45)
Release Year: 1969; *Chart:* #1 *Billboard* Hot 100
Cover Artist: the Nylons
Label: Open Air Records; *Recording:* Open Air #0022 (45)
Release Year: 1987; *Chart:* #12 *Billboard* Hot 100

Originally intended as the B-side of the single, "Na Na Hey Hey (Kiss Him Goodbye)" brought a studio group of musicians known as Steam to the top of the charts. We never heard from Steam again after this, but the song had many lives.

Bananarama recorded a remake of the Steam song in 1983 on their *Deep Sea Skiving* album (#810102), and it became a Top 10 hit in several foreign countries, including the United Kingdom, but it made little inroads in the United States.

A 1987 rendition by the Nylons, a Canadian doo-wop group, was a partially a cappella remake, and it peaked at number 12 on the Pop charts.

The original Steam rendition of "Na Na Hey Hey (Kiss Him Goodbye)" has become a staple at many sporting events and sports arenas.

"NEEDLES AND PINS"
Composers: Sonny Bono and Jack Nitzsche
Original Artist: Jackie DeShannon
Label: Liberty Records; *Recording:* Liberty #55563 (45)
Release Year: 1963; *Chart:* #84 *Billboard* Hot 100
Cover Artist: the Searchers

An original promotional copy of the original "Na Na, Hey Hey (Kiss Him Goodbye)" by Steam.

Label: Kapp Records; *Recording:* Kapp #577 (45)
Release Year: 1964; *Chart:* #13 *Billboard* Hot 100

"Needles and Pins" is a song about karma. The singer still loves a certain girl, and that love is reinforced when their paths cross. However, he is secretly hoping that someone will treat her the way she treated him so she can experience the "needles and pinza," too, and get a taste of her own medicine. The song was co-written by Sonny Bono and songwriter/arranger Jack Nitzsche, and a great singer/songwriter in her own right, Jackie DeShannon recorded it first and had a minor hit in 1963.

The following year, the British Invasion was in full swing, and a group from Liverpool (no, not that one) named the Searchers covered the tune and had the definitive hit version. It didn't make Top 10, but it did come very close.

A 1977 remake by a group called Smokie (RSO #881) and one from 1986 by Stevie Nicks and Tom Petty (MCA #52772) kept the song alive for several decades.

Needles and Pins was also the title of a short-lived NBC sitcom from 1973.

"NEVER MY LOVE"
Composers: Donald and Richard Addrisi
Original Artist: the Association
Label: Warner Brothers Records; *Recording:* Warner Brothers #7074 (45)
Release Year: 1967; *Chart:* #2 *Billboard* Hot 100
Cover Artist: Blue Swede
Label: EMI Records; *Recording:* EMI #3938 (45)
Release Year: 1974; *Chart:* #7 *Billboard* Hot 100

"Never My Love" is a tender song about unconditional love. "Never My Love" is the answer to a series of questions from the singer's significant other, such as "Will there come a time when I grow tired of you?" The Association recorded it first and most famously in 1967, and the song reached number 2 and sold a million copies. It was kept out of the number 1 spot by the Box Tops' classic "The Letter" (Mala #565).

Four years later, Marilyn McCoo and the Fifth Dimension remade the song for Bell Records (#134) and just missed the Top 10 with their version. They took the same approach to the song as had the Association, but the next version of the song was totally unique.

A group from Sweden known as Blue Swede had previously recorded the catchy "Oogah chocka" take on "Hooked on a Feeling" and hit number 1 on the Pop charts. They succeeded again in 1974 with an up-tempo rendition of "Never My Love," which brought the song into the Top 10 in the United States as well as numerous foreign countries.

The song's composers, the Addrisi Brothers, opted to record their own version in 1977 (Buddah #587). This time around, the tried-and-true song only reached number 80 on the charts. The Addrisi Brothers recorded a lot of records, but are probably best known for singing the theme to the early 1970s TV sitcom called *Nanny and the Professor.*

"NINETY-NINE WAYS"
Composer: Anthony September
Original Artist: Charlie Gracie
Label: Cameo Records; *Recording:* Cameo #105 (45 and 78)
Release Year: 1957; *Chart:* did not chart
Cover Artist: Tab Hunter
Label: Dot Records; *Recording:* Dot #15548 (45 and 78)
Release Year: 1957; *Chart:* #11 *Billboard* Hot 100

The original "Ninety-Nine Ways" on the flip side of Charlie Gracie's number 1 smash "Butterfly." When covered by Tab Hunter, it became a hit.

"Ninety-Nine Ways" was written by Anthony September—alias Anthony Mammarella—one of the producers of *American Bandstand*. The Charlie Gracie original was on the B-side of his number 1 million-seller titled "Butterfly."

The biggest hit version of "Ninety-Nine Ways" came from actor/singer Tab Hunter, who remembered, "Once again, as with 'Young Love,' we used the Jordanaires in the background. I don't recall ever hearing the Charlie Gracie original version of the song. I got to be on *American Bandstand* a few times as the recordings started moving up the charts. I'm very proud of my two gold records."

Hunter had successfully conquered movies and music. TV was next, and a sitcom titled *The Tab Hunter Show* spent one season on the NBC Sunday night lineup.

"NO, NOT MUCH"
Composers: Robert Allan and Al Stillman
Original Artist: the Four Lads
Label: Columbia Records; *Recording:* Columbia #40629 (45 and 78)
Release Year: 1956; *Chart:* #2 *Billboard* Hot 100
Cover Artist: the Vogues
Label: Reprise Records; *Recording:* Reprise #0803 (45)
Release Year: 1969; *Chart:* #34 *Billboard* Hot 100

"No, Not Much" is a song full of lies. The singer is trying to convince the listener, and himself, that he's not head over heels in love in lines such as, "You don't please me when you squeeze me, no, not much"—but his attempts are very transparent. The Four Lads recorded the song first and had a million-selling Top 3 smash in 1956.

After a long hiatus, "No, Not Much" was remade twice in 1969. Pittsburgh's Vogues had the bigger of the two versions, reaching the Top 40. The other version by Smoke Ring (Gold Dust #317 and Buddah #77) only made it to number 85.

"No, Not Much" was one of many songs of its ilk included in the Broadway musical titled *Forever Plaid*.

"NO LOVE AT ALL"
Composers: Wayne Carson Thompson and Johnny Christopher
Original Artist: Wayne Carson
Label: Monument Records; *Recording:* Monument #1192 (45)
Release Year: 1970; *Chart:* did not chart
Cover Artist: B. J. Thomas
Label: Scepter Records; *Recording:* Scepter #12307 (45)
Release Year: 1971; *Chart:* #16 *Billboard* Hot 100

The original version of "No Love at All" basically went unnoticed when recorded by one of the song's co-writers, Wayne Carson on the Monument Records label in 1970. B. J. Thomas remembered, "Wayne Carson was a good friend. I recorded a few of his songs. I wasn't aware of the fact that he had recorded the first version, but I loved the song. It was one of my favorites. I wish it had been an even bigger hit. I liked the song's message—even a little love is better than no love at all."

Thomas's rendition made Top 20 and was included on his *Most of All* album (Scepter #586).

O

"ONCE IN A WHILE"
Composers: Michael Edwards and Bud Green
Original Artist: Tommy Dorsey and His Orchestra

Label: RCA Victor Records; *Recording:* RCA Victor #25686 (78)
Release Year: 1937; *Chart:* #1 *Billboard* Music Hit Parade
Cover Artist: the Chimes
Label: Tag Records; *Recording:* Tag #444 (45)
Release Year: 1960; *Chart:* #11 *Billboard* Hot 100

"Once in a While" is a song that became a hit once in a while. Tommy Dorsey recorded it first in 1937 and had a number 1 hit with the ballad. Up next was Patti Page on the Mercury label (#5867) in 1952. The song's message is even though the guy is no longer first in the girl's heart, he hopes that once in a while he will fondly cross her mind.

There was also a big doo-wop rendition of the song by Lenny Cocco and the Chimes from Brooklyn, New York, on the tiny Tag Records label. The record caught on, and this rendition reached number 11 nationally and was even bigger in the New York area. The group quickly followed up "Once in a While" with another remake of an old standard, "I'm in the Mood for Love" (Tag #445). It was not as big a hit, but it did make the Top 40.

"ONE"
Composer: Harry Nilsson
Original Artist: Harry Nilsson
Label: RCA Victor Records; *Recording:* RCA Victor #9462 (45)
Release Year: 1968; *Chart:* did not chart
Cover Artist: Three Dog Night
Label: Dunhill Records; *Recording:* Dunhill #4191 (45)
Release Year: 1969; *Chart:* #5 *Billboard* Hot 100

Sometimes referred to as "One Is the Loneliest Number," Harry Nilsson wrote and recorded the first version of the song in 1968 on his *Aerial Ballet* album (RCA #3956). It was then released on a 45 that may not have ever gotten past the "promotional copy" phase.

Also in 1968, Al Kooper recorded a version of "One" on his *I Stand Alone* album (Columbia #9718). It was not a hit.

Both Nilsson and Kooper recorded renditions of the song that were rather staid. However, in 1969, a well-produced version by the up-and-coming Three Dog Night built in intensity as it went along. It became a Top 5 million-selling smash hit. Nilsson was just one of a long list of composers whose songs were recorded by Three Dog Night, along with Laura Nyro, Randy Newman, Hoyt Axton, Leo Sayer, and Russ Ballard.

"ONE LESS BELL TO ANSWER"
Composers: Burt Bacharach and Hal David
Original Artist: Keely Smith
Label: Atlantic Records; *Recording:* Atlantic #2429 (45)

Release Year: 1967; *Chart:* did not chart
Cover Artist: the Fifth Dimension
Label: Bell Records; *Recording:* Bell #940 (45)
Release Year: 1970; *Chart:* #2 *Billboard* Hot 100

"One Less Bell to Answer" is a song in which the female vocalist is attempting to convince herself that her life is better off now that she and her guy have broken up—one less egg to fry, one less bell to answer, and so on. Neither she nor the listener is convinced.

Written by Burt Bacharach and Hal David, the song was originally recorded by Keely Smith in 1967 for the Atlantic Records label. This original rendition went absolutely nowhere.

Just three years later, coincidentally, "One Less Bell to Answer" was released on the Bell Record label by Marilyn McCoo and the Fifth Dimension. It reached number 2 on the Pop charts and became a platinum single. It was included on the *Portrait* album (Bell #6045)—the group's first LP for the label—and it garnered them a gold record.

"OVER THE RAINBOW"

Composers: Harold Arlen and E. Y. Harburg
Original Artist: Judy Garland
Label: Decca Records; *Recording:* Decca #2672 (78)
Release Year: 1939; *Chart:* #1 *Billboard* Music Hit Parade
Cover Artist: the Demensions
Label: Mohawk Records; *Recording:* Mohawk #116 (45)
Release Year: 1960; *Chart:* #16 *Billboard* Hot 100

In *The Wizard of Oz*, Dorothy sings what became her portrayer's (Judy Garland's) signature song, "Over the Rainbow." Glenn Miller also had a big number 1 hit version of the song in the same year (Bluebird #10366). Since the movie's debut, it has been rerecorded countless times and was very popular fodder during the doo-wop era. It was rerecorded by the Moroccos (United #193), the Dell-Vikings (Luniverse #106), the Mustangs (#8005), and the Checkers (King #4719) to name but a few.

However, the biggest cover success during the doo-wop era came from the Bronx, New York, vocal group known as the Demensions. Their version, featuring a very long instrumental open, reached number 16 on the Pop charts on the small Mohawk Records label. It became their biggest hit.

An updated version by Gary Tanner in 1978 (20th Century #2373) broke onto the Hot 100, but not very high—peaking at number 69.

Judy Garland's "Over the Rainbow" was inducted into the Grammy Hall of Fame in 1981.

P

"PAPER ROSES"
Composers: Fred Spielman and Janice Torre
Original Artist: Anita Bryant
Label: Carlton Records; *Recording:* Carlton #528 (45)
Release Year: 1960; *Chart:* #5 *Billboard* Hot 100
Cover Artist: Marie Osmond
Label: MGM/Kolob Records; *Recording:* MGM #14609 (45)
Release Year: 1973; *Chart:* #5 *Billboard* Hot 100

Not to be confused with (although the message was identical) the 1955 song of the same name by Lola Dee (Wing #90015), this "Paper Roses" was a hit twice, more than a decade apart. The lyrics compare imitation flowers with the imitation love this couple used to share.

In 1973, a remake similar to the Anita Bryant original became the biggest solo hit for Marie Osmond on the MGM label. It sold over a million copies. Both hit versions peaked at number 5, coincidentally. After numerous marginally successful TV ventures, Marie Osmond became a longtime spokesperson for Nutrisystem weight loss plans.

"PASS THE DUTCHIE"
Composers: Jackie Mittoo, Leroy Ferguson, and Fitzroy Simpson
Original Artist: the Mighty Diamonds
Label: Music Works Records; *Recording:* Music Works #003 (45)
Release Year: 1982; *Chart:* did not chart
Cover Artist: Musical Youth
Label: MCA Records; *Recording:* MCA #52149 (45)
Release Year: 1982; *Chart:* #10 *Billboard* Hot 100

"Pass the Dutchie" began as "Pass the Kouchie"—a reggae song about sharing a marijuana cigarette. The originators of the song were the Mighty Diamonds (and *Diomonds* was indeed spelled with two *o*'s and no *a*).

The song was covered by a young reggae act known as Musical Youth, and all of the drug references were replaced with food and eating references. Additionally, "Kouchie" became "Dutchie." The song was included on *The Youth of Today* album (MCA #5389). It became their only hit in the United States.

"PATCHES"
Composers: Barry Mann and Larry Kolber
Original Artist: Jimmy Isle
Label: Everest Records; *Recording:* Everest #19383 (45)

Release Year: 1960; *Chart:* did not chart
Cover Artist: Dickey Lee
Label: Smash Records; *Recording:* Smash #1758 (45)
Release Year: 1962; *Chart:* #6 *Billboard* Hot 100

Like the "Patches" by Clarence Carter, this was also a very sad song, yet very different. It was originally recorded by Jimmy Isle on the Everest Records label in 1960, but this rendition was not a success. A girl nicknamed "Patches" hailed from the wrong side of town, and the guy's parents put the kibosh on their relationship as a result. Both "Patches" and the guy end their own lives as a result. Two years later, however, a very similar version caught on and became a Top 10 hit for Dickey Lee. He recorded yet another tearjerker—a song called "Laurie" (TCF Hall #102)—and it, too, became a big hit.

Coincidentally, both Jimmy Isle and Dickey Lee had previously recorded for the Sun Records label in Memphis.

"PENNIES FROM HEAVEN"
Composers: Arthur Johnston and Johnny Burke
Original Artist: Bing Crosby
Label: Decca Records; *Recording:* Decca #947 (78)
Release Year: 1936; *Chart:* #1 *Billboard* Music Hit Parade
Cover Artist: the Skyliners
Label: Calico Records; *Recording:* Calico #117 (45)
Release Year: 1960; *Chart:* #24 *Billboard* Hot 100

Bing Crosby starred in and recorded the title cut for the 1936 Columbia motion picture release of *Pennies from Heaven*. The very positive "glass half full" title song catapulted to number 1 on the charts and was covered countless times by Frank Sinatra, Andy Williams, Sarah Vaughan, Rosemary Clooney, Dean Martin, Billie Holiday, Tony Bennett, and Louis Armstrong to name but a few. In fact, Armstrong also had a role in the film as Henry.

In the rock and roll era, a smooth doo-wop group from the Pittsburgh area named the Skyliners was on a roll with ballad hits such as "Since I Don't Have You" and "This I Swear." As a change of pace in 1960, lead singer Jimmy Beaumont added an up-tempo song to the repertoire and remade the classic "Pennies from Heaven." It became a big national Top 30 hit and was far bigger on the East Coast. Although the Skyliners had the first doo-wop hit with the song, they weren't the first doo-wop group to record it—that honor would go to the Matadors (Sue #700) in 1957 (on the flip side of a ballad titled "Vengeance Will Be Mine").

In 1981, yet another motion picture with the title *Pennies from Heaven* was released. It stars Steve Martin and Bernadette Peters, and the title song appears twice in the film.

"PETER GUNN"

Composer: Henry Mancini
Original Artist: Ray Anthony
Label: Capitol Records; *Recording:* Capitol #4041 (45)
Release Year: 1959; *Chart:* #8 *Billboard* Hot 100
Cover Artist: Duane Eddy
Label: Jamie Records; *Recording:* Jamie #1168 (45)
Release Year: 1960; *Chart:* #27 *Billboard* Hot 100

Henry Mancini didn't only compose great music for the silver screen (*The Pink Panther, Breakfast at Tiffany's*); he also contributed to the small screen in a big way. Likely his most famous TV theme is "Peter Gunn" from the long-running Craig Stevens crime drama of the same name. The biggest recording of the theme came in 1959 as by Ray Anthony for Capitol Records. It was a Top 10 hit.

Just a year later, the theme received an update by "Mr. Twang," Duane Eddy, on Philadelphia's Jamie Record label. This version became a Top 30 hit. A quarter of a century later, Eddy teamed with Art of Noise for a new version of the TV theme (China #42986). Once again, Mancini's masterpiece was in the Top 50.

"THE PIED PIPER"

Composers: Steve Duboff and Artie Kornfeld
Original Artist: the Changing Times
Label: Philips Records; *Recording:* Philips #40320 (45)
Release Year: 1965; *Chart:* did not chart
Cover Artist: Crispian St. Peters
Label: Jamie Records; *Recording:* Jamie #1320 (45)
Release Year: 1966; *Chart:* #4 *Billboard* Hot 100

Very liberally based upon *The Pied Piper of Hamelin*, the song titled "The Pied Piper" was originally released in 1965 by a "garage rock" group known as the Changing Times on the Philips Records label. It was all but ignored at this juncture.

One year later, a singer from Kent, England, named Crispian St. Peters covered the song, and this time around the United States followed the piper. The song became a Top 5 sensation, and also became St. Peters's biggest hit. He also recorded a Top 40 rendition of We Five's "You Were on My Mind" in 1967 (see the entry for that song).

"PLEASE DON'T GO"

Composers: Harry Wayne Casey and Richard Finch
Original Artist: KC and the Sunshine Band

Label: T. K. Records; *Recording:* T. K. #1035 (45)
Release Year: 1979; *Chart:* #1 *Billboard* Hot 100
Cover Artist: KWS
Label: New Plateau Records; *Recording:* New Plateau #339 (CD)
Release Year: 1992; *Chart:* #6 *Billboard* Hot 100

After a long string of disco hits, KC and the Sunshine Band released their first ballad in 1979, and it was a whopping success. "Please Don't Go" was co-written by KC (under his real name, Harry Wayne Casey). It became the group's fifth of five number 1 hits.

Over a dozen years later, "Please Don't Go" was remade by a British group known as KWS. KWS stood for the members' names—King, Williams, and St. Joseph. The beginning of this version was like the original ballad, but the tempo speeds up about a minute in. It was a hit in several foreign countries, and it was their only hit in the United States.

"Please Love Me Forever"

Composers: Johnny Malone and Ollie Blanchard
Original Artist: Tommy Edwards
Label: MGM Records; *Recording:* MGM #12688 (45 and 78)
Release Year: 1958; *Chart:* #61 *Billboard* Hot 100
Cover Artist: Cathy Jean and the Roommates
Label: Valmor Records; *Recording:* Valmor #007 (45)
Release Year: 1961; *Chart:* #12 *Billboard* Hot 100

"Please Love Me Forever" began its life as the B-side of "It's All in the Game"—a number 1 hit for Tommy Edwards in 1958. The lyrics of the song beg for everlasting love, and this original version only reached number 61 on the Pop charts, but better days were ahead.

The second time around, "Please Love Me Forever" became a doo-wop hit by the Roommates on the Valmor Records label, featuring the memorable and rather shrill lead vocals of Cathy Jean. This rendition of the song just missed the Top 10 in 1961. An even bigger version was still to come.

Nicknamed "the Polish Prince," Bobby Vinton added his take on "Please Love Me Forever" to the fray in 1967, and had the only Top 10 hit with it (Epic #10397). Vinton's version garnered him a gold record.

"Portrait of My Love"

Composers: David West and Cyril Ornadel
Original Artist: Steve Lawrence
Label: United Artists Records; *Recording:* United Artists #291 (45)
Release Year: 1961; *Chart:* #9 *Billboard* Hot 100

Cover Artist: the Tokens
Label: Warner Brothers Records; *Recording:* Warner Brothers #5900 (45)
Release Year: 1967; *Chart:* #36 *Billboard* Hot 100

"Portrait of My Love" is a romantic song—a love song to the *n*th power. The singer muses that if someone attempted to paint a portrait of his love, the artist could never capture all of her assets and attributes on one canvas. The lyrics go on to state that even Michelangelo would need assistance to fully capture her essence. The original artist, Steve Lawrence, had a Top 10 hit with this well-crafted composition, and it became his only hit with United Artists Records (he also had hits for Columbia, Coral, and ABC-Paramount).

Kai Winding recorded a cover version in 1964 (Verve #10303), but it didn't chart. The portrait was repainted in 1967 by the prolific Tokens, and once again the song was in the Top 40. The Tokens produced their own records under the name Bright Tunes Productions, and "Portrait of My Love" was no exception. The name of one of the composers was spelled differently on this release—*Orndell*, as opposed to *Ornadel* on the Steve Lawrence original. The song was included on the Tokens' *It's a Happening World* album (Warner Brothers #1685).

"THE POWER OF LOVE"
Composers: Candy DeRouse, Gunther Mende, Jennifer Rush, and Mary S. Applegate
Original Artist: Air Supply
Label: Arista Records; *Recording:* Arista #9391 (45)
Release Year: 1985; *Chart:* #68 *Billboard* Hot 100
Cover Artist: Celine Dion
Label: 550 Music/Epic Records; *Recording:* 550 Music/Epic #77230 (CD)
Release Year: 1993; *Chart:* #1 *Billboard* Hot 100

"The Power of Love" was not, by any means, an overnight success. In the beginning, the song bore the title "The Power of Love (You Are My Lady)." The original 45 version by Air Supply, released at the nadir of their career, barely cracked the charts.

One of the song's composers, Jennifer Rush, released the next version (Epic #05754) early in 1986, and it fared only slightly better—peaking at number 57 on the Pop charts.

Laura Branigan took a stab at the song (Atlantic #89191) late in 1987. Each rendition of the song sold better than its predecessor, and this one was no exception. It reached the Top 30 early in 1988.

Bigger things were still ahead for "The Power of Love." The red-hot Celine Dion managed to put it over in a huge way in 1993. Her version reached number 1 early in 1994 and stayed there for four weeks.

This song is not to be confused with the Luther Vandross or Huey Lewis and the News hits of the same name.

"PUPPET MAN"
Composers: Neil Sedaka and Howard Greenfield
Original Artist: the Fifth Dimension
Label: Bell Records; *Recording:* Bell #880 (45)
Release Year: 1970; *Chart:* #24 *Billboard* Hot 100
Cover Artist: Tom Jones
Label: Parrot Records; *Recording:* Parrot #40062 and #40064 (45)
Release Year: 1971; *Chart:* #26 *Billboard* Hot 100

During "the hungry years"—a down period in Neil Sedaka's storied musical career—he and songwriting partner Howard Greenfield landed a couple of songs in the hands of the Fifth Dimension. "Puppet Man" followed a decent-sized hit titled "Working on a Groovy Thing," and it, too, made the Top 30. The subject matter of "Puppet Man" bears a resemblance to that of a previous hit by James and Bobby Purify called "I'm Your Puppet"—just pull my string and I'll do my thing.

Just one year later, Tom Jones recorded his take on the same song, but with more of an edge than the very smooth original. It, too, made the Top 30, and for some reason was released twice on 45 with different B-sides. "Puppet Man" was included on the *She's a Lady* album (Parrot #71046) in 1971.

"PUPPY LOVE"
Composer: Paul Anka
Original Artist: Paul Anka
Label: ABC-Paramount Records; *Recording:* ABC-Paramount #10082 (45)
Release Year: 1960; *Chart:* #2 *Billboard* Hot 100
Cover Artist: Donny Osmond
Label: MGM Records; *Recording:* MGM #14367 (45)
Release Year: 1972; *Chart:* #3 *Billboard* Hot 100

"Puppy Love" was written by Paul Anka. In the lyrics, he claimed to be seventeen, but at this time in 1960 he was really nineteen. The song is all about the opinions of others that he and his girl were too young to be in love, and thus the title. The song just missed the top spot on the charts, kept out of number 1 by "Theme from a Summer Place" by Percy Faith (Columbia #41490).

A dozen years later, fourteen-year-old Donny Osmond remade the Anka classic and introduced the tune to a whole new generation of young lovers. This new version hit number 3 on the Pop charts and sold over a million copies.

"Put a Little Love in Your Heart"
Composers: Jackie DeShannon, Jimmie Holiday, and Randy Myers
Original Artist: Jackie DeShannon
Label: Imperial Records; *Recording:* Imperial #66385 (45)
Release Year: 1969; *Chart:* #4 *Billboard* Hot 100
Cover Artists: Al Green and Annie Lennox
Label: A & M Records; *Recording:* A & M #1255 (45)
Release Year: 1988; *Chart:* #9 *Billboard* Hot 100

"Put a Little Love in Your Heart" was a socially conscious song, co-written by Jackie DeShannon. It urges all to "think of your fellow man, lend him a helping hand, put a little love in your heart." It became DeShannon's biggest hit, and earned her a gold record.

Almost twenty years later, the world was a better place for you and me when the song was remade by Annie Lennox and Al Green. It was Green's first appearance in the Top 10 in almost fifteen years. It was produced by Lennox's Eurythmics cohort, Dave Stewart, and was included in the soundtrack for the Bill Murray Paramount Studios holiday film *Scrooged*—an update of the Charles Dickens classic "A Christmas Carol."

"Puttin' on the Ritz"
Composer: Irving Berlin
Original Artist: Harry Richman
Label: Brunswick Records; *Recording:* Brunswick #4677 (78)
Release Year: 1930; *Chart:* #1 *Billboard*
Cover Artist: Taco
Label: RCA Victor Records; *Recording:* RCA Victor #13574 (45)
Release Year: 1983; *Chart:* #4 *Billboard* Hot 100

Introduced in the musical *Puttin' on the Ritz*, the star of the film, Harry Richman (a much better singer than actor), had a number 1 hit with the title song. Leo Reisman recorded a rendition in that same year (RCA Victor #22306). Fred Astaire performed the song in the 1946 Paramount musical titled *Blue Skies*. The title was inspired by the very upscale Ritz Hotel in New York, and the title "Puttin' on the Ritz" came to mean dressing up "to the nines."

A bizarre remake of "Puttin' on the Ritz" complete with a synthesizer brought the song back in a big way in 1983. The artist called himself simply Taco, and this uniquely updated rendition reached the Top 5 and sold over a million copies. Although Taco never had another hit, "Puttin' on the Ritz" was included on his *After Eight* album (RCA #4818), which reached the Top 30. And, yes, his name was really Taco—Taco Ockerse.

A very memorable performance of the song by Peter Boyle (the monster) and Gene Wilder (Dr. Frankenstein) was featured in Mel Brooks's 1974 classic *Young Frankenstein*.

R

"RED, RED WINE"
Composer: Neil Diamond
Original Artist: Neil Diamond
Label: Bang Records; *Recording:* Bang #556 (45)
Release Year: 1968; *Chart:* #62 *Billboard* Hot 100
Cover Artist: UB40
Label: A & M Records; *Recording:* A & M #2800 and #1244 (45)
Release Year: 1988; *Chart:* #1 *Billboard* Hot 100

Neil Diamond wrote and originally recorded "Red, Red Wine." Produced by Jeff Barry and Ellie Greenwich, this was Diamond's final release for the Bang Records label, and it wasn't a big hit. Performed in a medium tempo, the lyrics tell the age-old story of a man who turns to wine to help get over a breakup. It was included on his *Just for You* album (Bang #217).

The next version to chart in the United States was by UB40 and had a reggae beat. The year was 1984, and this time around it was a modest hit, reaching number 34 on the Pop charts. Their rendition was reworked in 1988 with a rap line inserted ("Red, red wine makes me feel so fine"), and this time it reached number 1. The group hit number 1 once more in 1993 with a reggae interpretation of Elvis Presley's "Can't Help Falling in Love" (see the entry for that song).

"RED ROSES FOR A BLUE LADY"
Composers: Sid Tepper and Roy C. Bennett
Original Artist: Vaughn Monroe
Label: RCA Victor Records; *Recording:* RCA Victor #3319 (78)
Release Year: 1948; *Chart:* #4 *Billboard* Music Popularity Chart
Cover Artist: Vic Dana
Label: Dolton Records; *Recording:* Dolton #304 (45)
Release Year: 1965; *Chart:* #10 *Billboard* Hot 100

The roses in "Red Roses for a Blue Lady" were definitely perennials—the song was covered many times successfully. Vaughn Monroe got it started late in 1948 and was quickly covered by Guy Lombardo (Decca #24549), and both versions made Top 10. The song tells the tale of a young man who, having had a big quarrel with his significant other, asks a florist to deliver a bouquet of roses to the girl as an apology. Roses were a lot less expensive in 1948.

The tune enjoyed quite a revival in 1965 with three renditions in the Top 30. Vic Dana had the biggest and reached Top 10. Bert Kaempfert's version just missed the Top 10 (Decca #31722), and even Wayne Newton joined the fray. Newton reached number 23 (Capitol #5366).

"RELEASE ME"

Composers: Eddie Miller, Dub Williams, and Robert Gene Yount
Original Artist: Eddie Miller and the Oklahomans
Label: 4-Star Records; *Recording:* 4-Star #1407 (78)
Release Year: 1949; *Chart:* did not chart
Cover Artist: Little Esther Phillips
Label: Lenox Records; *Recording:* Lenox #5555 (45)
Release Year: 1962; *Chart:* #8 *Billboard* Hot 100 and #1 R&B

"Release Me" is a song about a man who has come to the realization that his relationship is over. It was co-written by Eddie Miller, who also recorded the first version of the song as "Release Me (and Let Me Love Again)." It was covered in 1954 by Jimmy Heap who turned it into a Top 5 country hit.

The 1960s were kind to "Release Me." Little Esther Phillips had a Top 10 hit with the song in 1962 on both the Pop and R&B charts. Five years later it became the first hit single and also the biggest hit single for Engelbert Humperdinck on the Parrot Records label (#40011), kicking off a storied career with amazing longevity. *Release Me* was also the title of Humperdinck's first hit album (Parrot #71012). It spent over two years on the charts.

"RHINESTONE COWBOY"

Composer: Larry Weiss
Original Artist: Larry Weiss
Label: 20th Century Records; *Recording:* 20th Century #2084 (45)
Release Year: 1974; *Chart:* #24 *Billboard* Adult Contemporary
Cover Artist: Glen Campbell
Label: Capitol Records; *Recording:* Capitol #4095 (45)
Release Year: 1975; *Chart:* #1 *Billboard* Hot 100

"Rhinestone Cowboy" is a song about a country singer trying and trying to make it big—trying to persevere until things finally break his way. Despite years of frustration and rejection, he is very confident of fulfilling his dream and becoming a "rhinestone cowboy." The song was written by Larry Weiss, who recorded the original rendition both on a 45 and on his *Black and Blue Suite* album (20th Century #428). This version of the song reached number 24 on the Adult Contemporary charts, but just like the cowboy in the song, it wasn't an overnight success.

In 1975, Glen Campbell recorded his take for Capitol Records, and it clicked almost instantly. Glen Campbell was back in the Top 10 on the Pop charts for the first time in five years. In fact, "Rhinestone Cowboy" became his first number 1 hit.

Peter Griffin sang part of the song at a wedding in the *Family Guy* episode titled "There's Something about Paulie."

"RHYTHM OF THE RAIN"
Composer: John Claude Gummoe
Original Artist: the Cascades
Label: Valiant Records; *Recording:* Valiant #6026 (45)
Release Year: 1962; *Chart:* #3 *Billboard* Hot 100
Cover Artist: Gary Lewis and the Playboys
Label: Liberty Records; *Recording:* Liberty #56093 (45)
Release Year: 1969; *Chart:* #63 *Billboard* Hot 100

The original Cascades, famous for "Rhythm of the Rain"—left to right, John Claude Gummoe, Dave Szabo, Eddy Snyder, Dave Wilson (foreground), and David Stevens. *Courtesy of John Claude Gummoe*

John Claude Gummoe wrote a song in 1962 that had many more than nine lives—truly one of the most-covered songs of all time. Gummoe was a member of a vocal group called the Cascades who hailed from San Diego, where it rarely rains. And yet, his biggest hit was a song titled "Rhythm of the Rain," which was released in 1962 and peaked at number 3 on the Pop charts early in 1963. It was also a big hit in the United Kingdom. Gummoe said, "It was released on a branch of Warner Brothers Records called Valiant Records. The single was arranged by Perry Botkin Jr. and produced by Barry DeVorzon. It was DeVorzon who came up with the group's name. We had previously been known as the Thundernotes, but at a brainstorming session, DeVorzon was inspired by a package of Cascade dish soap on the counter, and the Cascades were born." Gummoe added, "We were supposed to record a song called 'I Wonder What She's Doing Tonight' as a follow-up, but at the time we had become disillusioned with Valiant Records and left to go to RCA Victor. The follow-up song was written by Barry DeVorzon, and he was not pleased about our leaving, and decided to record the song himself—as Barry and the Tamerlanes." That song, also on the Valiant label (#6034), just missed the Top 20 late in 1963.

About the bevy of versions of his song, Gummoe said, "It's been covered dozens of times by famous names such as Lawrence Welk, Bobby Darin, Johnny Rivers, Neil Sedaka, Percy Faith, Johnny Tillotson, Sarah Brightman, Jan and Dean, Jacky Ward, Stephen Bishop, the Browns, and artists from almost every country in the world. Our version of the song was used in the soundtrack for the film *Quadrophenia*."

A 1969 remake by Gary Lewis and the Playboys made the Hot 100 and it became the final chart record for that group. Dan Fogelberg's rendition received heavy airplay on adult contemporary and soft rock radio stations in 1990. Fogelberg's take on the classic song was included on his *The Wild Places* album (Full Moon #45059).

"RIGHT OR WRONG"
Composer: Wanda Jackson
Original Artist: Wanda Jackson
Label: Capitol Records; *Recording:* Capitol #4553 (45)
Release Year: 1960; *Chart:* #29 *Billboard* Hot 100 and #9 Country
Cover Artist: Ronnie Dove
Label: Diamond Records; *Recording:* Diamond #173 (45)
Release Year: 1964; *Chart:* #14 *Billboard* Hot 100

Wanda Jackson was born in Maud, Oklahoma, and early in her career toured with an up-and-coming Elvis Presley. Her early rockabilly singles like "Fujiama Mama," "Mean, Mean Man," and "Hot Dog, That Made Him Mad" are treasured among collectors. She finally crossed over to the Pop charts in 1960 with a great rocker called "Let's Have a Party" (which was included in the *Dead Poets Society* soundtrack), but it is her crossover ballads for which she is best known. Among them are "In the Middle of a Heartache" (Capitol #4635) and "Right or Wrong," and both were released in 1961.

Just three years later amidst the British Invasion, popular cover artist Ronnie Dove released his take on "Right or Wrong" and made it an even bigger hit on the pop charts—peaking at number 14. Dove had five songs reach the Top 20, but was never able to penetrate the Top 10.

As of this writing, Wanda Jackson still tours and was inducted into the Rock and Roll Hall of Fame in 2009 as an "early influence."

"RING OF FIRE"
Composers: Merle Kilgore and June Carter Cash
Original Artist: Anita Carter
Label: Mercury Records; *Recording:* Mercury #20770 (LP)
Release Year: 1963; *Chart:* did not chart
Cover Artist: Johnny Cash
Label: Columbia Records; *Recording:* Columbia #42788 (45)
Release Year: 1963; *Chart:* #17 *Billboard* Hot 100

"Ring of Fire" was definitely a family affair. It was co-written by Mrs. Johnny Cash and was originally an album cut by Johnny's sister-in-law, Anita, on the Mercury label very early in 1963. "Ring of Fire" is a song about falling in love—falling into the ring of fire and getting burned as a result.

A short time after Anita Carter's original album version, which was not a hit, "the Man in Black," Johnny Cash, recorded his own single version for Columbia Records, with a mariachi-inspired horn section. It became one of his biggest crossover hits.

Johnny Cash's "Ring of Fire" was included in the 1993 MGM motion picture *Suture*, but the Carter family put the kibosh on Pfizer's plans to use the song in a series of commercials for Preparation H in 2004. The song was performed by Joaquin Phoenix and Reese Witherspoon in the Johnny Cash biopic *Walk the Line* in 2005. A commemorative Johnny Cash postage stamp was issued on June 5, 2013, and the entire sheet of stamps was in the shape of a 45 rpm record.

"ROCK AND ROLL HEAVEN"
Composers: Alan O'Day and John Stevenson
Original Artist: Climax
Label: Rocky Road Records; *Recording:* Rocky Road #30072 (45)
Release Year: 1972; *Chart:* did not chart
Cover Artist: the Righteous Brothers

Label: Haven Records; *Recording:* Haven #7002 (45)
Release Year: 1974; *Chart:* #3 *Billboard* Hot 100

"Rock and Roll Heaven" is a song that pays homage to the legends of rock and roll no longer with us. Sonny Geraci and Climax, most famous for "Precious and Few" (Carousel #30055), recorded the original rendition but it was not a hit.

Two years later, the song served as a comeback hit for Bill Medley and Bobby Hatfield—the Righteous Brothers. The "late greats" referenced in the lyrics include Jim Morrison, Janis Joplin, Bobby Darin, Otis Redding, Jimi Hendrix, and Jim Croce. The song became a Top 3 smash, and it was included on their *Give It to the People* album (Haven #9201). In the early 1990s, the Righteous Brothers recorded an updated version of the song. Sadly, on November 5, 2003, Bobby Hatfield himself ascended to "rock and roll heaven."

"ROSE GARDEN"
Composer: Joe South
Original Artist: Joe South
Label: Capitol Records; *Recording:* Capitol #108 (LP)
Release Year: 1968; *Chart:* did not chart
Cover Artist: Lynn Anderson
Label: Columbia Records; *Recording:* Columbia #45252 (45)
Release Year: 1970; *Chart:* #3 *Billboard* Hot 100

Sometimes called "I Never Promised You a Rose Garden," the famous song was penned by the prolific Joe South, who recorded it first on his *Introspect* album in 1968. The lyrics seem to work better from the male perspective because of the rose garden and diamond ring references in the lyrics, and yet, it was a female who popularized the song.

Lynn Anderson, famous for her big blonde beehive hairdo, also became popular for her million-selling take on "Rose Garden." It was a huge crossover hit in 1970 on the Columbia label, and it reached Top 3 on the Pop charts early in 1971. The song was included on Anderson's platinum *Rose Garden* album (Columbia #30411) in 1971, and the popularity of this song briefly made her the darling of the variety show circuit. Along with that "rose garden" came some thorns, as Anderson never again reached the Top 50 on the Pop charts.

"RUBY, DON'T TAKE YOUR LOVE TO TOWN"
Composer: Mel Tillis
Original Artist: Johnny Darrell
Label: United Artists Records; *Recording:* United Artists #50126 (45)
Release Year: 1967; *Chart:* #9 *Billboard* Country
Cover Artist: Kenny Rogers and the First Edition

Label: Reprise Records; *Recording:* Reprise #0829 (45)
Release Year: 1969; *Chart:* #6 *Billboard* Hot 100

Mel Tillis wrote this timely song about a paralyzed veteran who is bedridden but fully cognizant of the fact that his wife "goes to town" often looking for love. The first version of the song by Johnny Darrell was a Top 10 hit on the Country charts. It was performed rather slowly with the lyrics delivered in a very staccato, over-enunciated manner.

Two years later, it was recorded at a speedier tempo and delivered with a lot more emotion by Kenny Rogers and the First Edition. It became the group's second Top 10 hit and was included on the *Ruby, Don't Take Your Love to Town* album (Reprise #6352). A short time after this big hit, Rogers got his own syndicated variety series titled *Rollin' with Kenny Rogers and the First Edition.*

"RUNAROUND"
Composer: Cirino Colacrai
Original Artist: the Three Chuckles
Label: Boulevard Records: *Recording:* Boulevard #100 (45 and 78)
Release Year: 1954; *Chart:* #20 *Billboard* Hot 100
Cover Artist: the Fleetwoods
Label: Dolton Records; *Recording:* Dolton #22 (45)
Release Year: 1960; *Chart:* #23 *Billboard* Hot 100

"Runaround" was originally recorded on the tiny Boulevard Records label by the Three Chuckles in 1954. When the record caught on, the song was leased to RCA Victor's short-lived subsidiary—the "X" record label (X #0066)—eventually cracking the national Top 20.

Gretchen Christopher of the Fleetwoods recalled, "Barbara Ellis and I were freshman cheerleaders in 1954 when 'Runaround' first hit. I loved it. Six years later, in the midst of our own recording successes, we recorded it with my leading the vocal arranging, including singing 'waited and waited and waited and waited' in 6/8 time, with Barbara in close harmony, against Gary Troxel's 4/4 melody. Ironically, it became one of my dad's favorite Fleetwoods' hits, even though he'd previously told me he didn't like the poundingly repetitive 6/8 of rock and roll and rhythm and blues."

Teddy Randazzo of the Three Chuckles became a prolific songwriter and record producer in the 1960s, working mostly with Little Anthony and the Imperials. The writer of "Runaround," Cirino Colacrai, made a few records with his own group, Cirino and the Bowties, on New York's Royal Roost Records label. Both Randazzo and Colacrai appeared in Alan Freed's early rock and roll movies.

Speaking of movies, Christopher added, "In the Alan Freed biopic *American Hot Wax*, the Fleetwoods are portrayed as Timmy and the Two Lips singing 'Mr. Blue' on one of Freed's concerts. In reality, we sang 'Come Softly to Me' on his New York TV show."

"RUNAWAY"
Composers: Max Crook and Charles Westover
Original Artist: Del Shannon
Label: Big Top Records; *Recording:* Big Top #3067 (45)
Release Year: 1961; *Chart:* #1 *Billboard* Hot 100
Cover Artist: Lawrence Welk
Label: Dot Records; *Recording:* Dot #16336 (45)
Release Year: 1962; *Chart:* #56 *Billboard* Hot 100

His given name was Charles Westover, but he was known on record as Del Shannon, and he reached number 1 on the charts with his very first release, "Runaway" in 1961, featuring the haunting and unique sound of a musitron in the song's instrumental break. Shannon scored other hits such as "Hats Off to Larry," "Keep Searchin' (We'll Follow the Sun)," and "Little Town Flirt," but never again topped the charts.

One year after the original Del Shannon version, a cover version emerged from a very unexpected source—Lawrence Welk. Welk's version was instrumental, except for an occasional "Ooh" or "Ahh" from a female chorus and a male bass singer. Welk's rendition barely penetrated the Top 60. A couple of other versions of "Runaway" by Bonnie Raitt and Tony Orlando and Dawn reached the Top 100 in the 1970s.

Del Shannon was poised for a big comeback in the early 1980s when he released a version of Phil Phillips's "Sea of Love" (produced by Tom Petty), but despite a lot of airplay it peaked at number 33. Career disappointment led Del Shannon to take his own life on February 8, 1990.

Shannon's "Runaway" has been included in countless movie soundtracks, including *American Graffiti*, *Good Will Hunting*, and *Eddie and the Cruisers*.

S

"SAD MOVIES (MAKE ME CRY)"
Composer: John D. Loudermilk
Original Artist: Sue Thompson
Label: Hickory Records; *Recording:* Hickory #1153 (45)
Release Year: 1961; *Chart:* #5 *Billboard* Hot 100
Cover Artist: the Lennon Sisters
Label: Dot Records; *Recording:* Dot #12265 (45)
Release Year: 1961; *Chart:* #57 *Billboard* Hot 100

John D. Loudermilk wrote songs that became hits for artists such as Eddie Cochran, George Hamilton IV, the Raiders, the Casinos, the Nashville Teens, Bobby Vee, and Johnny Tillotson, but no one had more success with his compositions than Sue Thompson—"Norman," "Paper Tiger," "James (Hold the Ladder Steady)," and "Sad Movies (Make Me Cry)." The latter was a cheating song about a girl whose boyfriend tells her he has to work and can't take her to the movies. She goes alone, only to see her boyfriend walk into the theater with her best friend. One of the best lines in the song is, "In the middle of the color cartoon, I started to cry."

Only three weeks after Thompson's version started moving up the charts, the Lennon Sisters (from *The Lawrence Welk Show*) released almost a Xerox copy of the tune on the Dot Records label, but didn't manage to penetrate the Top 40. Even though she was almost forty at the time, Thompson had a youthful voice and reached the Top 5 on the pop charts. "Sad Movies" and "Norman"— her biggest hits—both appear on the *Meet Sue Thompson* album (Hickory #104).

"SAVE YOUR HEART FOR ME"
Composers: Gary Geld and Peter Udell
Original Artist: Brian Hyland
Label: ABC-Paramount Records; *Recording:* ABC-Paramount #10452 (45)
Release Year: 1963; *Chart:* did not chart
Cover Artist: Gary Lewis and the Playboys
Label: Liberty Records; *Recording:* Liberty #55809 (45)
Release Year: 1965; *Chart:* #2 *Billboard* Hot 100

"Save Your Heart for Me" became a big hit in 1965, but it was first recorded by Brian Hyland, who recalled, "The song was written by the same writers/producers (Geld and Udell) I had been working with. They were writing some pop country songs. This was an ABC single session in 1963 at New York's RKO Studios along with 'I'm Afraid to Go Home,' which ended up being the A-side release with 'Save Your Heart for Me' as the B-side. 'I'm Afraid to Go Home' was later recorded by Cliff Richard and also Gene Pitney. For the whistler on the record they brought in the guy who whistled on the John Wayne movie theme, *The High and the Mighty*." The name of the whistler, by the way, was Muzzy Marcellino.

Brian Hyland's version did not make the charts, but a very similar version two years later also utilized a whistler and soared to number 2 on the Pop charts. Hyland remembered, "Gary Lewis's version with Leon Russell's arrangement made it a Pop hit." It was Lewis's third of seven consecutive Top 10 hits. Lewis also performed the theme song for the DePatie/Freleng Enterprises cartoon series *The Super Six*, which ran on Saturday mornings from 1966 to 1969 and is now available on a DVD box set.

"SEALED WITH A KISS"
Composers: Gary Geld and Peter Udell
Original Artist: the Four Voices
Label: Columbia Records; *Recording:* Columbia #41699 (45)

The ageless Brian Hyland continues to perform to sell-out crowds wherever he goes. *Courtesy of Brian Hyland*

Release Year: 1960; *Chart:* did not chart
Cover Artist: Brian Hyland
Label: ABC-Paramount Records; *Recording:* ABC-Paramount #10336 (45)
Release Year: 1962; *Chart:* #3 *Billboard* Hot 100

"Sealed with a Kiss" is a song with longevity, but the first version by the Four Voices on the Columbia label in 1960 was quite lackluster and did not chart. Brian Hyland said, "I don't remember actually hearing the earlier version, but I was under the impression it was done in the folk genre, like the Brothers Four." Indeed, that describes the Four Voices original perfectly.

Next time around, however, the Gary Geld and Peter Udell composition was a monster hit. Hyland recalled, "Gary and Peter had a specific arrangement in mind for this song, and taught it to me at the piano as they wanted it. I recorded the lead vocal and then the harmony vocal myself. They were great writers, and as producers they knew how to get the best out of their songs." ABC-Paramount wisely released the song about being apart for the summer just as the summer of 1962 was coming on. A lot of young lovers were able to connect, and it became a Top 3 smash. The B-side, "Summer Job," also cleverly tied in to the season. Both sides were included on the *Sealed with a Kiss* album (ABC-Paramount #431).

Once again, perfectly timed for summertime of 1968, Gary Lewis and the Playboys (Liberty #56037) had a Top 20 hit with a remake of the song. Bobby Vinton released his rendition (Epic #10861) during the summer of 1972, and like the Gary Lewis version, it, too, peaked at number 19 on the Pop charts. It was included on Vinton's *Sealed with a Kiss* album (Epic #31642)—his last for Epic Records after a long run.

"SECRET LOVE"
Composers: Sammy Fain and Paul Webster
Original Artist: Doris Day
Label: Columbia Records; *Recording:* Columbia #40108 (45 and 78)
Release Year: 1953; *Chart:* #1 *Billboard* Hot 100
Cover Artist: Freddy Fender
Label: ABC/Dot Records; *Recording:* ABC/Dot #17585 (45)
Release Year: 1975; *Chart:* #20 *Billboard* Hot 100

"Secret Love" made its debut in the Warner Brothers musical motion picture *Calamity Jane* in 1953 as by Doris Day. When released as a single, the secret was out and it reached number 1 on the Pop charts. The song also won an Oscar for Best Original Song. A flurry of cover versions followed.

For the R&B audience, the smooth-as-silk Moonglows recorded their vocal group rendition on Chicago's legendary Chance Records label (#1152) in 1954. Connie Francis recorded a version for the pop market, Mel Williams and also Marvin Gaye and Tammi Terrell released soulful versions in the 1960s, but it was a 1975 remake by Freddy Fender that brought "Secret Love" back into the Top 20 on the Pop charts. It became Fender's final Top 20 hit and was included on the *Are You Ready for Freddy* album (ABC/Dot #2044).

"SEE YOU IN SEPTEMBER"
Composers: Sherman Edwards and Sid Wayne
Original Artist: the Tempos
Label: Climax Records; *Recording:* Climax #102 (45)

Release Year: 1959; *Chart:* #23 *Billboard* Hot 100
Cover Artist: the Happenings
Label: B. T. Puppy Records; *Recording:* B. T. Puppy #520 (45)
Release Year: 1966; *Chart:* #3 *Billboard* Hot 100

"See You in September" was co-written by Sid Wayne, who also co-wrote "I'm Gonna Knock on Your Door," "It's Impossible," and numerous tunes for Elvis Presley's movies. He was also the musical director for the TV game show *Video Village* in the early 1960s. For this song Wayne was paired with songwriter Sherman Edwards. "See You in September" was originally recorded by a Pittsburgh group known as the Tempos with a slow, Latin beat, and it became a Top 30 hit for them in 1959. But there was more to this September song.

Bob Miranda, lead singer of the Happenings from New Jersey, recalled, "I first heard the song as by the Tempos. I felt it was a great song, but the Tempos recorded it slow and laid back. I envisioned the tune having more guts. We recorded the song with a 'Happenings spin,' lots of hooks, and kind of a Motown beat. Herb Bernstein embellished it all with the horn section. It came out really good and became our first Top 10 hit."

About the origins and meaning of the name of their record label, B. T. Puppy, Miranda said, "I think Jay Siegal of the Tokens was emulating the RCA dog, Nipper in a cartoonish way. Maybe the B. T. part of the name stood for Brooklyn Tokens. This was the Tokens' own record company, and Jay Siegal, is a great talent and has always been a great friend. We still work together quite often. He can still sing 'The Lion Sleeps Tonight' exactly like the day he first recorded it."

"Share Your Love with Me"

Composers: Alfred Braggs and Deadric Malone
Original Artist: Bobby Bland
Label: Duke Records; *Recording:* Duke #377 (45)
Release Year: 1964; *Chart:* #42 *Billboard* Hot 100 and #5 R&B
Cover Artist: Kenny Rogers
Label: Liberty Records; *Recording:* Liberty #1430 (45)
Release Year: 1981; *Chart:* #14 *Billboard* Hot 100

"Share Your Love with Me" was one of Bobby Bland's most pop-oriented singles and a great performance. Likely, coming in 1964, it got lost in the shuffle, what with all the British Invasion and Motown music that usurped the United States charts in that year. It failed to make Top 40 on the Pop charts, but it did reach Top 5 R&B.

In 1969 Aretha Franklin remade the tune. The single (Atlantic #2650) reached number 13 on the Pop charts and number 1 R&B, and it was included on the *This Girl's in Love with You* album (Atlantic #8248) in 1970. The single won Aretha a Grammy for Best Female R&B Vocal. As of this writing, Aretha was seen most recently in *Muscle Shoals*—a 2013 Magnolia Pictures release about the legendary Fame Recording Studio in Muscle Shoals, Alabama.

The next time around, the song sounded a bit different as it was adapted as a country single by Kenny Rogers. This version peaked at number 14 on the Pop charts and was included on Rogers's *Share Your Love* album (Liberty #1108). The album was produced by Lionel Richie, and if one listens to "Share Your Love with Me" very carefully, one can hear Gladys Knight providing some of the background vocals.

Sadly, Bobby "Blue" Bland died at the age of eighty-three on June 23, 2013.

"She Cried"

Composers: G. Richards and Teddy Daryll
Original Artist: Teddy Daryll
Label: Utopia Records; *Recording:* Utopia #501 (45)
Release Year: 1961; *Chart:* did not chart
Cover Artist: Jay and the Americans
Label: United Artists Records; *Recording:* United Artists #415 (45)
Release Year: 1962; *Chart:* #5 *Billboard* Hot 100

"She Cried" was co-written in 1960 by Ted Meister (a.k.a. Teddy Daryll), and he also recorded the first version of the song on the tiny Utopia label in 1961. This version of the teary ballad wasn't a hit.

In 1962, produced by Jerry Leiber and Mike Stoller for United Artists Records, Jay and the Americans took a shot at that same Teddy Daryll song and had a Top 5 smash. Mind you, at this time, the original Jay (Jay Traynor) was the front man for the group. After this hit, Traynor opted to pursue a solo career (which, sadly, never took off) and was replaced by Jay Black for the duration.

A female take on the song was released by the Shangrilas in 1966 as "He Cried" for Leiber and Stoller's Red Bird label (#053). This time around the song didn't crack the Top 50.

"She's a Lady"

Composer: Paul Anka
Original Artist: Paul Anka
Label: RCA Victor Records; *Recording:* RCA Victor #4309 (LP)
Release Year: 1970; *Chart:* did not chart
Cover Artist: Tom Jones
Label: Parrot Records; *Recording:* Parrot #40058 (45)
Release Year: 1971; *Chart:* #2 *Billboard* Hot 100

Canada's Paul Anka wrote this song in a period before his big comeback in the middle 1970s. Anka recorded the original version on a 1970 album titled *Paul*

Anka '70s. The album didn't chart, but the song called "She's a Lady" would soon go on to bigger and better things.

In 1971, Tom Jones rerecorded the song a bit faster, louder, and with much more oomph. This became the definitive version—a Top 3 million-selling smash. It's Jones's biggest hit of a long and storied career.

"She's a Lady" has been included in the soundtracks for such films as *Wilder Napalm* from 1993 and *To Wong Foo, Thanks for Everything! Julie Newmar* from 1995. One of the lyrics in the song, "she always knows her place," renders the song a bit archaic today.

"SHOULD I DO IT?"
Composer: Layng Martine Jr.
Original Artist: Tanya Tucker
Label: MCA Records; *Recording:* MCA #51131 (45)
Release Year: 1981; *Chart:* #50 *Billboard* Country
Cover Artist: the Pointer Sisters
Label: Planet Records; *Recording:* Planet #47960 (45)
Release Year: 1982; *Chart:* #13 *Billboard* Hot 100

"Should I Do It?" was a very retro-sounding single by Tanya Tucker in 1981. It was also the title cut from her 1981 MCA album (#5228). Neither the single nor the album fared very well on the Country charts. The song finds the singer on the horns of a dilemma—should she reconnect and allow herself to fall in love again with a guy from her past who treated her badly, or should she just move on and forget him?

"Should I Do It?" was covered in 1982 by Oakland, California's, red-hot Pointer Sisters on Planet Records and it became a Top 20 hit. It was included on the gold album *Black and White.* Turnabout is fair play, and a song by the Pointer Sisters, "Slow Hand" (Planet #47929), was covered by Conway Twitty (Elektra #47443), and it became a hit on the Country chart.

"SILENCE IS GOLDEN"
Composers: Bob Crewe and Bob Gaudio
Original Artist: the Four Seasons
Label: Philips Records; *Recording:* Philips #40211 (45)
Release Year: 1964; *Chart:* did not chart
Cover Artist: the Tremeloes
Label: Epic Records; *Recording:* Epic #10184 (45)
Release Year: 1967; *Chart:* #11 *Billboard* Hot 100

"Silence Is Golden" is a ballad about a guy who loves a girl who belongs to someone else. This other guy treats her badly, cheats on her and lies to her, but she doesn't see it. Should he tell her? No, "silence is golden." The first version of the song was by the Four Seasons, and was the B-side of a number 1 hit called "Rag Doll."

"Silence Is Golden" was far too good a song to remain merely a B-side, an also-ran. It was covered three years after the original by a British group called the Tremeloes. It was very similar to the Four Seasons original, but most people were hearing the song for the first time. It just missed the Top 10 in the late summer of 1967.

"SINCE I DON'T HAVE YOU"
Composers: Joe Rock and the Skyliners
Original Artist: the Skyliners
Label: Calico Records; *Recording:* Calico #103 (45)
Release Year: 1959; *Chart:* #12 *Billboard* Hot 100 and #3 R&B
Cover Artist: Don McLean
Label: Millennium Records; *Recording:* Millennium #11804 (45)
Release Year: 1981; *Chart:* #23 *Billboard* Hot 100

"Since I Don't Have You" is a durable, timeless ballad originally recorded in 1959 by Jimmy Beaumont and the Skyliners. The lyrics of the song were written in an automobile by the group's manager, Joe Rock, who had just suffered a painful breakup with a stewardess. Jimmy Beaumont then composed the music around the lyrics the next day. The group shopped the song around to several labels that turned the song down saying it was too sad or there were too many yous at the end. They finally landed at Calico Records, which was run by a group of doctors and lawyers who started the label as an investment. The group was originally called the Crescents, but the record label came up with the name Skyliners from the old Charlie Barnet jazz classic called "Skyliner." Despite the thirteen yous at the end, the song became a major doo-wop hit in 1959, and many, many cover versions followed.

Trini Lopez was among the first to cover the song (King #5187), but did not have a hit with it. The list is amazing, but Jay and the Americans, Art Garfunkel, and Barbra Streisand all released versions. Some of the more unusual takes on the song came from Patti LaBelle, Ronnie Milsap, and, believe it or not, Guns N' Roses.

However, the biggest cover came from the "American Pie" guy, Don McLean, during his 1980s comeback. His 1981 version (a follow-up to "Crying"—Millennium #11799) just missed the Top 20.

The Skyliners' original has been included in numerous movie soundtracks, including *American Graffiti* from 1973 and *Lethal Weapon 2* from 1989.

"SINGING THE BLUES"
Composer: Melvin Endsley
Original Artist: Guy Mitchell

Label: Columbia Records; *Recording:* Columbia #40769 (45 and 78)
Release Year: 1956; *Chart:* #1 *Billboard* Hot 100
Cover Artist: Marty Robbins
Label: Columbia Records; *Recording:* Columbia #21508 and #21545 (45 and 78)
Release Year: 1956; *Chart:* #17 *Billboard* Hot 100

Columbia had the market sewn up with "Singing the Blues" in 1956 with two hit renditions. The lyrics tell the tale of a guy who is really knocked for a loop by a breakup and feels like "singing the blues." Guy Mitchell was first and his rendition, replete with whistling, reached number 1 on the Pop charts.

For some reason, the Marty Robbins rendition of the song was released twice in 1956—as Columbia number 21508 and as number 21545. Robbins's version did not contain any whistling, but it did reach the Top 20.

"Sittin' in the Balcony"
Composer: John D. Loudermilk
Original Artist: Johnny Dee
Label: Colonial Records; *Recording:* Colonial #430 (45 and 78)
Release Year: 1957; *Chart:* #38 *Billboard* Hot 100
Cover Artist: Eddie Cochran
Label: Liberty Records; *Recording:* Liberty #55056 (45 and 78)
Release Year: 1957; *Chart:* #18 *Billboard* Hot 100

"Sittin' in the Balcony" is a song about a guy who's enjoying the last row of the theater with his significant other. He's oblivious as to whether there's a movie on the screen or a symphony playing—he's there to kiss his girlfriend and hold hands in the balcony. The song was composed by the prolific John D. Loudermilk, who also performed the original version of the song under the alias Johnny Dee on the Colonial Records label.

Dee's own version made Top 40, but the cover version by an up-and-coming Eddie Cochran did better. Buried in echo and complemented by some fine guitar work, Cochran's rendition peaked at number 18. His biggest hit, "Summertime Blues" (Liberty #55144), came in 1958.

"Sleep"
Composers: Adam Geibel and Tom Waring
Original Artist: Fred Waring and His Pennsylvanians
Label: RCA Victor Records; *Recording:* RCA Victor #19172 (78)
Release Year: 1924; *Chart:* #6 *Billboard*
Cover Artist: Little Willie John
Label: King Records; *Recording:* King #5394 (45)
Release Year: 1960; *Chart:* #13 *Billboard* Hot 100 and #10 R&B

The original version of "Sleep" was, for all intents and purposes, a lullaby. Fred Waring and His Pennsylvanians recorded, rerecorded, and rereleased the song numerous times on a myriad of record labels. The most readily available of those is the Decca pressing from 1950.

The best-known rendition of the song came from Little Willie John in 1960. This time around, "Sleep" was a vocal, and it was anything but sleepy. It had a quick, catchy tempo that might give one "restless leg syndrome." It peaked at number 13 on the Pop charts and Top 10 R&B. "Sleep" was included on John's 1961 album titled *Sure Things* (King #739).

"SLOOP JOHN B"

Composers: Carl Sandburg and Lee Hays
Original Artist: the Weavers
Label: Decca Records; *Recording:* Decca #27332 (45 and 78)
Release Year: 1950; *Chart:* did not chart
Cover Artist: the Beach Boys
Label: Capitol Records; *Recording:* Capitol #5602 (45)
Release Year: 1966; *Chart:* #3 *Billboard* Hot 100

This folk song, first popularized in the Bahamas in the 1930s, has many different titles and a rather confusing history. The poem/lyrics first appeared as "The John B. Sails" in a book titled *Pieces of Eight* by Richard Le Gallienne in 1917. Carl Sandburg, in 1927, included it in a book of songs titled *The American Songbag*.

Carl Sandburg, oddly, got co-writing credits on the Weavers' rendition of the song on the Decca label in 1950. At this time, the song was called "The Wreck of the John B." The Kingston Trio, Johnny Cash, Jimmie Rodgers, and even Dick Dale recorded versions of the song under various titles, but none made a big impact.

On a suggestion by Al Jardine, the Beach Boys changed a few of the lyrics in 1966. Now the song was titled "Sloop John B," and the only credit under the song's title on this record stated, "arranged by Brian Wilson." The record peaked at number 3 on the Pop charts and was a big hit in many foreign countries as well. It was included on the legendary Platinum *Pet Sounds* album (Capitol #2358), which was inducted into the Grammy Hall of Fame in 1998.

"SOLITAIRE"

Composers: Neil Sedaka and Phil Cody
Original Artist: Neil Sedaka
Label: RCA Victor Records; *Recording:* RCA Victor #1790 (LP)
Release Year: 1972; *Chart:* did not chart
Cover Artist: the Carpenters
Label: A & M Records; *Recording:* A & M #1721 (45)
Release Year: 1975; *Chart:* #17 *Billboard* Hot 100

This Neil Sedaka song was about a lonely man—not unlike the lonely man in "Fool on the Hill" by the Beatles. Sedaka's version was introduced on the *Solitaire* album in 1972 during a career lull. It was not a hit. Andy Williams released the song as a single in 1973 (Columbia #45936), and it was a minor hit on the Easy Listening chart.

With the help of Elton John, Sedaka was back in 1974, and "Solitaire" was reissued on the *Sedaka's Back* album (Rocket #463), but not released as a single.

The Carpenters released the song on their *Horizons* album (A & M #4530) in 1975. This platinum LP yielded "Please, Mr. Postman," "Only Yesterday," and "Solitaire." This time around, "Solitaire" was a Top 20 hit.

"SOME ENCHANTED EVENING"
Composers: Richard Rodgers and Oscar Hammerstein II
Original Artist: Perry Como
Label: RCA Victor Records; *Recording:* RCA Victor # 2896 (45 and 78)
Release Year: 1949; *Chart:* #1 *Billboard* Hot 100
Cover Artist: Jay and the Americans
Label: United Artists Records; *Recording:* United Artists #919 (45)
Release Year: 1965; *Chart:* #13 *Billboard* Hot 100

"Some Enchanted Evening" originated in the 1949 Rodgers and Hammerstein Broadway musical *South Pacific*. It was quite a success, and Ezio Pinza performed the song and won a Tony Award in that original production for his role as Emile de Becque. The 1949 recording of the tune by Perry Como on RCA Victor became a number 1 smash. In 1958, the 20th Century Fox movie version starring Rossano Brazzi in the de Becque role debuted in theaters.

Dozens of cover versions followed from the likes of Frank Sinatra, Jo Stafford, and Bing Crosby. The biggest version during the rock and roll era came from Jay and the Americans. As a follow-up to the operatic "Cara Mia" (United Artists #881), "Some Enchanted Evening" was perfect and almost reached the Top 10.

"SOMETHING"
Composer: George Harrison
Original Artist: the Beatles
Label: Apple Records; *Recording:* Apple #2654 (45)
Release Year: 1969; *Chart:* #3 *Billboard* Hot 100
Cover Artist: Shirley Bassey
Label: United Artists Records; *Recording:* United Artists #50698 (45)
Release Year: 1970; *Chart:* #55 *Billboard* Hot 100

There were only so many opportunities for George Harrison to shine in the Beatles, and this was one of them. Harrison wrote and sang lead on "Something"—one side of a two-sided hit single. "Something" was covered dozens of times and became a staple on TV variety shows. The song was included on the *Abbey Road* album (Apple #383). Harrison performed the song at the Concert for Bangladesh.

Shirley Bassey is best known as the singer of "Goldfinger" (United Artists #790) from 1965. After a lull on the charts, Bassey released her own take on "Something" and made it a hit all over again in 1970.

"Something Stupid"
Composer: C. Carson Parks
Original Artist: Carson and Gaile
Label: Kapp Records; *Recording:* Kapp #3516 (LP)
Release Year: 1966; *Chart:* did not chart
Cover Artist: Frank and Nancy Sinatra
Label: Reprise Records; *Recording:* Reprise #0561 (45)
Release Year: 1967; *Chart:* #1 *Billboard* Hot 100

"Something Stupid" was written by C. Carson Parks, the younger brother of composer/arranger/singer/author/actor Van Dyke Parks. Clarence Carson Parks teamed with Gaile Foote and recorded and released the original rendition of the song on the *San Antonio Rose* album in 1966 on the Kapp Records label. It wasn't a hit, but it soon would be.

Early in 1967, Frank Sinatra and producer Lee Hazlewood discovered the song. Hazlewood recommended that Frank should team with Nancy, Frank concurred, and magic happened. The song zoomed to number 1 on the Pop charts and it became the first father–daughter duet to reach number one. Neil Sedaka and his daughter, Dara, recorded "Should've Never Let You Go" (Elektra #46615) in 1980, but it didn't reach number 1. Frank Sinatra included "Something Stupid" on his *The World We Knew* album (Reprise #1022).

"Somewhere in the Night"
Composers: Richard Kerr and Will Jennings
Original Artist: Batdorf and Rodney
Label: Arista Records; *Recording:* Arista #0159 (45)
Release Year: 1975; *Chart:* #69 *Billboard* Hot 100
Cover Artist: Helen Reddy
Label: Capitol Records; *Recording:* Capitol #4192 (45)
Release Year: 1976; *Chart:* #19 *Billboard* Hot 100

"Somewhere in the Night" was first recorded by an obscure duo known as Batdorf and Rodney in 1975. Their full names were John Batdorf and Mark Rodney. This first time around, the song only reached number 69 on the Pop charts. However, the song had two great lives ahead.

Late in 1976, Australian sensation Helen Reddy remade "Somewhere in the Night" for Capitol Records. This time around, the song cracked the Top 20, and it was included on her *No Way to Treat a Lady* album (Capitol #11418), but there's still more to the story.

The first version of the song was released on Arista Records, and Arista released yet another version—the biggest one—late in 1978. It took Barry Manilow to make the song a Top 10 hit (Arista #0381). It was included on his *Even Now* album (Arista #4164). The album went triple platinum.

"SPEEDY GONZALES"
Composers: Buddy Kaye, David Hill, and Ethel Lee
Original Artist: David Dante

David Dante did "Speedy Gonzales" first, before a big boost from Pat Boone.

Label: RCA Victor Records; *Recording:* RCA Victor #7860 and #8056 (45)
Release Year: 1960; *Chart:* did not chart
Cover Artist: Pat Boone
Label: Dot Records; *Recording:* Dot #16368 (45)
Release Year: 1960; *Chart:* #6 *Billboard* Hot 100

This song was based upon the popular Warner Brothers cartoon mouse, Speedy Gonzales—the fastest mouse in all of Mexico. The song did not become a hit very speedily, however. "Speedy Gonzales" was originally recorded by David Dante for RCA Victor Records in 1960, and was produced by the legendary Hugo Peretti and Luigi Creatore. It was RCA number 7860 the first time around. When a cover version started to catch on in 1962, RCA rereleased Dante's rendition as RCA number 8056. Both RCA releases are identical, and both open with the "La la las" of a young Mexican girl.

That cover version was by one of the most prolific cover artists in history, Pat Boone, on the Dot label. Unlike Dante's original, this one opens with a short narration by Boone to set the scene. Also featured were some vocal inserts from the genuine cartoon voice of Speedy Gonzales, the amazing genius of Mel Blanc, and that made all the difference in the world. It reached Top 10 in 1962, and has the significance of being Boone's final Top 10 entry.

Kid's show star Soupy Sales remade the song in 1965 for ABC-Paramount (#10681), but it didn't chart.

David Dante used the names David Hill and David Hess when writing songs. He co-wrote "Speedy Gonzales."

Times have changed, and the cartoon and the song are not really deemed to be politically correct in the current day.

"SPOOKY"
Composers: Mike Shapiro, Harry Middlebrooks Jr., Buddy Buie, and James Cobb
Original Artist: Mike Sharpe
Label: Liberty Records; *Recording:* Liberty #55922 (45)
Release Year: 1967; *Chart:* #57 *Billboard* Hot 100
Cover Artist: Dennis Yost and Classics IV
Label: Imperial Records; *Recording:* Imperial #66259 (45)
Release Year: 1967; *Chart:* #3 *Billboard* Hot 100

Songwriter Mike Shapiro, under the name Mike Sharpe, released the original, seldom-heard rendition of "Spooky" very early in 1967. It was an instrumental one can easily envision being played on a "smooth jazz–formatted" radio station. It was a very minor hit and didn't crack the Top 50.

Lyrics were added by Classics IV guitarist James Cobb and the group's producer, Buddy Buie. This "new" rendition of the song was released very late in 1967 and reached number 3 on the Pop charts early in 1968. It became the first of four Top 20 hits for Dennis Yost and Classics IV. Some members of the group—James Cobb, Dean Daughtry, and Bob Nix—later became the Atlanta Rhythm Section and rerecorded "Spooky" (Polydor #2001). Once again, the song was a hit, peaking at number 17 in 1979.

The Classics IV and Atlanta Rhythm Section versions of "Spooky" are favorites of classic hits radio stations around Halloween.

"STAND BY YOUR MAN"

Composers: Tammy Wynette and Billy Sherrill
Original Artist: Tammy Wynette
Label: Epic Records; *Recording:* Epic #10398 (45)
Release Year: 1968; *Chart:* #19 *Billboard* Hot 100 and #1 Country
Cover Artist: Candi Staton
Label: Fame Records; *Recording:* Fame #1472 (45)
Release Year: 1970; *Chart:* #24 *Billboard* Hot 100 and #4 R&B

Tammy Wynette and Billy Sherrill wrote "Stand by Your Man" in 1968 and instantly had an inkling that the song would define Wynette's career. Their intuition proved accurate, and the song reached number 1 on the Country chart, but also crossed over onto the Pop charts in a big way. Some members of Women's Lib, however, grumbled and griped about the tune's message.

A 1970 remake almost sounded like a different song. The artist was Candi Staton, and her "Stand by Your Man" was a Top 5 hit on the R&B charts; it, too, crossed over to the Pop charts.

Wynette's original has been added to the Library of Congress's National Recording Registry. It has also been included in the soundtracks of countless motion pictures, such as *Sleepless in Seattle*, *Four Weddings and a Funeral*, and *Five Easy Pieces*.

"STAR DUST"

Composer: Hoagy Carmichael
Original Artist: Hoagy Carmichael
Label: Gennett Records; *Recording:* Gennett #6311 (78)
Release Year: 1927; *Chart:* did not chart
Cover Artist: the Dominoes
Label: Liberty Records; *Recording:* Liberty #55071 (45 and 78)
Release Year: 1957; *Chart:* #12 *Billboard* Hot 100 and #5 R&B

"Star Dust" (sometimes combined as "Stardust") began as an instrumental when first recorded in an up-tempo jazz mode by its composer, Hoagy Carmichael, in 1927—but it was not a big hit. Versions by Isham Jones (Brunswick

#1083), Benny Goodman (RCA Victor #25320), and Artie Shaw (RCA Victor #27230)—all instrumentals—all reached the Top 3. When lyrics were added by Mitchell Parish, the song became even more popular.

Nat King Cole released a version (with lyrics) in May of 1957 (Capitol EP #824) that made the Hot 100, but only a month later, a future million-selling version by an R&B vocal group known as the Dominoes was released. Often called Billy Ward and His Dominoes, the group boasted some of the greatest lead vocalists of all time—first Clyde McPhatter, then Jackie Wilson, and on "Star Dust," the amazing Eugene Mumford (formerly of the Larks on the Apollo and Lloyds record labels). It was a hit on both the Pop and R&B charts.

Still more versions cracked the Hot 100 in the 1960s from the likes of Frank Sinatra (Reprise #20059 in 1962), and Nino Tempo and April Stevens (Atco #6286 in 1964).

"STONEY END"
Composer: Laura Nyro
Original Artist: the Blossoms
Label: Ode Records; *Recording:* Ode #101, #106, and #125 (45)
Release Year: 1967; *Chart:* did not chart
Cover Artist: Barbra Streisand
Label: Columbia Records; *Recording:* Columbia #45236 (45)
Release Year: 1970; *Chart:* #6 *Billboard* Hot 100

"Stoney End" is just one of a long list of popular Laura Nyro compositions. The little-known original version was by Darlene Love's Blossoms on the Ode Records label in 1967. The girl group performed the song flawlessly, but their version did not catch on. The Blossoms released the song three times with three different flip sides and three different Ode label numbers, to no avail.

A year later, Peggy Lipton, the actress who portrayed Julie Barnes on the hit and hip new series *The Mod Squad*, utilized the exact same track the Blossoms had used—also on Ode Records (#114)—and released her vocal version. It, too, failed to catch on.

Late in 1970, a brief change in direction for Barbra Streisand had her recording a new version of this up-tempo tune. This time around it clicked in a big way, and Streisand's take on the song returned her to the Top 10 for the first time in six years. It was included on Barbra's Top 10 platinum *Stoney End* album (Columbia # 30378).

"STRAWBERRY LETTER 23"
Composer: Shuggie Otis
Original Artist: Shuggie Otis
Label: Epic Records; *Recording:* Epic #30752 (LP)

Both the Blossoms and Peggy Lipton (Julie on _The Mod Squad_) did "Stoney End" before Barbra Streisand.

Release Year: 1971; _Chart:_ did not chart
Cover Artist: the Brothers Johnson
Label: A & M Records; _Recording:_ A & M #1949 (45)
Release Year: 1977; _Chart:_ #5 _Billboard_ Hot 100 and #1 R&B

Produced by his dad, Johnny Otis, John Alexander "Shuggie" Otis recorded several albums for the Epic label in the 1970s. A cut he wrote for his 1971 _Freedom Flight_ LP titled "Strawberry Letter 23" went unnoticed for six years.

   In 1977, the song was unearthed and rerecorded by the Brothers Johnson on the _Right on Time_ album (A & M #4644). With Lee Ritenour on guitar, "Strawberry Letter 23" was released as a single and it reached number 5 on the charts and sold over a million copies. It was the group's second of three Top 10 hits.

"SUGAR AND SPICE"
Composer: Fred Nightingale
Original Artist: the Searchers
Label: Liberty Records; *Recording:* Liberty #55646 and #55689 (45)
Release Year: 1964; *Chart:* #44 *Billboard* Hot 100
Cover Artist: the Cryan' Shames
Label: Destination Records; *Recording:* Destination #624 (45)
Release Year: 1966; *Chart:* #49 *Billboard* Hot 100

Tony Hatch, under the alias of Fred Nightingale, wrote "Sugar and Spice" in 1963 for the Searchers. The lyrics were inspired by the children's rhyme, "Sugar and spice and all things nice—that's what little girls are made of." The Searchers had a bigger hit with the song in the United Kingdom than in the United States.

We hadn't heard the last of "Sugar and Spice." In 1966, a Chicago group called the Cryan' Shames covered the song very similarly with almost the same result—it, too, reached the Top 50.

The original version by the Searchers was included in the soundtrack for the 1987 hit Robin Williams Touchstone motion picture *Good Morning, Vietnam.*

"SUKIYAKI"
Composers: Ei Rokusuke and Nakamura Hachidai
Original Artist: Kyu Sakamoto
Label: Capitol Records; *Recording:* Capitol #4945 (45)
Release Year: 1963; *Chart:* #1 *Billboard* Hot 100
Cover Artist: A Taste of Honey
Label: Capitol Records; *Recording:* Capitol #4953 (45)
Release Year: 1981; *Chart:* #3 *Billboard* Hot 100 and #1 R&B

The year 1963 was definitely one of musical transition. The Beatles hadn't yet made an impact in the United States, and yet songs from foreign countries were big. "Dominique" by the Singing Nun (Philips #40152) and "Sukiyaki" by Kyu Sakamoto were number 1 hits in the States, even though not one word of English was spoken in the lyrics. The latter was performed in Japanese and, in fact, was originally titled "Ue O Muite Aruko" (translating to "I Have My Head Held High" or "I Look Up When I Walk"), but was retitled "Sukiyaki" for the U.S. audience—even though "Sukiyaki" is never mentioned in the lyrics. The record reached number 1 and stayed there for three weeks.

Eighteen years later, A Taste of Honey, the same R&B group who had given us "Boogie Oogie Oogie" (Capitol #4565), remade "Sukiyaki." Well, technically it was a remake—the melody and the title were the same, but it was now a song about lost love with new English lyrics. This new rendition reached number 3 on the Pop charts and number 1 on the R&B charts, and it sold over a million copies. Jewel Akens also had a unique take on the song on the Era Records label (#3164) titled "My First Lonely Night." The Akens song, one of his follow-ups to the smash hit "The Birds and the Bees," was not a hit, but it used the "I hold my head up high" line and was much closer to the original in its message.

"THE SUN AIN'T GONNA SHINE (ANYMORE)"
Composers: Bob Crewe and Bob Gaudio
Original Artist: Frankie Valli
Label: Smash Records; *Recording:* Smash #1995 (45)
Release Year: 1965; *Chart:* did not chart
Cover Artist: the Walker Brothers
Label: Smash Records: *Recording:* Smash #2032 (45)
Release Year: 1966; *Chart:* #13 *Billboard* Hot 100

Composed by Bob Crewe and Bob Gaudio, "The Sun Ain't Gonna Shine (Anymore)" was originally released as a solo venture by Frankie Valli in 1965 on the Philips Record subsidiary, Smash Records. It was anything but a smash and never made the Hot 100.

On that very same Smash label one year later, the song was remade by the Walker Brothers of "Make It Easy on Yourself" fame (see the entry for that song), and it became a Top 20 smash. This recording had a Righteous Brothers sound to it and led to *The Sun Ain't Gonna Shine Anymore* album (Smash #27082).

A 1968 attempt at making the song a hit again, this time in psychedelic fashion by a group called the Fuzzy Bunnies (Decca #32364) fell flat.

"A SUNDAY KIND OF LOVE"
Composers: Barbara Belle, Anita Leonard, Stan Rhodes, and Louis Prima
Original Artist: Fran Warren (with the Claude Thornhill Orchestra)
Label: Columbia Records; *Recording:* Columbia #37219 (78)
Release Year: 1947; *Chart:* #15 *Billboard* Music Popularity Chart
Cover Artist: the Harptones
Label: Bruce Records; *Recording:* Bruce #101 (45 and 78)
Release Year: 1953; *Chart:* did not chart

"A Sunday Kind of Love" is a song about trying to find a lasting love—one that lasts past Saturday night, one that's more than a casual date. Singer Fran Warren recorded it first as the vocalist for the Claude Thornhill Orchestra in 1947. The song was quickly covered by Louis Prima (Majestic #1113), Jo Stafford (Capitol #388), Ella Fitzgerald (Decca #23866), Frankie Laine (Mercury #5018), and Jimmy Dorsey (Mercury #10023).

The song became a popular choice by many groups during the doo-wop era. It was recorded by Bobby Hall and the Kings (Jax #320), the Dell-Vikings

The flawless R&B interpretation of Fran Warren's "A Sunday Kind of Love" by Willie Winfield and the Harptones on the Bruce label.

(Mercury EP #3359), Rudy Lampert (Rhythm #128), and most notably by Willie Winfield and the Harptones on the Bruce Records label. This version of versions has long been an R&B vocal group collector favorite, and Raoul Cita of the original Harptones said, "We were singing in a hallway at 1650 Broadway and we were asked if we would like to record for a new record label called Bruce Records. 'A Sunday Kind of Love' was our first release and our first hit, but both sides of the record got considerable airplay in the New York area. I'm actually partial to the ballad on the flip side called 'I'll Never Tell.'" As well as providing a harmony voice, Mr. Cita was playing piano on that record, but who was playing the very prominent organ? Cita said, "That was a gentleman named Ram Ramirez." Did "A Sunday Kind of Love" inspire the group to record "On Sunday Afternoon" (Rama #214) a few years later? Cita said, "No, it was totally a coincidence that we recorded two songs with Sunday in the title. It wasn't intended to be an answer or a follow-up at all."

Other versions of note include ones by Jan and Dean, Lenny Welch, Dinah Washington, the Four Seasons, and Jerry Lee Lewis.

"Susie Darlin'"

Composer: Robin Luke
Original Artist: Robin Luke
Label: Bertram International Records; *Recording:* Bertram International #206 (45)
Release Year: 1958; *Chart:* #5 *Billboard* Hot 100
Cover Artist: Tommy Roe
Label: ABC-Paramount Records; *Recording:* ABC-Paramount #10362 (45)
Release Year: 1962; *Chart:* #35 *Billboard* Hot 100

Robin Luke was a sixteen-year-old young man going to school in Hawaii when he wrote a song with his sister Susie's name in the title. It was originally released on the tiny Bertram International Records label in 1958—a rare pressing that is worth several hundred dollars today. When the song started getting airplay, it was sold to the much larger Dot Records label (#15781) and this bouncy song with a cha-cha beat became a Top 5 million-selling smash. It became Luke's only hit—in fact none of his follow-up singles ever made the Hot 100 again.

The song, however, has had a few afterlives. Tommy Roe released a version slower than the original as the follow-up to his number 1 classic "Sheila," and this remake became a Top 40 hit.

There was also a 1965 rendition by Mike Curb—later a famous songwriter, producer, and record company executive—on Capitol's Tower Records label (Tower #202). A few of the lyrics were changed in this version; thus Robin Luke and M. Libert are listed as the composers of Curb's "Susie Darlin'."

"Suspicion"

Composers: Doc Pomus and Mort Shuman
Original Artist: Elvis Presley
Label: RCA Victor Records; *Recording:* RCA Victor #2523 (LP)
Release Year: 1962; *Chart:* did not chart
Cover Artist: Terry Stafford
Label: Crusader Records; *Recording:* Crusader #101 (45)
Release Year: 1964; *Chart:* #3 *Billboard* Hot 100

The prolific songwriting team of Doc Pomus and Mort Shuman composed "(Marie's the Name) His Latest Flame," "Little Sister," "Viva Las Vegas," and "Suspicion" for Elvis Presley. For whatever reason, "Suspicion" was buried on a 1962 Presley album titled *Pot Luck with Elvis.*

Two years later, an artist named Terry Stafford who sounded quite a bit like Presley remade "Suspicion" on a small Southern California label known as Crusader Records. The song caught on and became a big Top 3 hit. Several years after this monster hit, Stafford surfaced in a Casey Kasem motion picture titled *Wild Wheels*.

RCA Victor then released Presley's "Suspicion" on a 45 for the first time, but it was the flip side, "Kiss Me, Quick" (RCA #0639), that made the charts. "Suspicion" is not to be confused with Presley's later number 1 hit "Suspicious Minds" (RCA Victor #9764; see the entry for that song).

"SUSPICIOUS MINDS"

Composer: F. Zambon (a.k.a. Mark James)
Original Artist: Mark James
Label: Scepter Records; *Recording:* Scepter #12221 (45)
Release Year: 1968; *Chart:* did not chart
Cover Artist: Elvis Presley
Label: RCA Victor Records; *Recording:* RCA Victor #9764 (45)
Release Year: 1969; *Chart:* #1 *Billboard* Hot 100

Singer/songwriter/producer Mark James wrote a few songs for both B. J. Thomas and Elvis Presley during his career. James wrote and originally recorded a song titled "Suspicious Minds" in 1968, and he used the alias F. Zambon for the composer credits. The tune tells the tale of lovers who both think the other is cheating. It was released on the Scepter Records label and produced by the great Chips Moman, but the record went absolutely nowhere.

Moman then brought the song to Elvis Presley and made history. It became Presley's eighteenth and final number 1 hit on the Pop charts and incited Presleymania all over again. It solidified Presley's comeback in 1969. The false fade at about three minutes and thirty seconds was not present on the Mark James original. With a total run time of about four minutes and twenty seconds, "Suspicious Minds" became Presley's longest number 1 hit.

The closest Elvis Presley ever came to number 1 again was "Burning Love" (RCA number 0769) in 1972. It peaked at number 2.

"SWAY"

Composers: Pablo Beltran Ruiz and Norman Gimbel
Original Artist: Dean Martin
Label: Capitol Records; *Recording:* Capitol #2818 (45 and 78)
Release Year: 1954; *Chart:* #15 *Billboard* Hot 100
Cover Artist: Bobby Rydell
Label: Cameo Records: *Recording:* Cameo #182 (45)
Release Year: 1960; *Chart:* #14 *Billboard* Hot 100

Pablo Beltran Ruiz wrote and performed the true original version of this song in 1953 under the original Mexican title "Quien Sera?" English lyrics were added to this mambo by Norman Gimbel, and Dean Martin recorded this song now known as "Sway," and Dino's rendition reached number 15 on the Pop charts.

One of the lyrics of the song says, "Hold me close, sway me more." The music world got more in 1960 when Bobby Rydell remade "Sway" for Cameo Records in Philadelphia, and did Dean Martin one better by reaching number 14 on the Pop charts. Rydell also had success covering Dino's "Volare" (see the entry for that song).

The song was a natural for Michael Bublé, and "Sway" was included on his *Michael Bublé* album (143 Records #48376) in 2003.

"Swayin' to the Music"
Composer: Jack Tempchin
Original Artist: the Funky Kings
Label: Arista Records; *Recording:* Arista #0209 (45)
Release Year: 1976; *Chart:* #61 *Billboard* Hot 100
Cover Artist: Johnny Rivers
Label: Big Tree Records; *Recording:* Big Tree #16094 (45)
Release Year: 1977; *Chart:* #10 *Billboard* Hot 100

The Funky Kings released the original version of this song as "Slow Dancing." The composer, Jack Tempchin, was a member of the Funky Kings. The group's name was rather deceiving, however—they were anything but funky, and the song peaked at number 61 on the Pop charts.

The "King of the Covers," Johnny Rivers, jumped on the song in 1977. The title was changed to "Swayin' to the Music (Slow Dancin')," and this rendition reached the Top 10. In fact, it became the final Top 10 hit for Rivers, and was included on his *Outside Help* album (Big Tree #76004).

"Sweet and Innocent"
Composers: Billy Sherrill and Rick Hall
Original Artist: Bobby Denton
Label: Judd Records; *Recording:* Judd #1001 (45)
Release Year: 1958; *Chart:* did not chart
Cover Artist: Donny Osmond
Label: MGM Records; *Recording:* MGM #14227 (45)
Release Year: 1971; *Chart:* #7 *Billboard* Hot 100

"Sweet and Innocent" has a message not unlike "Go Away, Little Girl." Written by Billy Sherrill and Rick Hall, the first and least-known rendition of the song came from Bobby Denton in 1958 on the Judd Records label. It was not a hit.

Also in 1958, Roy Orbison released a version on RCA Victor (#7381) on the flip side of "Seems to Me." Once again, "Sweet and Innocent" did not chart.

Then, the song was overhauled a bit with some new lyrics and a revamped melody, while keeping intact the "Sweet and Innocent" refrain and melody from the original. This updated and more upbeat rendition became the first solo hit for Donny Osmond of the Osmond Brothers in 1971. The song finally charted, peaking at number 7 and selling over a million copies.

"A Swingin' Safari"

Composer: Bert Kaempfert
Original Artist: Bert Kaempfert
Label: Decca Records; *Recording:* Decca #74305 (LP)
Release Year: 1962; *Chart:* did not chart
Cover Artist: Billy Vaughn
Label: Dot Records; *Recording:* Dot #16374 (45)
Release Year: 1962; *Chart:* #13 *Billboard* Hot 100

"A Swingin' Safari" is an extremely familiar instrumental song, but few know the song's title. It was composed by Bert Kaempfert, and his original 1962 version was released on the *That Happy Feeling* album on the Decca label in the United States, and on the *A Swingin' Safari* album (Polydor #30060) overseas.

The catchy tune became a hit later in 1962 when it was covered by Billy Vaughn on a Dot label 45. This version peaked at number 13 on the Pop charts and became Vaughn's final trip into the Top 20.

The original Bert Kaempfert version was utilized as the theme song for *The Match Game*—the original NBC version—hosted by Gene Rayburn from 1962 to 1969. This version of the Mark Goodson and Bill Todman show was recorded in New York City.

T

"Take Good Care of Her"

Composers: Arthur Kent and Ed Warren
Original Artist: Adam Wade
Label: Coed Records; *Recording:* Coed #546 (45)
Release Year: 1961; *Chart:* #7 *Billboard* Hot 100
Cover Artist: Elvis Presley
Label: RCA Victor Records; *Recording:* RCA Victor #0196 (45)
Release Year: 1974; *Chart:* did not chart

"Take Good Care of Her" originated with African American singer Adam Wade. Wade had a sound that was similar to that of Johnny Mathis, and this was his first of three Top 10 hits on the Coed Records label, which also released hits by the Duprees, the Crests, Trade Martin, and the Rivieras. In "Take Good Care of Her," boy loses girl, but still loves her and asks her new beau and future husband to "treat her well."

This ballad was remade numerous times. Balladeer Mel Carter (Imperial #66208) recorded a rendition in 1966 that reached number 78 on the Pop charts. Sonny James, "the Southern Gentleman," also recorded a version of the song in 1966 (Capitol #5612) and had a hit on the Country chart.

Even "the King of Rock and Roll" released it on a single. It was on the B-side of his Top 40 hit "I've Got a Thing about You, Baby." "Take Good Care of Her" was included on Elvis Presley's *Good Times* album (RCA #0475)—one of his least successful albums, peaking only at number 90.

Adam Wade made history in 1975 when he became the first black game show host on CBS's short-lived *Musical Chairs*, which often featured the Tokens, the Spinners, and Irene Cara.

"TAKE GOOD CARE OF MY BABY"
Composers: Carole King and Gerry Goffin
Original Artist: Bobby Vee
Label: Liberty Records; *Recording:* Liberty #55354 (45)
Release Year: 1961; *Chart:* #1 *Billboard* Hot 100
Cover Artist: Bobby Vinton
Label: Epic Records; *Recording:* Epic #10305 (45)
Release Year: 1968; *Chart:* #33 *Billboard* Hot 100

"Take Good Care of My Baby" was one of the first compositions by the prolific Brill Building team of Carole King and Gerry Goffin. Bobby Vee had numerous Top 20 hits, but this proved to be his only number 1.

Because of the similarity in their names, Bobby Vee and Bobby Vinton were sometimes confused in the early 1960s. Adding to the confusion, Bobby Vinton released his own version of "Take Good Care of My Baby" in 1968. Performed as a slow shuffle, as opposed to the bouncy medium tempo of the original, Vinton brought the song to a new generation of Top 40 radio listeners. It was also included on the *Take Good Care of My Baby* album (Epic #26382).

"TALK BACK TREMBLING LIPS"
Composer: John D. Loudermilk
Original Artist: Ernest Ashworth
Label: Hickory Records; *Recording:* Hickory #1214 (45)
Release Year: 1963; *Chart:* #1 *Billboard* Country
Cover Artist: Johnny Tillotson
Label: MGM Records; *Recording:* MGM #13181 (45)
Release Year: 1963; *Chart:* #7 *Billboard* Hot 100

John D. Loudermilk wrote a lot of very popular songs—many of which became hits more than once. Such is the case with "Talk Back Trembling Lips," a song about "manning up." The singer is repeatedly mistreated by his girlfriend, but he loves her too much to break it off and is too timid to let her know that his heart is breaking. Ernest Ashworth recorded it first in 1963 and had the Country chart sewn up, reaching number 1.

A cover for the Pop charts by Johnny Tillotson very late in 1963 peaked at number 7. Tillotson had just signed with MGM Records after a long stay at Archie Bleyer's Cadence label. It was an auspicious beginning for Tillotson's new venture, but only weeks later four lads from Liverpool effectively put the kibosh on his and many other pop singers' careers. It was Tillotson's last Top 30 hit.

"TALL PAUL"
Composers: Dick Sherman, Bob Roberts, and Bob Sherman
Original Artist: Judy Harriet
Label: Surf Records; *Recording:* Surf #5027 (45)
Release Year: 1958; *Chart:* did not chart
Cover Artist: Annette and the Afterbeats
Label: Disneyland Records; *Recording:* Disneyland #118 (45)
Release Year: 1959; *Chart:* #7 *Billboard* Hot 100

Judy Harriet had the original version of "Tall Paul" on the small Surf Records label in 1958, but for all intents and purposes it went unnoticed. The song was composed by Bob Roberts along with the Sherman Brothers, Bob and Dick. Those same Sherman Brothers later went on to have success for Walt Disney, writing original music for the 1964 smash hit, *Mary Poppins*.

The Shermans achieved their first Disney success when Annette Funicello covered "Tall Paul" in 1959 as Annette and the Afterbeats, and had a Top 10 Smash on Disneyland Records. Truly one of the shortest Top 10 hits, the record was just barely over ninety seconds in length. Appropriately, the boy's name in the song was Paul, and Annette Funicello and Paul Anka were an item at the time. In 1989, Funicello sang a piece of "Tall Paul" in the film *Troop Beverly Hills*. Three more Top 20 Funicello hits followed ("Pineapple Princess," "O Dio Mio," and "First Name Initial") on Disney's Buena Vista label. This recording career served as a bridge between Funicello's Mousketeer years and her beach movie years. Funicello died on April 8, 2013, at the age of seventy after a long battle with multiple sclerosis.

"TAMMY"
Composers: Jay Livingston and Ray Evans
Original Artist: Debbie Reynolds
Label: Coral Records; *Recording:* Coral #61851 (45 and 78)
Release Year: 1957; *Chart:* #1 *Billboard* Hot 100
Cover Artist: the Ames Brothers

Label: RCA Victor Records; *Recording:* RCA Victor #6930 (45 and 78)
Release Year: 1957; *Chart:* #5 *Billboard* Hot 100

"Tammy" is a sentimental ballad from the Debbie Reynolds motion picture *Tammy and the Bachelor* that starred Reynolds, Leslie Nielsen, and Walter Brennan. Reynolds's rendition of the song reached number 1 on the Pop charts for five weeks and sold well over a million copies.

There was a big cover version, however. The Ames Brothers jumped on the "Tammy" bandwagon and peaked at number 5 on the Pop charts. Ed Ames later broke off from his brothers for a solo career. He also portrayed Mingo for six seasons on NBC's *Daniel Boone*, which starred Fess Parker.

Speaking of television, Jay Livingston and Ray Evans, who wrote "Tammy" also wrote the theme song for *Bonanza* and *Mister Ed*. *Tammy* also became a single season sitcom on ABC in 1965, starring Debbie Watson.

"A TASTE OF HONEY"
Composers: Ric Marlow, Bobby Scott, and Lee Morris
Original Artist: Lenny Welch
Label: Cadence Records; *Recording:* Cadence #1428 (45)
Release Year: 1963; *Chart:* did not chart
Cover Artist: the Beatles
Label: Vee Jay Records; *Recording:* Vee Jay #1062 (LP)
Release Year: 1964; *Chart:* did not chart

"A Taste of Honey" was written as an instrumental for the Broadway show titled *A Taste of Honey* in 1960. Not too long afterward, lyrics were added and the first artist to record this "new and improved" version was Lenny Welch on Archie Bleyer's Cadence Records label. Welch recalled, "It wasn't a big hit in the United States, but I performed it in clubs in England. The Beatles then covered it on their *Introducing the Beatles* album and it sold millions of copies."

Even though it was recorded by the Fab Four, the song is most readily associated with Herb Alpert and the Tijuana Brass (A & M #775), who had a Top 10 hit with the song in 1965. It was also included on Alpert's popular *Whipped Cream & Other Delights* album (A & M #110), which was number 1 for five weeks in that same year. It's interesting to note that Alpert's version returned the song to its roots—an instrumental. The Herb Alpert School of Music is part of the UCLA campus.

"A TEAR FELL"
Composers: Eugene Randolph and Dorian Button
Original Artist: Teresa Brewer
Label: Coral Records; *Recording:* Coral #61590 (45 and 78)
Release Year: 1956; *Chart:* #5 *Billboard* Hot 100
Cover Artist: Ivory Joe Hunter

Label: Atlantic Records; *Recording:* Atlantic #1086 (45 and 78)
Release Year: 1956; *Chart:* #15 *Billboard* R&B

"A Tear Fell" could also easily be called "A Fool Am I in Love" (a line uttered frequently in the song). It's all about a young lady who observes her lover in the arms of someone new, and thus "A Tear Fell." Teresa Brewer shed the first tear and had a Top 5 hit, but there were more.

For the R&B charts, Ivory Joe Hunter released his rendition for Atlantic Records only weeks after Brewer's. It reached number 15.

Another R&B version from Ray Charles (ABC-Paramount #10571) in 1964 introduced the song to a whole new generation. It peaked at number 13.

"A Teenage Prayer"

Composers: Bix Reichner and Bernie Lowe
Original Artist: Gloria Mann
Label: Sound Records; *Recording:* Sound #126 (45 and 78)
Release Year: 1955; *Chart:* #19 *Billboard* Hot 100
Cover Artist: Gale Storm
Label: Dot Records; *Recording:* Dot #15436 (45 and 78)
Release Year: 1955; *Chart:* #6 *Billboard* Hot 100

"A Teenage Prayer" is a song about unrequited love. The singer is pining for a guy who doesn't know she exists, but she has faith that one day her teenage prayer will be answered. Gloria Mann recorded the song first on the small Sound Records label of Philadelphia. This is likely why the cover version became the bigger hit—it was on a bigger label with much better distribution.

That cover version was one side of a two-sided Top 10 smash by TV's *My Little Margie* and *Oh, Susanna*, Gale Storm. Released on Christmas Eve of 1955, Storm's rendition eclipsed Mann's early in 1956 and became the definitive hit.

"Tell Me Why"

Composers: Marshall Helfand and Don Carter
Original Artist: Norman Fox and the Rob Roys
Label: Back Beat Records; *Recording:* Back Beat #501 (45 and 78)
Release Year: 1957; *Chart:* did not chart
Cover Artist: the Belmonts
Label: Surprise Records; *Recording:* Surprise #1000 (45)
Release Year: 1961; *Chart:* #18 *Billboard* Hot 100

Not to be confused with the Four Aces' song nor the Beatles' song of the same name, this "Tell Me Why" was pure vocal group harmony. The original rendition of the song came from the Bronx, New York, via Houston, Texas. Norman Fox, longtime lead singer for the Rob Roys said,

Named for the popular alcoholic beverage, the Rob Roys, featuring Norman Fox, recorded the original "Tell Me Why" before the Belmonts made it a national hit.

We had an audition at a tiny record store in the Bronx, and the interviewers had connections to Don Carter of Back Beat Records in Houston, Texas. Even though Marshall Helfand and I wrote the song "Tell Me Why," my name was removed from the credits on the record. The group's name at the time was the Velvetones, but we found out that there was another group who recorded a song called "Glory of Love" on Aladdin Records in 1957, so we had to change it. Carter also thought the name was a bit corny, so I attempted to come up with a cool, up-to-date name. At the time, the Rob Roy was a very popular drink and, upon my suggestion, we became Norman Fox and the Rob Roys. Even though our version of "Tell Me Why" didn't make the national charts, it sold well in New York, Philadelphia, Boston, and, as I found out years later, Southern California.

Four years later, after Dion pursued a solo career, the Belmonts were on their own and opted to rerecord "Tell Me Why" in 1961—originally on the tiny Surprise Records label. When the record caught on, it was reissued on the Sabrina label (#500) and it made the national Top 20. Had Norman Fox been listed as composer, he would have received some royalties, but Fox said, "In the long run, the Belmonts' remake benefitted us—it re-popularized 'Tell Me Why' and the Rob Roys and I continue to get a lot of work today as a result."

Marshall Helfand's name in the credits on the Belmonts' 45 was mistakenly listed as "Helford." The Rob Roys performed on the PBS fundraising special titled *Doo Wop Discoveries*.

"TENNESSEE WALTZ"

Composers: Cowboy Copas, Redd Stewart, and Pee Wee King
Original Artist: Cowboy Copas
Label: King Records; *Recording:* King #696 (78)
Release Year: 1948; *Chart:* #6 *Billboard* Country
Cover Artist: Patti Page
Label: Mercury Records; *Recording:* Mercury #5534 (78)
Release Year: 1950; *Chart:* #1 *Billboard* Hot 100

"Tennessee Waltz" is a song about losing your significant other to an old friend. The singer was dancing with his sweetheart and, while dancing, ran into an old friend who cut in, and the rest is history. Cowboy Copas co-wrote the song and had a Top 10 hit with it on the Country chart on the King Record label.

Many artists covered the song—Pee Wee King, Guy Lombardo, Les Paul and Mary Ford, and Jo Stafford, to name a few—but none did as well as Patti Page. Her "Tennessee Waltz" defined her career and stayed at number 1 for nine weeks.

To round out the 1950s, a rock and roll rendition of "Tennessee Waltz" by Bobby Comstock and the Counts (Blaze #349) just missed the Top 50.

"THAT OLD BLACK MAGIC"

Composers: Johnny Mercer and Harold Arlen
Original Artist: Glenn Miller Band
Label: RCA Victor Records; *Recording:* RCA Victor #1523 (78)
Release Year: 1942; *Chart:* #1 *Billboard* Music Popularity Chart
Cover Artist: Bobby Rydell
Label: Cameo Records; *Recording:* Cameo #190 (45)
Release Year: 1961; *Chart:* #21 *Billboard* Hot 100

"That Old Black Magic" is a song about the magic of love and being in its spell. Glenn Miller started the magic with the first version of this Johnny Mercer and

Harold Arlen standard. The Modernaires provided the vocals. It was a number 1 hit—Glenn Miller's final chart topper.

Among the artists who covered "That Old Black Magic" were Judy Garland, Frank Sinatra, Margaret Whiting, Sammy Davis Jr., and Ella Fitzgerald. Even Philadelphia teen idol Bobby Rydell took a stab at it and just missed the Top 20 in 1961.

"THAT'S LIFE"
Composers: Kelly Gordon and Dean Kay
Original Artist: Marion Montgomery
Label: Capitol Records; *Recording:* Capitol #5321 (45)
Release Year: 1963; *Chart:* did not chart
Cover Artist: Frank Sinatra
Label: Reprise Records; *Recording:* Reprise #0531 (45)
Release Year: 1966; *Chart:* #4 *Billboard* Hot 100

"That's Life" started its life in 1963 when it was recorded by Marion Montgomery, who was discovered by Peggy Lee, who brought her to Capitol Records. Despite a world of talent, Montgomery's career never got into gear—the record was not a success by any stretch of the imagination, at least not yet.

"Old Blue Eyes" was next in line. Late in 1966, Sinatra remade the song and made it his own. The alliterative line "I've been a puppet, a pauper, a pirate, a poet, a pawn and a king" is legendary (in Montgomery's original, the line ended with "a pawn and a queen"). It was included on the *That's Life* album (Reprise #1020).

A few of the many who have covered the song include Aretha Franklin, Della Reese, Shirley Bassey, David Lee Roth, Michael Bolton, and Michael Bublé.

"THAT'S WHEN YOUR HEARTACHES BEGIN"
Composers: Fred Fisher, Billy Hill, and William Raskin
Original Artist: Shep Fields & His Rippling Rhythm Orchestra
Label: Bluebird Records; *Recording:* Bluebird #7015 (78)
Release Year: 1937; *Chart:* did not chart
Cover Artist: Elvis Presley
Label: RCA Victor Records; *Recording:* RCA Victor #6870 (45 and 78)
Release Year: 1957; *Chart:* #58 *Billboard* Hot 100

"That's When Your Heartaches Begin" in its original form resembles a Lawrence Welk record, with its bubbly presentation and accordion accompaniment. Vocals are provided by Bob Goday, under the heading of Shep Fields & His Rippling Rhythm Orchestra on RCA's Bluebird Records label. The song tells of the pain one feels upon discovering the significant other in the arms of a good and trusted friend.

The Ink Spots had success with a cover version in 1941 (Decca #3720). Their smooth-as-silk vocals were emulated a decade later by Billy Bunn and the Buddies on RCA Victor (#4657)—featuring Bunn's unusual and intense vibrato on lead vocals.

Bunn's version of "That's When Your Heartaches Begin" was not a hit on RCA Victor, but another version was five years later on the flip side of "All Shook Up"—a number 1 smash for Elvis Presley. It only reached number 58 on the Hot 100 on its own, but with a chart topper on the flip and inclusion on the 1958 *Elvis' Gold Records* album (RCA #1707), the Presley version is the best known. Like the Ink Spots' take on the song, Presley's also features a spoken bridge in the middle.

"THEN YOU CAN TELL ME GOODBYE"
Composer: John D. Loudermilk
Original Artist: Don Cherry
Label: Verve Records; *Recording:* Verve #10270 (45)
Release Year: 1962; *Chart:* did not chart
Cover Artist: the Casinos
Label: Fraternity Records; *Recording:* Fraternity #977 (45)
Release Year: 1967; *Chart:* #6 *Billboard* Hot 100

Don Cherry had a huge hit in 1956 with "Band of Gold" on the Columbia label (see the entry for that song). However, finding a follow-up proved elusive. Cherry recorded the original rendition of John D. Loudermilk's "Then You Can Tell Me Goodbye" in 1962, but this version was not a hit. Several other versions (Johnny Nash—Argo #5479; Frank Ifield—Hickory #1486) also failed to chart. The lyrics beg patience through the bad times and giving one's relationship the old college try.

It took a vocal group from Cincinnati fronted by Gene Hughes named the Casinos to finally put the song over in a big way. The record was released very early in 1967 on the Fraternity label, and it possessed a retro doo-wop sound. It became the group's only Top 10 hit. The song was included on the *Then You Can Tell Me Goodbye* album (Fraternity #1019). The album contained numerous doo-wop ballads, including "Maybe," "Gee Whiz," "Talk to Me," and "To Be Loved."

Eddy Arnold had a hit with the song on the Country chart in 1968 (RCA Victor #9606).

"THERE, I'VE SAID IT AGAIN"
Composers: Redd Evans and David Mann
Original Artist: the Benny Carter Orchestra
Label: Bluebird Records; *Recording:* Bluebird #11090 (78)

Release Year: 1941; *Chart:* did not chart
Cover Artist: Bobby Vinton
Label: Epic Records; *Recording:* Epic #9638 (45)
Release Year: 1963; *Chart:* #1 *Billboard* Hot 100

"There, I've Said It Again" is a beautifully written classic that was born in 1941 by the Benny Carter Orchestra on RCA's Bluebird subsidiary. This version wasn't a whopping success, but RCA's next shot at it was. As by Vaughn Monroe, the tune reached number 1 in 1945, but there was still more in store.

A very smooth take on the song very late in 1959 from Sam Cooke (Keen #2105) dented the bottom of the Hot 100 (number 81), but a 1963 remake returned the song to the number 1 spot. Bobby Vinton's Epic rendition of "There, I've Said It Again" reached number 1 early in 1964 and stayed there for four weeks. It was the final number 1 hit in the United States before the Beatles hit with "I Want to Hold Your Hand," changing music forevermore. It was the end of a more innocent era. Epic, indeed.

"THERE'S A KIND OF HUSH"
Composers: Les Reed and Geoff Stephens
Original Artist: the New Vaudeville Band
Label: Fontana Records; *Recording:* Fontana #27560 (LP)
Release Year: 1966; *Chart:* did not chart
Cover Artist: Herman's Hermits
Label: MGM Records; *Recording:* MGM #13681 (45)
Release Year: 1967; *Chart:* #4 *Billboard* Hot 100

"There's a Kind of Hush" had its origins as an album cut. It was included on the *Winchester Cathedral* album in 1966, but not released as a single. It was not recorded in the retro style of the album's title cut, which became a number 1 smash as a single (Fontana #1562).

One year later, Peter Noone and Herman's Hermits covered "There's a Kind of Hush" much in the manner of the original. Produced by Mickie Most, this rendition sold over a million copies and reached the Top 5. It became the eleventh and final Top 10 hit for the group.

A decade later, Karen and Richard Carpenter remade "There's a Kind of Hush" and just missed the Top 10 (A & M #1800). Coincidentally, it was the Carpenters' final trip into the Top 15.

"THEY DON'T KNOW"
Composer: Kirsty MacColl
Original Artist: Kirsty MacColl
Label: Stiff Records; *Recording:* Stiff #47 (45)

Release Year: 1979; *Chart:* did not chart
Cover Artist: Tracey Ullman
Label: MCA/Stiff Records; *Recording:* MCA/Stiff #52347 (45)
Release Year: 1984; *Chart:* #8 *Billboard* Hot 100

The composer of "They Don't Know," Kirsty MacColl, also recorded the original version of the song in 1979. It's a song about ignoring the hearsay and the gossip, and instead following one's heart when it comes to love. This original version was a flop, but the love story doesn't end here.

The song was covered five years later in a very similar fashion by a British comedienne named Tracey Ullman, and this time around the song went Top 10. It was Ullman's only Top 40 hit, but bigger things were still ahead for this talented lady. In 1987, on the brand new Fox TV Network, Ullman got her own sketch show titled *The Tracey Ullman Show* and it had a three-year run. The most memorable thing about this show was the introduction of *The Simpsons*, who earned their own historically long-running spin-off. Ullman also had success on a similar HBO show a few years later titled *Tracey Takes On.*

"THIS DIAMOND RING"
Composers: Al Kooper, Bob Brass, and Irwin Levine
Original Artist: Sammy Ambrose
Label: Musicor Records; *Recording:* Musicor #1061 (45)
Release Year: 1964; *Chart:* did not chart
Cover Artist: Gary Lewis and the Playboys
Label: Liberty Records; *Recording:* Liberty #55756 (45)
Release Year: 1965; *Chart:* #1 *Billboard* Hot 100

"This Diamond Ring" was originally recorded by an obscure Miami-born singer named Sammy Ambrose. Released on Musicor Records, the song went largely unnoticed. This original version has become somewhat of a current-day collector's item.

The song was then offered to Bobby Vee, who turned it down. Vee was with Liberty Records, and the song was then passed down to another singer who was just getting started on the label—Jerry Lewis's son, Gary Lewis, and his group, the Playboys. This version was recorded a bit faster than the original more soulful Sammy Ambrose rendition, and it quickly became a chart topper and sold well over a million copies. "This Diamond Ring" was the first of seven consecutive Top 10 hits for the group. The *This Diamond Ring* album (Liberty #7408) also became a Top 30 hit.

"This Diamond Ring" became so popular that Liberty Records released an answer record by Wendy Hill titled "(Gary, Please Don't Sell) My Diamond Ring" (Liberty #55771). It wasn't a hit, but it did give us closure.

"THIS GUY'S IN LOVE WITH YOU"
Composers: Burt Bacharach and Hal David
Original Artist: Herb Alpert
Label: A & M Records; *Recording:* A & M #929 (45)
Release Year: 1968; *Chart:* #1 *Billboard* Hot 100
Cover Artist: Dionne Warwick
Label: Scepter Records; *Recording:* Scepter #12241 (45)
Release Year: 1969; *Chart:* #7 *Billboard* Hot 100

"This Guy's in Love with You" was basically a lost/discarded Bacharach and David composition uncovered by Herb Alpert, who decided to record the song himself. Alpert loved the lyrics and all the open places for a horn section to shine. The vocals were ideal for his limited vocal range, and the record was a whopping success—peaking at number 1 in 1968. It remained there at number 1 for an entire month.

A cover-slash-answer record in 1969 by Dionne Warwick, now titled "This Girl's in Love with You," returned the song to the Top 10. It was included on her *Promises, Promises* album (Scepter #571).

Alpert has a unique distinction—a number 1 hit as a vocalist and a number 1 hit instrumental ("Rise"—A & M #2151) in 1979.

"THIS MASQUERADE"
Composer: Leon Russell
Original Artist: Leon Russell
Label: Shelter Records; *Recording:* Shelter #7325 (45)
Release Year: 1972; *Chart:* did not chart
Cover Artist: George Benson
Label: Warner Brothers Records; *Recording:* Warner Brothers #8209 (45)
Release Year: 1976; *Chart:* #10 *Billboard* Hot 100

"This Masquerade" was composed by Leon Russell as the B-side of his biggest hit single, "Tight Rope," in 1972. This version has a long instrumental intro—well over a minute—before Russell's distinctive vocal stylings commence. This original rendition did not chart, but its placement on the flip of a hit single definitely got it noticed.

Numerous cover versions emerged—Shirley Bassey, the Carpenters, Willie Nelson, and Kenny Rogers among them—but none was bigger than that of George Benson. The Pittsburgh native truly made it his own, and it became Benson's first of four Top 10 singles. The 45 version was just a bit over three minutes in length, but the cut on the *Breezin'* album (Warner Brothers #2919) was in excess of eight minutes. The LP won a Grammy for Best Pop Instrumental Album, and this multiplatinum album was inducted into the Grammy Hall of Fame in 2008.

"THIS TIME"
Composer: Chips Moman
Original Artist: Thomas Wayne
Label: Mercury Records; *Recording:* Mercury #71287 (45 and 78)
Release Year: 1958; *Chart:* did not chart
Cover Artist: Troy Shondell
Label: Goldcrest Records; *Recording:* Goldcrest #161 (45)
Release Year: 1961; *Chart:* #6 *Billboard* Hot 100

Chips Moman was a very prolific producer, guitarist, and composer. Among his many compositions is "This Time," a song about a permanent and final breakup. The singer and his significant other had threatened to break it off in

Before Troy Shondell had a Top 10 hit with "This Time," Thomas Wayne did it first.

the past, but "this time" it was for real. The original artist was Thomas Wayne on the Mercury label in 1958. This version was not a hit, but Wayne did have one big hit the following year with "Tragedy" (see the entry for that song).

In 1961, a Fort Wayne, Indiana, singer whose real name was Gary Shelton remade "This Time" under the pseudonym Troy Shondell. Originally released on the tiny Goldcrest label, the record was leased to Liberty Records (#55353) after it caught on, where it became a Top 10 hit. There was no "next time" for this singer of "This Time"—Troy Shondell became a genuine one-hit wonder.

"TILL THEN"
Composers: Eddie Seiler, Sol Marcus, and Guy Wood
Original Artist: the Mills Brothers
Label: Decca Records; *Recording:* Decca #18599 (78)

In between the Mills Brothers and the Classics, Sonny Til did "Till Then."

Release Year: 1944; *Chart:* #8 *Billboard* Music Popularity Chart and #1 R&B
Cover Artist: the Classics
Label: Musicnote Records; *Recording:* Musicnote #1116 (45)
Release Year: 1963; *Chart:* #20 *Billboard* Hot 100

"Till Then" is a song about going off for a stint in the military and leaving a sweetheart behind. The singer asks his lover to wait for his return and remain faithful. The Mills Brothers got the ball rolling with their timely Top 10 version in 1944, while the United States was still embroiled in World War II.

Many other recording artists armed themselves with cover versions in the 1950s. It made perfect sense for Sonny Til to record "Till Then" (Jubilee #5107)—his name was in the title. Til was the lead singer for the R&B vocal group known as the Orioles, and they received considerable airplay on black radio stations. A pop group known as the Hilltoppers, famous for their cover songs, also had a hit with their rendition (Dot #15132) in 1954.

In 1963, the conflict in Vietnam was heating up. In a way, history was repeating itself. Emil Stucchio, the lead singer of a Brooklyn doo-wop group known as the Classics recalled,

> Because things were bubbling under in Southeast Asia, the owner of Musicnote Records, Andy Leonetti, thought it would be a smart idea for us to remake the Mills Brothers classic "Till Then." Coincidentally, that song was originally released the year I was born. From the very beginning, everything fell into place. Our brilliant arranger, Larry Lucie, gave the bass singer the starting line "Dome doo doo dome doo doo dome, doo doo dome wepp wedda weh," and then I come in with the lead vocals and the song's title. Musicnote was eager for us to do a ballad, and they certainly picked the right one. I'll never forget—we recorded it on January 25, 1963, the day before my dad's fiftieth birthday. When I heard the playback in the studio, I knew it was a hit. Everything just felt right about this one. It wasn't a lush arrangement, just a simple love song. There were a lot of smiling faces in the studio that day. My instincts were right—it was a big hit, especially in the Northeast. It was truly one of the most romantic records of 1963, and I'm so very grateful.

Unfortunately, success was short-lived because of the British Invasion only months later. Stucchio, however, isn't bitter: "Over fifty years later, I'm still performing 'Till Then.' We got to sing it on a couple of those wonderful PBS fundraising specials—*Doo Wop 51* and *Doo Wop Romance*. Recently, I was out with my grandsons and I was recognized and I felt like a rock star in front of those boys. I couldn't be happier."

"TILL THERE WAS YOU"
Composer: Meredith Willson
Original Artist: Sue Raney
Label: Capitol Records; *Recording:* Capitol #3847 (45 and 78)
Release Year: 1957; *Chart:* did not chart
Cover Artist: the Beatles
Label: Capitol Records; *Recording:* Capitol #2047 (LP)
Release Year: 1964; *Chart:* did not chart

"Till There Was You" is a romantic ballad with a beautiful and haunting melody plus myriad chord changes. The song was written for *The Music Man*. In the play and the movie of the same name, the song was performed by Marian the Librarian (portrayed by Barbara Cook on Broadway and Shirley Jones in the motion picture). The first recorded version came from the Nelson Riddle Orchestra with vocalist Sue Raney in 1957. Many cover versions followed from the likes of Anita Bryant, Peggy Lee, and Sergio Franchi.

Performed with a Latin beat, one of the most unusual renditions came from the early Beatles on their *Meet the Beatles* album in 1964 (*With the Beatles* on Parlophone in the United Kingdom). This remake featured Paul McCartney on lead vocals. It stands out as one of the group's most unusual choices in cover songs.

"TIME IS ON MY SIDE"
Composers: Norman Meade and Jimmy Norman
Original Artist: Kai Winding
Label: Verve Records; *Recording:* Verve #10307 (45)
Release Year: 1963; *Chart:* did not chart
Cover Artist: the Rolling Stones
Label: London Records; *Recording:* London #9708 (45)
Release Year: 1964; *Chart:* #6 *Billboard* Hot 100

Under the alias Norman Meade, arranger Jerry Ragovoy penned a song that was a real sleeper—it took some "time" to become a big hit. The lyrics were provided by Jimmy Norman, and the first version of "Time Is on My Side" came from Kai Winding (who was famous for the 1963 Top 10 hit "More" from *Mondo Cane* on Verve #10295). The background singers, not listed on the label, were Cissy Houston and the Warwick sisters—Dionne and Dee Dee. This rendition did not make the charts.

Next up was New Orleans legend Irma Thomas. Her intense "Time Is on My Side" (Imperial #66041) was arranged and conducted by the prolific H. B. Barnum, but this version also failed to make the charts. Thomas sang the National Anthem for the New Orleans Saints home opener in 2011.

Both Kai Winding and New Orleans great Irma Thomas did "Time Is on My Side" before it became the Rolling Stones' first Top 10 hit.

Then came the British Invasion of 1964, and in that year, time was finally on the side of this particular song. The Rolling Stones remade "Time Is on My Side," and historically, it became the group's very first Top 10 hit in the United States. The Stones were likely more influenced by the Irma Thomas rendition than the Kai Winding original.

"Tiptoe through the Tulips"
Composers: Al Dubin and Joe Burke
Original Artist: Nick Lucas
Label: Brunswick Records; *Recording:* Brunswick #4418 (78)
Release Year: 1929; *Chart:* #1 *Billboard*
Cover Artist: Tiny Tim
Label: Reprise Records; *Recording:* Reprise #0679 (45)
Release Year: 1968; *Chart:* #17 *Billboard* Hot 100

The 1929 motion picture musical *Gold Diggers of Broadway* marked the first appearance of a song titled "Tiptoe through the Tulips," written by Al Dubin and Joe Burke. Nick Lucas released the first recording of the song, and it blossomed into a number 1 hit and remained at the top for ten weeks.

Numerous cover versions emerged, but none was bigger than the one by the eccentric Tiny Tim in 1968. Tiny Tim was born Herbert Khaury, and appearances on the burgeoning *Rowan and Martin's Laugh-In* on NBC incited interest in his bizarre act. Tiny was anything but tiny, had long hair, played the ukulele, and sang in an extremely high register with intense vibrato. He was like a car wreck, and all of America was getting an eyeful. When he released "Tiptoe through the Tulips," the novelty song became a Top 20 hit and Tiny Tim's signature song. Tiny Tim wed Miss Vicki on a memorable and high-rated *Tonight Show Starring Johnny Carson* on December 21, 1969.

"To All the Girls I've Loved Before"
Composers: Albert Hammond and Hal David
Original Artist: Albert Hammond
Label: Music for Pleasure Records; *Recording:* Music for Pleasure #54962 (LP)
Release Year: 1979; *Chart:* did not chart
Cover Artist: Willie Nelson and Julio Iglesias
Label: Columbia Records; *Recording:* Columbia #04217 (45)
Release Year: 1984; *Chart:* #5 *Billboard* Hot 100 and #1 Country

It happened several times to Albert Hammond—a song he wrote and originally recorded became a hit for someone else. Such was the case with his original rendition of "To All the Girls I've Loved Before." It was released in the United States on an album titled *The Albert Hammond Collection* in 1979. In a few select European countries, the song was released as the B-side of "Down by the River" on an Epic Records single. It was not a hit.

In 1984, the song was remade as somewhat of a novelty duet featuring Willie Nelson and Julio Iglesias. The record created quite a buzz and became quite a sensation, reaching number 5 on the Pop charts. It went platinum.

"To Know Him Is to Love Him"
Composer: Phil Spector
Original Artist: the Teddy Bears
Label: Dore Records; *Recording:* Dore #503 (45)
Release Year: 1958; *Chart:* #1 *Billboard* Hot 100
Cover Artist: Peter and Gordon
Label: Capitol Records; *Recording:* Capitol #5461 (45)
Release Year: 1965; *Chart:* #24 *Billboard* Hot 100

This song's title was inspired by the words on Phil Spector's dad's tombstone. Spector wrote the song and sang harmony on the Teddy Bears' number 1 hit version of the song, released on the Dore Record label in 1958. Carol Connors (a.k.a. Annette Kleinbard) sang lead. The Teddy Bears never had another hit, but Phil Spector went on to bigger and better things (as did this song). Another version on the same Dore Records label (#663) five years later by the Darlings failed to make the charts, as did a cover by Evelyn Kingsley and the Towers (Capitol #4069).

In 1965, Peter and Gordon were riding high as part of the British Invasion. They remade the Teddy Bears' classic, but changed the title to "To Know You Is to Love You." It became a Top 30 hit. Four years later, Bobby Vinton used the Peter and Gordon song title and the song became popular again (Epic #10481), peaking at number 34 on the Pop charts.

A biopic titled *Phil Spector* focused upon the eccentric producer's legal battles and first aired on HBO March 24, 2013. The lead role was filled by Al Pacino.

"TONIGHT YOU BELONG TO ME"
Composers: Lee David and Billy Rose
Original Artist: Irving Kaufman
Label: Banner Records; *Recording:* Banner #1892 (78)
Release Year: 1926; *Chart:* did not chart
Cover Artist: Patience and Prudence
Label: Liberty Records; *Recording:* Liberty #55022 (45 and 78)
Release Year: 1956; *Chart:* #4 *Billboard* Hot 100

"Tonight You Belong to Me" has a long history. The first recorded version was released during the summer of 1926 by Irving Kaufman on the Banner Records label. This was just one of numerous releases by Kaufman in that same year.

Speaking of the same year, there were two hit versions of "Tonight You Belong to Me" in 1956. The first was by a very young duet with the last name of McIntyre. Known on record as Patience and Prudence, they were eleven and fourteen, respectively, and their youthful voices sold over a million records and reached Top 5 on the Pop charts.

To try their patience, a cover version by the Lennon Sisters (Dianne, Kathy, Janet, and Peggy) a month later rivaled the original sisters for airplay. The Lennons, very popular costars on *The Lawrence Welk Show* on ABC, reached number 15 on the Coral label (#61701).

"TOTAL ECLIPSE OF THE HEART"
Composer: Jim Steinman
Original Artist: Bonnie Tyler
Label: Columbia Records; *Recording:* Columbia #03906 (45)
Release Year: 1983; *Chart:* #1 *Billboard* Hot 100
Cover Artist: Nicki French
Label: Critique Records; *Recording:* Critique #15539 (CD)
Release Year: 1995; *Chart:* #2 *Billboard* Hot 100

"Total Eclipse of the Heart" was composed by Jim Steinman and originally offered to Meat Loaf. Steinman's work with Meat Loaf is legendary, as are his compositions and big, exorbitant productions. Meat Loaf didn't record the song, and it was offered next to gravelly voiced Welsh singer Bonnie Tyler. Tyler gave the song the edge to put it over in a big way; it became the biggest hit of her career, and it hit number 1 on the Pop charts and stayed there for four weeks. It sold well over a million copies in 1983. The version on the *Faster Than the Speed of Night* album (Columbia #38710) is almost three minutes longer than the single version played on radio.

A dozen years later, a British singer named Nicki French covered "Total Eclipse of the Heart." This rendition begins as a ballad, but takes on a dance beat in the second verse. Once again the song was a million-selling hit—reaching number 2 in 1995. It was French's only chart single in the United States.

"Total Eclipse of the Heart" has recently been included in TV commercials for Fiber One Nutrition Bars.

"TRAGEDY"
Composers: Fred Burch and Gerald Nelson
Original Artist: Thomas Wayne and the DeLons
Label: Fernwood Records; *Recording:* Fernwood #109 (45)
Release Year: 1959; *Chart:* #5 *Billboard* Hot 100
Cover Artist: the Fleetwoods
Label: Dolton Records; *Recording:* Dolton #40 (45)
Release Year: 1961; *Chart:* #10 *Billboard* Hot 100

Not to be confused with the Bee Gees' hit of the same name, this "Tragedy" was a Top 10 hit twice—two years apart. The first version by Thomas Wayne and a girl trio called the DeLons was released on a small Memphis label called Fernwood. This original version of the song became a Top 5 hit in 1959.

In 1961, "Tragedy" became the third Top 10 hit for the Fleetwoods from the state of Washington. Gretchen Christopher of the group remembered, "Tragedy was the first hit we recorded with a live orchestra at United Studios in Hollywood. All of our previous releases had been done a cappella and closer to home at Northwest Recorders and J. F. Boles Recording in Seattle."

Thomas Wayne was also the originator of the song "This Time," later made famous by Troy Shondell (see the entry for that song). Wayne's life was struck by "tragedy" with his untimely passing at the age of thirty-one in 1971 because of an automobile wreck.

"TRUE COLORS"
Composers: Billy Steinberg and Tom Kelly
Original Artist: Cyndi Lauper
Label: Portrait Records; *Recording:* Portrait #06247 (45)
Release Year: 1986; *Chart:* #1 *Billboard* Hot 100

Cover Artist: Phil Collins
Label: Atlantic Records; *Recording:* Atlantic #8686 (CD)
Release Year: 1998; *Chart:* #66 *Billboard* Hot 100

"True Colors" was the first hit released from Cyndi Lauper's platinum second album, *True Colors* (Portrait #40313). The single reached number 1 on the Pop charts, and it was nominated for (but didn't win) a Grammy for Best Pop Female Vocal Performance. At times, the aforementioned vocal performance takes on an Elmer Fudd–esque quality when Lauper sounds as though she's singing, "Twue colors are beautiful like a wainbow."

Phil Collins released his version of "True Colors" in 1998—the nadir of his long and seemingly invincible run. Collins's version was a wee bit more upbeat than the original and it received considerable airplay, but only attained number 66 on the Pop charts.

Before digital cameras and cell phone cameras, "True Colors" was utilized in TV commercials for Kodak film. More recently, the Cyndi Lauper version was part of the soundtrack for the 2010 motion picture *Sex and the City 2*.

"TRUE LOVE WAYS"
Composers: Buddy Holly and Norman Petty
Original Artist: Buddy Holly
Label: Coral Records; *Recording:* Coral #62210 (45)
Release Year: 1960; *Chart:* did not chart
Cover Artist: Peter and Gordon
Label: Capitol Records; *Recording:* Capitol #5406 (45)
Release Year: 1965; *Chart:* #14 *Billboard* Hot 100

"True Love Ways" is a beautifully orchestrated Buddy Holly ballad, recorded just a few months before his untimely passing. For some reason, it was not released as a single until 1960. Like Holly's song "Everyday," this one never charted, and yet is very familiar and very popular.

Regardless of its failure to chart, "True Love Ways" has influenced many— among them, Peter and Gordon, who remade the song in 1965 for Capitol Records and had a Top 20 hit. Country singer Mickey Gilley revered the song as well, and his own 1980 version (Epic #50876) became a crossover hit, reaching number 66 on the Pop charts and number 1 Country.

"TRY A LITTLE TENDERNESS"
Composers: Jim Campbell, Reg Connelly, and Harry Woods
Original Artist: Ray Noble and His Orchestra
Label: RCA Victor Records; *Recording:* RCA Victor #24263 (78)
Release Year: 1933; *Chart:* did not chart

Cover Artist: Otis Redding
Label: Volt Records; *Recording:* Volt #141 (45)
Release Year: 1967; *Chart:* #25 *Billboard* Hot 100

Most music fans only know "Try a Little Tenderness" as an intense, soulful ballad. It certainly didn't start out that way. The first version from way back in 1933 was by Ray Noble and His Orchestra, featuring Val Rosing on vocals. A rendition by Ted Lewis later that same year reached number 6 on the Pop charts (Columbia #2748). Like the Noble rendition, this was a big band arrangement. Others who covered the song include Bing Crosby, Jimmy Durante, Frank Sinatra, and Mel Torme.

One could see that the song was headed in a more soul-oriented direction in the early 1960s when it was covered by Aretha Franklin and performed live in concert by Sam Cooke. The tune really turned the corner late in 1966 when Otis Redding truly made it his own. This and the Three Dog Night (Dunhill #4177) 1969 interpretation of the song are the two best-known renditions.

Redding's version was included in the soundtrack for Paramount Pictures' 1986 classic *Pretty in Pink*. A similarly soulful rendition was also featured in 20th Century Fox's 1991 musical hit *The Commitments*.

"TURN AROUND, LOOK AT ME"
Composer: Jerry Capehart
Original Artist: Glen Campbell
Label: Crest Records; *Recording:* Crest #1087 (45)
Release Year: 1961; *Chart:* #62 *Billboard* Hot 100
Cover Artist: the Vogues
Label: Reprise Records; *Recording:* Reprise #0686 (45)
Release Year: 1968; *Chart:* #7 *Billboard* Hot 100

"Turn Around, Look at Me" is a song about unrequited love—falling for someone who doesn't even know you exist. Written and produced by Jerry Capehart, the original version of the song became the first chart single in Glen Campbell's solo career. It only reached number 62 on the Pop charts, but it was a start—bigger things were ahead for the song. The song was very quickly covered by an African American artist named Tommy Butler (Roulette #4399), but his excellent version was not a hit, although it did make the Top 30 in Bozeman, Montana. The Lettermen and the early Bee Gees took a crack at it with very little success.

In 1968, after a two-year lull on the charts, the Vogues of Pittsburgh remade "Turn Around, Look at Me." This time around, the song was a Top 10 hit and sold over a million copies. It was also the title cut from the group's album (Reprise #6314) released in that same year.

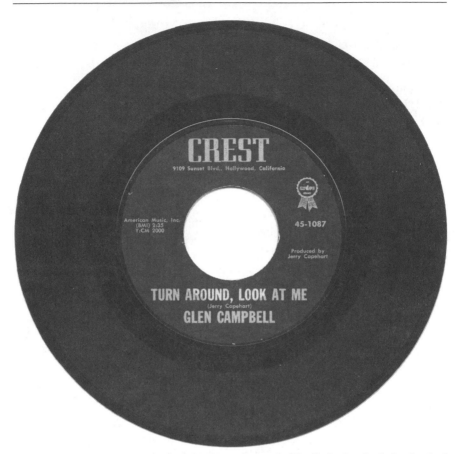

"Turn Around, Look at Me" was Glen Campbell's first charted single, but the remake six years later by the Vogues became the definitive hit version.

"TURN THE BEAT AROUND"
Composers: Gerald and Peter Jackson
Original Artist: Vicki Sue Robinson
Label: RCA Victor Records; *Recording:* RCA Victor #10562 (45)
Release Year: 1976; *Chart:* #10 *Billboard* Hot 100
Cover Artist: Gloria Estefan
Label: Crescent Moon Records; *Recording:* Crescent Moon #77630 (CD)
Release Year: 1994; *Chart:* #13 *Billboard* Hot 100

"Turn the Beat Around" was a million-selling disco hit in the Bicentennial Year, 1976. Written by the Jackson Brothers, Gerald and Peter, it became the only Top 10 hit for Vicki Sue Robinson and was included on her *Never Gonna Let You Go* album (RCA #1256).

Almost twenty years later, the song was revived by Gloria Estefan, and once again it sold over a million copies. This rendition was included in the soundtrack for the Sylvester Stallone and Sharon Stone Warner Brothers motion picture titled *The Specialist.*

"TWILIGHT TIME"
Composer: Buck Ram
Original Artist: the Three Suns
Label: Majestic Records; *Recording:* Majestic #1041 (78)
Release Year: 1946; *Chart:* #8 *Billboard* Music Popularity Chart
Cover Artist: the Platters
Label: Mercury Records; *Recording:* Mercury #71289 (45 and 78)
Release Year: 1958; *Chart:* #1 *Billboard* Hot 100

In 1946, Morty Nevins, Al Nevins, and Artie Dunn entered the "Twilight Zone" while performing in a musical trio known as the Three Suns. They recorded the first version of a Buck Ram composition—"Twilight Time." This version, on the Majestic label, was an instrumental hit. Al Nevins later partnered with Don Kirshner and formed the very successful Aldon Music publishing company, which set the cornerstone for the Brill Building sound of the late 1950s and early 1960s.

A dozen years after the Three Suns version, Buck Ram brought the song to the R&B vocal group he managed, Tony Williams and the Platters. This time around, the song reached number 1 and sold well over a million copies.

U

"UNCHAINED MELODY"
Composers: Alex North and Hy Zaret
Original Artist: Les Baxter
Label: Capitol Records; *Recording:* Capitol #3055 (45 and 78)
Release Year: 1955; *Chart:* #1 *Billboard* Hot 100
Cover Artist: the Righteous Brothers
Label: Philles Records; *Recording:* Philles #129 (45)
Release Year: 1965; *Chart:* #4 *Billboard* Hot 100

"Unchained Melody" originated as part of the soundtrack for a 1955 Warner Brothers prison film titled *Unchained.* Thus, it was called "Unchained Melody." In the film, Todd Duncan performed the song and his performance of the song was nominated for an Academy Award, but he lost to "Love Is a Many Splendored Thing."

Les Baxter and His Orchestra recorded the first version of the song for Capitol Records, and it reached number 1 on the Pop charts in 1955 and is the only version that makes any reference to the song's title ("Unchain me, unchain me"). There were numerous cover versions in that same year, and both Al Hibbler (Decca #29441) and Roy Hamilton (Epic #9102) had Top 10 hits with theirs, but June Valli's on RCA Victor #6078 missed the Top 20.

By far, the most unusual and yet endearing version came from a doo-wop group from Brooklyn called Vito and the Salutations (Herald #583). Performed up-tempo, it was quite an innovative update of the old standard, akin to the Marcels' take on "Blue Moon." This rendition reached number 66 on the Pop charts late in 1963 and was huge in the New York area.

Without question, the most important and enduring interpretation came from Bill Medley and Bobby Hatfield, collectively the Righteous Brothers. It ·became a Top 5 hit in 1965 for Phil Spector's Philles label, but its afterlife was uncanny. The song was included in the soundtrack for the Patrick Swayze, Demi Moore, and Whoopi Goldberg megahit 1990 Paramount motion picture *Ghost*. Almost overnight there were two Righteous Brothers' renditions of the song on the charts at the same time (one old, one new), and each made Top 20. The Righteous Brothers' original rendition was inducted into the Grammy Hall of Fame in 2000.

V

"Venus in Blue Jeans"
Composers: Jack Keller and Howard Greenfield
Original Artist: Bruce Bruno
Label: Roulette Records; *Recording:* Roulette #4427 (45)
Release Year: 1961; *Chart:* did not chart
Cover Artist: Jimmy Clanton
Label: Ace Records; *Recording:* Ace #8001 (45)
Release Year: 1962; *Chart:* #7 *Billboard* Hot 100

Roulette recording artist Bruce Bruno's biggest claim to fame was being the opening act for Ronnie Hawkins and the Hawks in the early 1960s. The New Rochelle, New York, native recorded a song called "Venus in Blue Jeans" in 1961, and it became the B-side of a 45 titled "Dear Joanne."

Neither side of the Bruce Bruno 45 became a hit. In fact, Jimmy Clanton said,

> I was totally unaware of that rendition. My recording came at the end of a recording session. We usually recorded three songs each time we recorded—an A-side, a B-side, and a throwaway. It was done in New York and there was a pile of demo records in the corner which had been rejected by other recording artists. "Venus in Blue Jeans" was one of them and I just loved the chord changes in the song. We

utilized this wonderful horn section in the studio, and that part was arranged by Carole King. That throwaway song turned out really good and became my third Top 10 hit. To this day, the audience always knows what's coming by that wonderful horn part at the beginning of the song.

It's interesting to note that Neil Sedaka is credited for writing the song on the hit version. Clanton added, "I don't know how that happened. Sedaka did write a few songs for me ('Another Sleepless Night' and 'All the Words in the World'), but not that one. It was written by Jack Keller and Howard Greenfield."

"VOLARE"
Composers: Domenico Modugno and Franco Migliacci
Original Artist: Domenico Modugno
Label: Decca Records; *Recording:* Decca #30677 (45 and 78)
Release Year: 1958; *Chart:* #1 *Billboard* Hot 100
Cover Artist: Bobby Rydell
Label: Cameo Records; *Recording:* Cameo #179 (45)
Release Year: 1960; *Chart:* #4 *Billboard* Hot 100

The original title was "Nel Blu Dipinto di Blu (Volare)," and that translates to something akin to "Paint the Sky Blue." It was co-written and first performed by Domenico Modugno on the Decca label, and it was a sensation, reaching number 1 (for five weeks) and selling over a million copies.

Modugno's rendition was performed completely in Italian, but the next version that same year by Dean Martin (Capitol #4018) was half Italian and half English. Dino's version retained the slow opening verse of the original. The song was now simply titled "Volare," and it peaked at number 12 on the Pop charts.

In 1960, "Volare" was updated by one of Philadelphia's "Boys of Bandstand," Bobby Rydell. This time around, the slow opening verse was completely extracted, and even though Rydell was of Italian descent, all of the lyrics were in English (except for the "Volare, cantare" part). "Nel blu dipinto di blu" became "your love has given me wings"—this was long before Red Bull had been invented. This hit was followed by two more remakes of old standards—"Sway" and "That Old Black Magic" (see the entries for those songs).

W

"WALK AWAY, RENEE"
Composers: Tony Sansone, Bob Calilli, and Michael Brown
Original Artist: Sylvie Vartan
Label: RCA Victor Records; *Recording:* RCA Victor #187 (EP)

Release Year: 1966; *Chart:* did not chart
Cover Artist: the Left Banke
Label: Smash Records; *Recording:* Smash #2041 (45)
Release Year: 1966; *Chart:* #5 *Billboard* Hot 100

"Walk Away, Renee" began as "Quand un Amour Renait" by Sylvie Vartan on a French extended play (EP) for RCA Victor in 1966. Later that year, the Anglicized rendition by the Left Banke was released on Smash Records and became a smash record. Now known as "Walk Away, Renee," the song told the tale of a man who was attempting to get over a breakup, but not having a great deal of success. The song, however, was quite a success and reached number 5 on the Pop charts.

A remake just two years later by the Four Tops (Motown #1119) peaked at number 14 on the Pop charts and number 15 R&B.

"WASTED DAYS AND WASTED NIGHTS"

Composers: Baldemar Huerta and Wayne Duncan
Original Artist: Freddy Fender
Label: Duncan Records; *Recording:* Duncan #1001 (45)
Release Year: 1959; *Chart:* did not chart
Cover Artist: Freddy Fender
Label: ABC Dot Records; *Recording:* ABC Dot #17558 (45)
Release Year: 1975; *Chart:* #8 *Billboard* Hot 100

His real name was Baldemar Huerta, but on record he was Freddy Fender, a Latino singer/songwriter who got his start in the 1950s. Despite a lot of releases on a lot of labels, Fender was not an instant success story. Perseverance paid off, with one song in particular. "Wasted Days and Wasted Nights" was released on numerous record labels between 1959 and 1962—Duncan, Imperial, and Talent Scout—but to no avail.

Fender landed at ABC Dot Records in 1975 and, as a follow-up to his number 1 smash titled "Before the Next Teardrop Falls" (see the entry for that song), he opted to give "Wasted Days and Wasted Nights" one more try. The original had much more of a New Orleans feel to it, but now, with a face-lift, the tune caught on and reached the Top 10 and garnered Fender his second consecutive gold record. It was included on the *Before the Next Teardrop Falls* album (ABC Dot #2020) and that, too, earned the singer a gold record.

"WAY DOWN YONDER IN NEW ORLEANS"

Composers: John Turner Layton and Henry Creamer
Original Artist: the Peerless Quartet
Label: RCA Victor Records; *Recording:* RCA Victor #26827 (78)
Release Year: 1922; *Chart:* #9 *Billboard*

Freddy Fender recorded "Wasted Days and Wasted Nights" numerous times on numerous labels before it became a big hit. All those days and nights weren't wasted at all.

Cover Artist: Freddy Cannon
Label: Swan Records; *Recording:* Swan #4043 (45)
Release Year: 1959; *Chart:* #3 *Billboard* Hot 100

"Way Down Yonder in New Orleans" began in a Broadway show titled *Spice of 1922*. It's a song about the beautiful girls of "the crescent city." The first recording of the song was by the Peerless Quartet on the RCA Victor label, and it became a Top 10 hit.

The song was covered by Louis Armstrong, Jo Stafford, the Andrews Sisters, and Frankie Laine. However, likely the best known rendition of the song came about in the rock and roll era. Freddy "Boom Boom" Cannon remade the tune in 1959 for Philadelphia's Swan Records label, and it became a Top 3 million-selling smash early in 1960. It was included on *The Explosive Freddy Cannon* album (Swan #502).

"THE WAY OF LOVE"

Composers: Jack Dieval and Al Stillman
Original Artist: Kathy Kirby
Label: Parrot Records; *Recording:* Parrot #9775 (45)
Release Year: 1965; *Chart:* did not chart
Cover Artist: Cher
Label: Kapp Records; *Recording:* Kapp #2158 (45)
Release Year: 1972; *Chart:* #7 *Billboard* Hot 100

Based upon a French song titled "J'ai le Mal de Toi," "The Way of Love" is a warning to proceed with caution when it comes to affairs of the heart—one can get hurt. The original English version came from British blonde bombshell vocalist Kathy Kirby. Released on London's Parrot Records label, the song failed to chart but did get some U.S. airplay in 1965.

In 1972, the ballad was remade in very similar fashion by Cher on the Kapp label, and this time it became a Top 10 hit, aided by exposure on *The Sonny and Cher Comedy Hour* on CBS. It was included on the *Gypsies, Tramps and Thieves* album (Kapp #5549).

"THE WAY YOU LOOK TONIGHT"

Composers: Jerome Kern and Dorothy Fields
Original Artist: Fred Astaire
Label: Brunswick Records; *Recording:* Brunswick #7717 (78)
Release Year: 1936; *Chart:* #1 *Billboard* Music Hit Parade
Cover Artist: the Lettermen
Label: Capitol Records; *Recording:* Capitol #4586 (45)
Release Year: 1961; *Chart:* #13 *Billboard* Hot 100

This classically tinged ballad first appeared in the RKO Ginger Rogers and Fred Astaire film *Swing Time* in 1936. In that same year, Astaire released the song on a Brunswick 78, and there were covers galore from the likes of Bing Crosby, Billie Holliday, Perry Como, Doris Day, Peggy Lee, Tony Bennett, and Mel Torme. "The Way You Look Tonight" won an Oscar for Best Original Song in 1936.

This beautiful song also made the transition into the doo-wop realm. A racially integrated vocal group from California called the Jaguars had a very popular rendition in 1956 (R-Dell #11). The Jarmels (Laurie #3098) released a unique upbeat version with a Latin beat in 1961 on the B-side of their big hit "A Little Bit of Soap."

The smooth doo-wop version of the old standard "The Way You Look Tonight" by California's Jaguars on the R-Dell record label.

Also in 1961, a smooth remake of the song by the Lettermen on the Capitol label just missed the Top 10. This rendition was likely inspired by the Jaguars' 1956 hit, as it features an almost identical classical piano introduction.

This song has a very strong association with Frank Sinatra, who released it on his Top 10 1964 album titled *Days of Wine and Roses, Moon River, and Other Academy Award Winners* (Reprise #1011).

"THE WEDDING"
Composers: Fred Jay and Joaquin Prieto
Original Artist: Anita Bryant
Label: Columbia Records; *Recording:* Columbia #42148 (45)
Release Year: 1961; *Chart:* did not chart

Cover Artist: Julie Rogers
Label: Mercury Records; *Recording:* Mercury #72332 (45)
Release Year: 1964; *Chart:* #10 *Billboard* Hot 100

Originally an Argentinian melody titled "La Novia," the Anglicized version was titled "The Wedding," and the first version was by the former Miss Oklahoma Anita Bryant on Columbia Records. Bryant had success on the small Carlton record label in 1960, but her switch to the much bigger Columbia label did not prove fruitful. Bryant's version of "The Wedding" was mostly ignored.

Very late in 1964, British singer Julie Rogers covered "The Wedding." The song possessed extremely vivid lyrics that allowed the listener to fully envision the entire wedding ceremony. Early in 1965, Rogers's version peaked at number 10 and became her only U.S. hit.

Anita Bryant and her popular TV commercials for orange juice disappeared from public view after causing outrage because of her antigay crusade in 1977.

"WEDDING BELL BLUES"

Composer: Laura Nyro
Original Artist: Laura Nyro
Label: Verve Folkways Records; *Recording:* Verve Folkways #5024 (45)
Release Year: 1966; *Chart:* bubbled under #103
Cover Artist: the Fifth Dimension
Label: Soul City Records; *Recording:* Soul City #779 (45)
Release Year: 1969; *Chart:* #1 *Billboard* Hot 100

Laura Nyro wrote and originally recorded the song, "Wedding Bell Blues" in 1966 for the Verve Folkways Record label—a subsidiary of MGM. The song tells the story of a young lady who wonders if her beau will ever propose. It was released on a single and was also included on her *More Than a New Discovery* album (Verve Forecast #3020, later reissued as *The First Songs*). The single "bubbled under" the Hot 100 for a few weeks, but stalled at number 103.

A couple of years later, the Fifth Dimension found great success with Nyro's compositions such as "Stoned Soul Picnic" and "Sweet Blindness," so they opted to remake "Wedding Bell Blues," too. The song was ideal for Marilyn McCoo because the guy mentioned in the song was named Bill, and nothing needed to be changed because she had recently married group member Billy Davis Jr. Once again, they were successful covering one of Laura's songs, and "Wedding Bell Blues" became the group's second number 1 hit in 1969—the first was "Aquarius/Let the Sunshine In" (Soul City #772).

McCoo and Davis Jr. were wed on July 26, 1969.

"WEEKEND IN NEW ENGLAND"
Composer: Randy Edelman
Original Artist: Randy Edelman
Label: 20th Century Records; *Recording:* 20th Century #494 (LP)
Release Year: 1975; *Chart:* did not chart
Cover Artist: Barry Manilow
Label: Arista Records; *Recording:* Arista #0212 (45)
Release Year: 1976; *Chart:* #10 *Billboard* Hot 100

Randy Edelman wrote and also recorded the original version of "Weekend in New England" on his *Farewell, Fairbanks* album on the 20th Century label. The song is about a romantic weekend in New England, even though the word *weekend* is never mentioned in the lyrics. The singer ponders about how long it will be until he gets to see his lover again.

Edelman's original from 1975 was not a hit, but when covered late in 1976 by Barry Manilow, it took off in a big way. Early in 1977 it reached the Top 10. "Weekend in New England" was included on Manilow's *This One's for You* album (Arista #4090).

"WE'RE ALL ALONE"
Composer: Boz Scaggs
Original Artist: Boz Scaggs
Label: Columbia Records; *Recording:* Columbia #33920 (LP)
Release Year: 1976; *Chart:* did not chart
Cover Artist: Rita Coolidge
Label: A & M Records; *Recording:* A & M #1965 (45)
Release Year: 1977; *Chart:* #7 *Billboard* Hot 100

"We're All Alone" was written and originally performed by Boz Scaggs on his hugely successful *Silk Degrees* album. It went multiplatinum and remained on the charts for over two years. Scaggs released "We're All Alone" as the B-side of the hit single "Lido Shuffle" (Columbia #10491), but it didn't chart.

Frankie Valli had the first rendition to crack the Hot 100 (Private Stock #088), but it only got as high as number 78 in 1976.

"We're All Alone" finally reached Top 10 in 1977 when covered by Rita Coolidge. She had a lot of success covering "Higher and Higher" and "The Way You Do the Things You Do," and this was no exception. It sold over a million copies and was included on her *Anywhere, Anytime* album (A & M #4616).

"WE'VE GOT TONIGHT"
Composer: Bob Seger
Original Artist: Bob Seger

Label: Capitol Records; *Recording:* Capitol #4653 (45)
Release Year: 1978; *Chart:* #13 *Billboard* Hot 100
Cover Artist: Kenny Rogers and Sheena Easton
Label: Liberty Records; *Recording:* Liberty #1492 (45)
Release Year: 1983; *Chart:* #6 *Billboard* Hot 100

"We've Got Tonight" is a song about "living in the now." Even though the relationship alluded to in the song isn't going anywhere, the singer thinks that they should take advantage of the fact that they're together tonight. Bob Seger wrote and recorded the original version, which reached number 13 on the Pop charts in 1978. It was included on his multiplatinum *Stranger in Town* album (Capitol #11698).

Just five years later, the song was remade as a duet by Kenny Rogers and Sheena Easton, and this time around it cracked the Top 10. The song can also be found on Rogers's *We've Got Tonight* album (Liberty #51143).

"WHAT A DIFFERENCE A DAY MAKES"
Composers: Maria Grever and Stanley Adams
Original Artist: the Dorsey Brothers
Label: Decca Records; *Recording:* Decca #38914 (78)
Release Year: 1934; *Chart:* #5 *Billboard*
Cover Artist: Dinah Washington
Label: Mercury Records; *Recording:* Mercury #71435 (45)
Release Year: 1959; *Chart:* #8 *Billboard* Hot 100

Written by Mexican songwriter Maria Grever, the original title was "Cuando Vuelva a Tu Lado." It translated to something akin to "When I Return to You," and with Anglicized lyrics from Stanley Adams the song morphed into "What a Difference a Day Made." The Dorsey Brothers recorded it in 1934 and had a Top 5 hit on 78 for Decca Records.

The "Made" in the title became "Makes" in the remake by the brilliant Dinah Washington in 1959. The lyric "It's heaven when you find romance on your menu" is clever and memorable. This exquisite version became Washington's very first Top 10 hit on the Pop charts, although she had previously had more than two dozen on the R&B charts. The song garnered her a 1959 Grammy for Best Rhythm and Blues Performance. Her rendition was inducted into the Grammy Hall of Fame in 1998. *What a Difference a Day Makes* was also the title of a Top 40 album by Ms. Washington (Mercury #20479).

Previously a ballad, the song became a disco hit when Esther Phillips remade it in 1975 (Kudu #925). It reached the Top 20 on the Pop charts and Top 10 R&B.

"WHEEL OF FORTUNE"
Composers: George David Weiss and Bennie Benjamin
Original Artist: Johnny Hartman
Label: RCA Victor Records; *Recording:* RCA Victor #47-4349 (45 and 78)

Release Year: 1951; *Chart:* did not chart
Cover Artist: Kay Starr
Label: Capitol Records; *Recording:* Capitol #1964 (45 and 78)
Release Year: 1952; *Chart:* #1 *Billboard* Hot 100

Written by George David Weiss and Bennie Benjamin, this song is not about fortune at all, but rather the quest for true love. There were so many versions of "Wheel of Fortune" released in 1952 the exact order is unclear. The first charted version came from the Eddie Wilcox Orchestra, with Sunny Gale on vocals. Released on the Derby label, it reached number 2 on the R&B chart. Dinah Washington reached number 3 R&B with her version, too (Mercury #8267). Earlier versions by both Johnny Hartman (RCA Victor #47-4349) and Al Costello with the Walter Scott Orchestra (Crescendo Records) were released late in 1951 but did not chart.

Meanwhile, Kay Starr hit number 1 on the Pop charts with her interpretation on the Capitol label. Starr's version was the only one that utilized the sound of a real spinning game wheel in the beginning.

Another R&B version came next from the smooth vocal group from Baltimore and Washington, D.C., known as the Cardinals. Released on the Atlantic label (#958), the song reached number 6 on the R&B chart in the spring of 1952. The Four Flames (Specialty #423) released their take on the song in 1952 as well, but their version didn't chart. Lavern Baker attempted a revival of the song in 1959 (Atlantic #2059) but was met with only marginal success.

The song shares a title with one of the most successful game shows of all time, which began its amazing run with Chuck Woolery as host on January 6, 1975.

"WHEN I FALL IN LOVE"

Composers: Victor Young and Eddie Heyman
Original Artist: Doris Day
Label: Columbia Records; *Recording:* Columbia #37986 (45 and 78)
Release Year: 1952; *Chart:* #20 *Billboard* Hot 100
Cover Artist: the Lettermen
Label: Capitol Records; *Recording:* Capitol #4658 (45)
Release Year: 1961; *Chart:* #7 *Billboard* Hot 100

In "When I Fall in Love," the singer avers that when she falls in love, it will be the real thing and it will be forever. The song was first heard in the RKO motion picture *One Minute to Zero*. It starred Robert Mitchum and Ann Blyth, and Doris Day had the first hit with the song, reaching Top 20.

A doo-wop group called the Flamingos had quite a bit of success with a remake of the old standard "I Only Have Eyes for You," so a few other standards followed, including "When I Fall in Love" (End #1079) in 1960. One year later, a vocal trio called the Lettermen recorded the biggest chart version of the song for the Capitol label. It peaked at number 7 and was included on the album titled *A Song for Young Love* (Capitol #1669).

Nat King Cole released a version of the song as an album cut (*Love Is the Thing*—Capitol #824), and his daughter Natalie released hers thirty years later as a single (EMI/Manhattan #50138).

Celine Dion reached the Top 30 with a remake in 1993 (Epic Soundtrax #77021) that was used in the Tom Hanks and Meg Ryan motion picture classic *Sleepless in Seattle*.

"WHEN I NEED YOU"
Composers: Albert Hammond and Carole Bayer Sager
Original Artist: Albert Hammond
Label: Epic Records; *Recording:* Epic #35049 (LP)
Release Year: 1976; *Chart:* did not chart
Cover Artist: Leo Sayer
Label: Warner Brothers Records; *Recording:* Warner Brothers #8332 (45)
Release Year: 1977; *Chart:* #1 *Billboard* Hot 100

"When I Need You" is a song about a long-distance romance and fantasy. The singer just has to close his eyes and he's with the one he loves—she's only a heartbeat away. Composer Albert Hammond introduced the song, appropriately, on his *When I Need You* album in 1976.

A year later, the song was covered by the red-hot Leo Sayer, who had just come off of a number 1 single titled "You Make Me Feel Like Dancing" (Warner #8283). "When I Need You" followed suit and, like its predecessor, also sold over a million copies. This version was also a number 1 hit in the United Kingdom.

"WHISPERING"
Composers: John Schoenberger, Richard Coburn, and Vincent Rose
Original Artist: Paul Whiteman and His Ambassador Orchestra
Label: RCA Victor Records; *Recording:* RCA Victor #18690 (78)
Release Year: 1920; *Chart:* #1 *Billboard*
Cover Artist: Nino Tempo and April Stevens
Label: Atco Records; *Recording:* Atco #6281 (45)
Release Year: 1963; *Chart:* #11 *Billboard* Hot 100

"Whispering" by Paul Whiteman in 1920 was quite an instrumental sensation. It reached number 1 and remained there steadfastly for eleven weeks, selling well over a million copies. Only John Schoenberger is credited as composer on this version, but on later releases with lyrics, Richard Coburn and Vincent Rose come into the picture.

Very late in 1963, Nino Tempo and April Stevens released a vocal version as a follow-up to their number 1 smash "Deep Purple" (see the entry for that song). It may have been just a wee bit too similar to "Deep Purple," in fact; the harmonica in the background, the harmonizing, and Stevens's spoken bridge in the middle were all back for an encore. This version of "Whispering" just missed the Top 10 early in 1964. The song was included on the *Deep Purple* album (Atco #156). The Beatles hit it big in the United States at about the same time, and that put the kibosh on any more hits from this duo.

A disco medley version of "Whispering/Cherchez La Femme" by Dr. Buzzard's Original Savannah Band (RCA #10827) returned the song to the Top 30 in 1976.

"Who's Sorry Now?"
Composers: Ted Snyder, Bert Kalmar, and Harry Ruby
Original Artist: the Original Memphis Five
Label: RCA Victor Records; *Recording:* RCA Victor #19052 (78)
Release Year: 1923; *Chart:* did not chart
Cover Artist: Connie Francis; *Label:* MGM Records; *Recording:* MGM #12588
    (45 and 78)
Release Year: 1958; *Chart:* #4 *Billboard* Hot 100

"Who's Sorry Now?" was written by Ted Snyder, Bert Kalmar, and Harry Ruby, and at least half a dozen versions cropped up in 1923—the first of which came from the Original Memphis Five on RCA Victor. This version is instrumental, and thus only Ted Snyder is credited as composer on the label. However, in that same year, renditions by the Ben Selvin Orchestra, Isham Jones, and Marion Harris were all vocals. In 1946, the song was included as part of the soundtrack for the United Artists Marx Brothers classic, *A Night in Casablanca*.

Early vocal versions of the song contain another verse, which began with the line, "You smiled when we parted, it hurt me somehow." This verse was eliminated in the immensely popular Connie Francis rendition of 1958. Francis was on the last legs of her recording contract and was about to be released from MGM after ten abysmal failures. Her father had been badgering her to record a new version of "Who's Sorry Now?" and, reluctantly, she acquiesced. Wouldn't you know, that became her first of a long string of big hits, aided by a big push from *American Bandstand*.

Fifteen years later, Marie Osmond brought the song back into the Top 40 (MGM/Kolob #14786), albeit briefly. Osmond's version was patterned after Connie Francis's and also doesn't contain the verse heard in the 1923 originals.

"Why Don't You Believe Me?"
Composers: Lew Douglas, King Raney, and Roy Rodde
Original Artist: Joni James
Label: MGM Records; *Recording:* MGM #11333 (45 and 78)
Release Year: 1952; *Chart:* #1 *Billboard* Hot 100
Cover Artist: the Duprees
Label: Coed Records; *Recording:* Coed #584 (45)
Release Year: 1963; *Chart:* #37 *Billboard* Hot 100

"Why Don't You Believe Me?" is the story of someone attempting to convince another of her love. Joni James had a number 1 hit with the song, written by King Raney, Roy Rodde, and Lew Douglas. Douglas also conducted the orchestra on James's record. Other versions competing for a piece of the pie in 1952 included one by Patti Page (Mercury #70025) that reached the Top 5, and one by Margaret Whiting (Capitol #2292) that peaked at number 29.

The first R&B/doo-wop version came from New York's Five Crowns on the Rainbow Records label (#202) in 1952. It wasn't a hit then, but this collector's item is quite a valuable treasure today. Over a decade later, a doo-wop group from Jersey City, New Jersey, named the Duprees loved the ballads of Joni James, and they had hits with remakes of two of her songs—"Why Don't You Believe Me?" and "Have You Heard?" (see the entry for that song) back-to-back. Both titles were questions, and both reached the Top 40 late in 1963. "Why Don't You Believe Me?" is cut three of side one on the *You Belong to Me* album (Coed #905).

"Wild World"

Composer: Cat Stevens
Original Artist: Cat Stevens
Label: A & M Records; *Recording:* A & M #1231 (45)
Release Year: 1971; *Chart:* #11 *Billboard* Hot 100
Cover Artist: Maxi Priest
Label: Virgin Records; *Recording:* Virgin #99269 (45)
Release Year: 1988; *Chart:* #25 *Billboard* Hot 100

"Wild World" is a message to a young lady after an amicable breakup. The singer is saying goodbye and passing along a gentle warning for his ex to proceed with caution because it's a "wild world" out there. Written and performed by Cat Stevens, it became his first chart hit in the United States in 1971, and just missed the Top 10.

In 1988, a reggae-infused version by Maxi Priest, coincidentally, became that group's first chart hit in the United States as well. Then, just five years later, the reggae beat was gone and a group known as Mr. Big (Atlantic #87308) recorded a version similar in texture to the Cat Stevens original. This version peaked at number 27 late in 1993.

"Wildwood Days"

Composers: Kal Mann and Dave Appell
Original Artist: the Dovells
Label: Parkway Records; *Recording:* Parkway #867 (45)
Release Year: 1963; *Chart:* did not chart
Cover Artist: Bobby Rydell
Label: Cameo Records; *Recording:* Cameo #252 (45)
Release Year: 1963; *Chart:* #17 *Billboard* Hot 100

Wildwood, New Jersey, was a rocking town on the Jersey Shore in the late 1950s and early 1960s. Recording artists from Philadelphia found a lot of club work there, and the prolific songwriting team of Kal Mann and Dave Appell attempted to cash in by writing a song about those good times. The result was "Wildwood Days," and the original version by the Dovells from the early spring of 1963 was hidden on the B-side of "You Can't Sit Down," one of their biggest.

The Dovells recorded for Parkway Records, while Bobby Rydell was on the sister label, Cameo, and just a month after the original, he released a version. This is the one that became a hit—reaching number 17 during the summer of 1963. Rydell went to the well again with a song about Atlantic City's famous "Steel Pier" (a Cameo one-sided 45 not assigned a number), but it failed to chart.

"Wind beneath My Wings"
Composers: Jeff Silbar and Larry Henley
Original Artist: Roger Whittaker
Label: RCA Victor Records; *Recording:* RCA Victor #1421 (LP)
Release Year: 1982; *Chart:* did not chart
Cover Artist: Bette Midler
Label: Atlantic Records; *Recording:* Atlantic #88972 (45)
Release Year: 1988; *Chart:* #1 *Billboard* Hot 100

Roger Whittaker had first dibs on "Wind beneath My Wings" in 1982, and he jumped at the opportunity. It was the title cut of his RCA Victor album but it failed to make the charts.

Lou Rawls was next in line (Epic #03758), and he was the first to make the charts with the tune in 1983 (number 65 on the Pop charts). For some reason, Gladys Knight and the Pips' version from late in 1983 (Columbia #04219) changed the title to "Hero." This version reached number 64 on the R&B chart.

However, when a version by "the Divine Miss M," Bette Midler, was included in the soundtrack for the hit 1988 Touchstone motion picture *Beaches*, magic transpired. Midler's rendition became her only number 1 single, and it stayed on the charts for over six months. Midler portrayed C. C. Bloom in the film.

"Without You"
Composer: Harry Nilsson
Original Artist: Harry Nilsson
Label: RCA Victor Records; *Recording:* RCA Victor #0604 (45)
Release Year: 1971; *Chart:* #1 *Billboard* Hot 100
Cover Artist: Mariah Carey
Label: Columbia Records; *Recording:* Columbia #77358 (CD)
Release Year: 1994; *Chart:* #3 *Billboard* Hot 100

Not to be confused with the Johnny Tillotson hit of the same name, this "Without You" is an intense ballad about giving up. The singer faces the fact he simply can't go on without his significant other. The song was written and originally performed by Harry Nilsson, who really got to display his vocal chops on this one. It became his only number 1 hit, and was included on his landmark *Nilsson Schmilsson* album in 1971 (RCA #4515), which spent almost a full year on the charts.

An equally fine performance was delivered by Mariah Carey on her remake of "Without You" in 1994. It reached number 3 on the Pop charts and was included on her multiplatinum album titled *Musicbox* (Columbia #53205).

"THE WONDER OF YOU"
Composer: Baker Knight
Original Artist: Ray Peterson

Both Ray Peterson and Elvis Presley recorded "The Wonder of You" on the RCA Victor label, but Peterson did it first.

Label: RCA Victor Records; *Recording:* RCA Victor #7513 (45)
Release Year: 1959; *Chart:* #25 *Billboard* Hot 100
Cover Artist: Elvis Presley
Label: RCA Victor Records; *Recording:* RCA Victor #9835 (45)
Release Year: 1970; *Chart:* #9 *Billboard* Hot 100

Baker Knight composed several Top 10 songs for Ricky Nelson in his Imperial Record days ("I Got a Feeling," "Lonesome Town," "Sweeter Than You," and "Never Be Anyone Else but You"). He also wrote a song with Perry Como in mind called "The Wonder of You," but it was instead recorded by Ray Peterson and it became his first chart hit in 1959, peaking at number 25 on the RCA Victor label.

Once again, on the RCA Victor label, the song was remade by Elvis Presley in his comeback years. It was recorded live in Las Vegas in February of 1970 and released as a single that spring. It reached number 9 on the Pop charts, and was even bigger in the United Kingdom. It sold well over a million copies and was included on the platinum *On Stage—February 1970* album (RCA #4362).

The Platters also recorded a version. It was the title cut of a British album they released on Pickwick Records (#896).

"WONDERFUL, WONDERFUL"

Composers: Sherman Edwards and Ben Raleigh
Original Artist: Johnny Mathis
Label: Columbia Records; *Recording:* Columbia #40784 (45 and 78)
Release Year: 1957; *Chart:* #14 *Billboard* Hot 100
Cover Artist: the Tymes
Label: Parkway Records; *Recording:* Parkway #884 (45)
Release Year: 1963; *Chart:* #7 *Billboard* Hot 100 and #23 R&B

Despite the title, "Wonderful, Wonderful" has no connection to Lawrence Welk. Written by Sherman Edwards and Ben Raleigh, the romantic song was presented to Johnny Mathis, who released it early in 1957 and had his first of a long string of Top 20 hits for Columbia Records.

Six years later, as the follow-up to their number 1 smash "So Much in Love," Philadelphia's Tymes remade the song and mimicked the Mathis original. This version actually charted higher than Mathis's, and peaked at number 7 on the Pop charts in 1963. Wonderful, indeed.

"WONDERLAND BY NIGHT"

Composers: Lincoln Chase and Gunter Newman Klaus
Original Artist: Bert Kaempfert
Label: Decca Records; *Recording:* Decca #31141 (45)
Release Year: 1960; *Chart:* #1 *Billboard* Hot 100

Cover Artist: Louis Prima
Label: Dot Records; *Recording:* Dot #16151 (45)
Release Year: 1960; *Chart:* #15 *Billboard* Hot 100

The original and biggest version of this trumpet-laden ballad was by German-born Bert Kaempfert on the Decca label. Released late in 1960, it scaled the charts, reaching the apex early in 1961.

Kaempfert's version was an instrumental, but two vocal versions also made Top 20 in 1961. Louis Prima's take on the song on the Dot label reached number 15, and Anita Bryant's (Carlton #537) peaked at number 18. Coincidentally, it was the final Top 20 hit for both Prima and Bryant. Engelbert Humperdinck recorded a vocal version on his *A Man without Love* album (Parrot #71022) in 1968.

"WOODEN HEART"

Composers: Bert Kaempfert, Ben Weisman, Fred Wise, and Kay Twomey
Original Artist: Elvis Presley
Label: RCA Victor Records; *Recording:* RCA Victor #2256 (LP)
Release Year: 1960; *Chart:* did not chart
Cover Artist: Joe Dowell
Label: Smash Records; *Recording:* Smash #1708 (45)
Release Year: 1961; *Chart:* #1 *Billboard* Hot 100

In the hit 1960 motion picture *G.I. Blues*, Elvis Presley portrayed Tulsa McLean and his costar was the leggy dancer Juliet Prowse as Lili. In the film, Presley sings the song "Wooden Heart," sometimes called "Muss I Denn." The song was included on the soundtrack album, but not released as a single in the United States, leaving the door wide open for a cover version.

Singer Joe Dowell jumped at the opportunity and his release on the Smash label became a smash hit. It hit number 1 for one week in 1961. Fame was fleeting for Dowell, as he was never again able to reach the Top 20.

Elvis Presley finally did release his version of "Wooden Heart" on a 45 in the United States, but it was lost in the shuffle as the B-side of an RCA Victor 45 rpm reissue of "Blue Christmas" (RCA #0720) in 1964.

An answer record by a young lady named Marie Ann (Epic #9465) was titled "(I Know That) Your Heart's Not Made of Wood." However, the writers on this 45 are listed as J. Brandon and K. Millet.

"WORKING MY WAY BACK TO YOU"

Composers: Sandy Linzer and Denny Randell
Original Artist: the Four Seasons
Label: Philips Records; *Recording:* Philips #40350 (45)
Release Year: 1966; *Chart:* #9 *Billboard* Hot 100

Cover Artist: the Spinners
Label: Atlantic Records; *Recording:* Atlantic #3637 (45)
Release Year: 1979; *Chart:* #2 *Billboard* Hot 100 and #6 R&B

"Working My Way Back to You" is the first Four Seasons record on which original member Nick Massi was replaced by Charles Calello. It's the story of a guy trying to win back a girl he lost, emphasizing that old chestnut, "You don't know what you've got until you lose it." It became a Top 10 hit early in 1966.

A lucky thirteen years later, the song was remade as a disco medley by the Spinners—paired with "Forgive Me, Girl." The two songs lyrically and melodically complemented one another extremely well, and the record sold well over a million copies and peaked at number 2 on the Pop charts, and number 6 R&B. A similar pairing of "Cupid" and "I've Loved You for a Long Time" also became a big hit for the group the following year.

Bobby Smith of the Spinners died March 16, 2013.

"A World without Love"
Composers: John Lennon and Paul McCartney
Original Artist: Peter and Gordon
Label: Capitol Records; *Recording:* Capitol #5175 (45)
Release Year: 1964; *Chart:* #1 *Billboard* Hot 100
Cover Artist: Bobby Rydell
Label: Cameo Records; *Recording:* Cameo #320 (45)
Release Year: 1964; *Chart:* #80 *Billboard* Hot 100

John Lennon and Paul McCartney wrote so many songs, some of them were given to other British acts such as Billy J. Kramer and the Dakotas, and Peter and Gordon. The latter recorded one of their compositions, "A World without Love" early in 1964 in the United Kingdom, where it instantly took off.

One of the "Boys of Bandstand," Bobby Rydell, tried to get a jump on the British by releasing "A World without Love" first in the United States, but he just wasn't quick enough. Both Rydell's version and Peter and Gordon's original were released in the States on May 9, 1964. Being British (which in 1964 rendered one extremely cool), Peter and Gordon, of course, prevailed and had a number 1 hit with the song. Rydell's version did get a lot of airplay in the New York, New Jersey, and Philadelphia radio markets, but only reached number 80 on the charts. The British Invasion was extremely hard on the teen idols, who earlier had ruled the Pop charts. Rydell never again reached the Top 50.

"Worst That Could Happen"
Composer: Jimmy Webb
Original Artist: the Fifth Dimension

Label: Soul City Records; *Recording:* Soul City #92001 (LP)
Release Year: 1968; *Chart:* did not chart
Cover Artist: the Brooklyn Bridge
Label: Buddah Records; *Recording:* Buddah #75 (45)
Release Year: 1968; *Chart:* #3 *Billboard* Hot 100

Written by the prolific Jimmy Webb, "Worst That Could Happen" is a song about someone who hears a rumor that his ex (whom he still loves) is marrying someone else. While the singer is happy for this person, it's the worst that could happen to him. The original version of the song appeared on a Fifth Dimension album that was originally titled *The Magic Garden*, but later retitled *The Worst That Could Happen* on Johnny Rivers's Soul City Label.

That album title was altered once the cover version of "Worst That Could Happen" by the Brooklyn Bridge became a hit early in 1969 to cash in on its success. The Brooklyn Bridge featured the Crests' former lead singer, Johnny Maestro. The other members of the group had previously recorded as the Del Satins, and besides making their own doo-wop records, they backed up many of Dion's solo hits after he and the Belmonts parted ways in 1960. "Worst That Could Happen" sold well over a million copies and was included on *The Brooklyn Bridge* album in 1969 (Buddah #5034).

Johnny Maestro died at the age of seventy on March 24, 2010.

Y

"Yesterday"

Composers: John Lennon and Paul McCartney
Original Artist: the Beatles
Label: Capitol Records; *Recording:* Capitol #5498 (45)
Release Year: 1965; *Chart:* #1 *Billboard* Hot 100
Cover Artist: Ray Charles
Label: ABC/TRC Records; *Recording:* ABC/TRC #11009 (45)
Release Year: 1967; *Chart:* #25 *Billboard* Hot 100 and #9 R&B

"Yesterday" is a song about how one's life can change in the blink of an eye. The singer's significant other has decided to leave, unexpectedly, and now he longs for "yesterday" when all was well. The Beatles reached number 1 with their rendition in the latter part of 1965. The B-side, "Act Naturally," also did well (see the entry for that song).

The biggest cover version of "Yesterday" was recorded by "the Genius of Soul," Ray Charles, in 1967, two years after the original. Charles's soulful version, complete with his trademarked "Now, wait a minute" added to the lyrics, reached Top 10 on the R&B charts and rose to number 25 on the Pop charts. It's included on the *Ray Charles Invites You to Listen* album (ABC/ TRC #595).

"YESTERDAY, WHEN I WAS YOUNG"
Composers: Charles Aznavour and Herbert Kretzmer
Original Artist: Charles Aznavour
Label: Barclay Records; *Recording:* Barclay #60500 (45)
Release Year: 1964; *Chart:* did not chart
Cover Artist: Roy Clark
Label: Dot Records; *Recording:* Dot #17246 (45)
Release Year: 1969; *Chart:* #19 *Billboard* Hot 100

French actor/singer Charles Aznavour wrote and recorded the original version of "Yesterday, When I Was Young." Written as "Hier Encore," which translates to something akin to "Yesterday," Aznavour recorded the song for Barclay Records in 1964. His version, all in French, sounds rather hurried, as if it were a relay race. It was not yet a hit in the United States.

The tune was Anglicized by Herbert Kretzmer and recorded by Roy Clark at the exact same time that his hosting duties on *Hee Haw* began on CBS during the early summer of 1969. Although Clark was famous for being a banjo virtuoso, no banjo was used on this tender ballad about a man who realizes late in life that opportunity knocked many times over the years, but he never answered the door. It became Clark's only Top 20 Pop hit—peaking at number 19. The song can also be found on the *Yesterday, When I Was Young* album (Dot #25953). Roy Clark performed the song on an episode of TV's *The Odd Couple*, which is still running in syndication.

"Yo Yo"
Composer: Joe South
Original Artist: Billy Joe Royal
Label: Columbia Records; *Recording:* Columbia #43883 (45)
Release Year: 1966; *Chart:* bubbled under #117
Cover Artist: the Osmonds
Label: MGM Records; *Recording:* MGM #14259 (45)
Release Year: 1971; *Chart:* #3 *Billboard* Hot 100

Singer/songwriter Joe South wrote "Down in the Boondocks" and "I Knew You When" for Billy Joe Royal, and he also composed this upbeat blue-eyed soul tune for him in 1966. One of the most memorable lyrics in the song is, "I used to be a swinger, until you wrapped me around your finger, just like a yo yo." Royal did a great job on the record, but it failed to catch on in a big way, and "bubbled under" the Hot 100, peaking at number 117. However, like a true "yo yo," the song bounced back.

Five years later, the red-hot Osmond Brothers remade the song in a very similar fashion, and this time it worked. It peaked at number 3 on the Pop charts and sold well over a million copies. It was included on the Top 10 *Phase III* album in 1971 (MGM #4796).

"YOU ALWAYS HURT THE ONE YOU LOVE"
Composers: Doris Fisher and Allan Roberts
Original Artist: the Mills Brothers
Label: Decca Records; *Recording:* Decca #18599 (78)
Release Year: 1944; *Chart:* #1 *Billboard* Music Popularity Chart and #5 R&B
Cover Artist: Clarence "Frogman" Henry
Label: Argo Records; *Recording:* Argo #5388 (45)
Release Year: 1961; *Chart:* #12 *Billboard* Hot 100 and #11 R&B

"You Always Hurt the One You Love" is a song about how we take things for granted. The Mills Brothers recorded a huge hit version in 1944 for the Decca label. "Till Then" (see the entry for that song) is on the flip side, and that's the side that hit number 1 on the R&B chart, while "You Always Hurt the One You Love" reached number 1 on the Pop charts. Either way, it was a huge two-sided smash.

Some seventeen years later, Clarence "Frogman" Henry recorded a very retro rendition of the tune as a follow-up to the similar-sounding "But I Do" (Argo #5378), his biggest hit. Although not as big, it just narrowly missed the Top 10 and sold a lot of copies in 1961. It was also the title cut of his *You Always Hurt the One You Love* album (Argo #4009).

Actor Ryan Gosling performed the song in the 2010 motion picture from the Weinstein Company titled *Blue Valentine*.

"YOU ARE MY SUNSHINE"
Composer: Paul Rice
Original Artist: the Pine Ridge Boys
Label: Bluebird Records; *Recording:* Bluebird #8263 (78)
Release Year: 1939; *Chart:* did not chart
Cover Artist: Ray Charles
Label: ABC-Paramount Records; *Recording:* ABC-Paramount #10375 (45)
Release Year: 1962; *Chart:* #7 *Billboard* Hot 100 and #1 R&B

"You Are My Sunshine" was first recorded by the Pine Ridge Boys on RCA's Bluebird label in August of 1939, and no composer was listed on the label. One month later, the Rice Brothers Gang version (Decca #5763) was released, and Paul Rice was listed as the composer. Then, in 1940, Jimmie Davis and the Charles Mitchell Orchestra released one of the most familiar versions of the song, also on Decca (#5813). This release once again failed to list a composer on the label. Jimmie Davis later became governor of Louisiana, and he pushed to have "You Are My Sunshine" included as one of the state songs. Some versions released after Davis's list him and Charles Mitchell as the composers. Such was the case on the Bing Crosby rendition, again on Decca (#3952), in 1941.

Davis and Mitchell are credited on one of the biggest hit versions of the song—the 1962 recording by Ray Charles on ABC-Paramount. As per usual, Ray made the song his own—and reached Top 10 on both the Pop and R&B charts. Margie Hendrix of the Raelettes performed an intense solo on this cut.

There were also a couple of R&B vocal group versions—on the flip side of the original "Louie Louie" by Richard Berry and the Pharaohs (Flip #321) in 1957, and on the Clover label (#1001) by Johnny and the Thunderbirds in 1959. Neither one made the charts.

"You Belong to Me" (1952)
Composers: Pee Wee King, Chilton Price, and Redd Stewart
Original Artist: Sue Thompson
Label: Mercury Records; *Recording:* Mercury #6407 (45 and 78)
Release Year: 1952; *Chart:* did not chart
Cover Artist: the Duprees
Label: Coed Records; *Recording:* Coed #569 (45)
Release Year: 1962; *Chart:* #7 *Billboard* Hot 100

"You Belong to Me" is sometimes erroneously called "See the Pyramids along the Nile." It is a song about faithfulness, and the original version was recorded for the country field by Sue Thompson on Mercury Records. Thompson enjoyed a great deal of success in the early 1960s with songs composed by John D. Loudermilk ("Sad Movies," "Norman," "James (Hold the Ladder Steady)," "Paper Tiger"), but this was almost a decade earlier. Shortly after Thompson released her version of "You Belong to Me," Patti Page followed suit—also on Mercury Records, but it was on the B-side of a big hit titled "I Went to Your Wedding" (#5899).

The first big hit version of the ballad came from Jo Stafford (Columbia #39811). It soared to number 1 in 1952, and Stafford's popularity led to her own eponymous CBS variety show in 1954.

A full decade later, a doo-wop vocal group from Jersey City, New Jersey, called the Duprees remade the ballad in retro fashion for Coed Records as their first release, and enjoyed a Top 10 hit right off the bat. This "You Belong to Me" is not to be confused with the Carly Simon hit of the same name from 1977 (see the entry for that song).

"You Belong to Me" (1977)
Composers: Carly Simon and Michael McDonald
Original Artist: the Doobie Brothers
Label: Warner Brothers Records; *Recording:* Warner Brothers #3045 (LP)

The 1982 version of the Duprees. Top left to right—Dwayne O'Hara, *Who Did It First?* author Bob Leszczak (top center), Bobby Wells; bottom left to right—Al Latta, original member Mike Arnone (center), and Richie Rosato.

Release Year: 1977; *Chart:* did not chart
Cover Artist: Carly Simon
Label: Elektra Records; *Recording:* Elektra #45477 (45)
Release Year: 1978; *Chart:* #6 *Billboard* Hot 100

Much like the Duprees/Jo Stafford song of the same name, this "You Belong to Me" is also a song about being faithful. The singer realizes that her significant other flirts a lot, but the song's title is a more-than-gentle reminder for him to remain faithful. The Doobie Brothers recorded the song first as a cut on the Top 10 *Livin' on the Fault Line* album in 1977, but it was not released as a single.

The co-writer of the tune, Carly Simon, opted to release the song on a 45 in 1977 and mounted her final trip into the Top 10 as a result. James Taylor can be heard singing harmony. "You Belong to Me" can also be found on her *Boys in the Trees* album (Elektra #128), which went platinum.

A live rendition of "You Belong to Me" was released as a Doobie Brothers' single in 1983 (Warner #29552), but it only reached number 79 on the Pop charts.

"You Can Depend on Me"
Composers: Charles Carpenter, Louis Dunlap, and Earl Hines
Original Artist: Louis Armstrong
Label: Okeh Records; *Recording:* Okeh #41538 (78)
Release Year: 1931; *Chart:* #4 *Billboard*
Cover Artist: Brenda Lee
Label: Decca Records; *Recording:* Decca #31231 (45)
Release Year: 1961; *Chart:* #6 *Billboard* Hot 100

This "You Can Depend on Me" is not to be confused with the Smokey Robinson and the Miracles song (Tamla #54028) of the same name. The song in the spotlight here dates back to the 1930s. Louis Armstrong recorded it in 1931, and it became a Top 10 hit for him in 1932 for the Okeh Records label. It's a song about a couple who part as friends. The singer wants the ex to know that, even though she has found someone new, she can always depend on an undying friendship.

An upbeat doo-wop version in 1955 by the Sabres (Bullseye #101) failed to make the charts, but a lush ballad version by the red-hot Brenda Lee in 1961 brought the standard back into the Top 10, and introduced it to a whole new generation of record buyers.

"You Cheated"
Composer: Don Burch
Original Artist: the Slades
Label: Domino Records; *Recording:* Domino #500 (45)
Release Year: 1958; *Chart:* #42 *Billboard* Hot 100
Cover Artist: the Shields
Label: Tender Records; *Recording:* Tender #513 (45)
Release Year: 1958; *Chart:* #12 *Billboard* Hot 100 and #11 R&B

This song was a true anomaly. In an era when white covers of black records were the norm, the complete opposite occurred with "You Cheated." Sometimes called "You Cheated, You Lied," the song was written by Austin, Texas's, Don Burch of the white vocal group called the Slades. They recorded the ballad for the tiny Domino Records label in 1958.

The Slades penetrated the Top 50, but a cover by a Southern California group called the Shields on the small Tender Records label began to garner more attention, more airplay, and more sales. The Shields' record was then leased to the much bigger Dot Records label (#15805), and it just missed the Top 10 on both the Pop and R&B charts. Anonymously singing the falsetto parts on the Shields single was the ubiquitous Jesse Belvin. Trying to cash in on the same theme, the Shields released "Play the Game Fair" in 1959 (Tender #521) as a follow-up, but it failed to chart.

The Shields' hit cover version of "You Cheated" on its original Tender record label.

A version of "You Cheated" by Beverly Noble and an unnamed girl group (Sparrow #100) in the early 1960s got some airplay on the West Coast, but failed to chart.

"You Don't Have to Be a Baby to Cry"
Composers: Bob Merrill and Terry Shand
Original Artist: Moon Mullican
Label: King Records; *Recording:* King #868 (78)
Release Year: 1950; *Chart:* did not chart
Cover Artist: the Caravelles
Label: Smash Records; *Recording:* Smash #1852 (45)
Release Year: 1963; *Chart:* #3 *Billboard* Hot 100

"You Don't Have to Be a Baby to Cry" dates back to 1950. A couple of versions with a country flair were released in that year—Moon Mullican on the King label, Ernest Tubb on the Decca label (a Top 10 Country hit), and even Jimmy Dorsey on Columbia. It's a song about a love gone wrong; thus the title.

A very gentle, whispery, airy version by a female British duet called the Caravelles in 1963 became a Top 3 Smash label smash. The girls soon had reason to cry—they never again came close to the Top 50.

"YOU DON'T HAVE TO SAY YOU LOVE ME"
Composers: Pino Donaggio, Vito Pallavicini, Vicki Wickham, and Simon Napier-Bell
Original Artist: Dusty Springfield
Label: Philips Records; *Recording:* Philips #40371 (45)
Release Year: 1966; *Chart:* #4 *Billboard* Hot 100
Cover Artist: Elvis Presley
Label: RCA Victor Records; *Recording:* RCA Victor #9916 (45)
Release Year: 1970; *Chart:* #11 *Billboard* Hot 100

"You Don't Have to Say You Love Me" began as an Italian song on an acetate demo record by Pino Donaggio from 1965. At that time, the song was titled "Lo Che Non Vivo (Senza Te)," and Dusty Springfield and the powers-that-be at Philips Records loved the melody but needed someone to write English lyrics. Vicki Wickham and Simon Napier-Bell got that assignment, and the result was Springfield's biggest hit, which peaked at number 4 on the Pop charts in 1966.

A soul version in 1968 by the Four Sonics of Detroit, Michigan, on the Sport Records label (#110) reached number 32 on the R&B charts and crossed over to the Pop charts at number 89.

The song had one more life in 1970 during Elvis Presley's comeback years. Recorded a wee bit faster than Springfield's, the single was taken from the *Elvis— That's the Way It Is* album (RCA #4445). Both the single and the album garnered gold records for "the King of Rock and Roll."

"YOU NEVER DONE IT LIKE THAT"
Composers: Neil Sedaka and Howard Greenfield
Original Artist: Neil Sedaka
Label: Elektra Records; *Recording:* Elektra #102 (LP)
Release Year: 1977; *Chart:* did not chart
Cover Artist: the Captain and Tennille
Label: A & M Records; *Recording:* A & M #2063 (45)
Release Year: 1978; *Chart:* #10 *Billboard* Hot 100

In the mid to late 1970s, Sedaka was back in a big way, and a good deal of his success came from the Captain and Tennille covering his songs "Lonely Night

(Angel Face)" and "Love Will Keep Us Together" (see the entries for those songs).

After both of those songs became whopping successes, the Captain and Tennille went to the well one more time in 1978, covering a song from Neil Sedaka's album titled *A Song* released in 1977. The album was not a huge success for Sedaka, and none of the singles he released from the album became hits. The song of choice for the Captain was a bouncy ditty called "You Never Done It Like That," which had more of an edge than the duo's previous releases. The song tells the tale of someone who reunited with an old lover and was pleasantly surprised and wowed by how romantically experienced she had become. It became a Top 10 hit for A & M Records and was included on the *Dream* album (A & M #4707).

"You Were on My Mind"
Composer: Sylvia Fricker
Original Artist: Ian and Sylvia
Label: Vanguard Records; *Recording:* Vanguard #35025 (45)
Release Year: 1964; *Chart:* did not chart
Cover Artist: We Five
Label: A & M Records; *Recording:* A & M #770 (45)
Release Year: 1965; *Chart:* #3 *Billboard* Hot 100

"You Were on My Mind" was written by Sylvia Fricker. Her married name was Tyson. She and Ian Tyson recorded the original rendition of that song on Vanguard Records, and it had a sound somewhere between the Seekers and the Rooftop Singers. It was a hit in Canada but not in the United States.

That was the job of We Five—a California group made up of Beverly Bivens, Pete Fullerton, Bob Jones, Mike Stewart, and Jerry Burgan. Burgan remembered, "Mike Stewart and I heard the song on Ian and Sylvia's *Northern Journey* album. Our vocal arrangement was Mike Stewart's brainchild, and the 12-string parts were Bob Jones's. We wanted it to have a 'rock feel,' so we used a drummer for the session. Our manager/producer, Frank Werber [head of the Kingston Trio's Trident Productions in San Francisco], shopped it around and it was released by Herb Alpert and Jerry Moss on A & M Records."

The We Five version eliminated the "I got drunk and I got sick" line heard in the Ian and Sylvia original. A version by Crispian St. Peters, which was a big hit in the United Kingdom, is also sans the "drunk" line and mirrors the We Five interpretation rather than the Ian and Sylvia original.

"Young Love"
Composers: Ric Cartey and Carole Joyner
Original Artist: Ric Cartey
Label: Stars Records; *Recording:* Stars #539 (45 and 78)

Release Year: 1956; *Chart:* did not chart
Cover Artist: Tab Hunter
Label: Dot Records; *Recording:* Dot #15533 (45 and 78)
Release Year: 1957; *Chart:* #1 *Billboard* Hot 100

There were two huge hit versions of this ballad titled "Young Love" in 1957, but few realize that the first version was on the B-side of a rockabilly 45 titled "Ooo-Eee" by the co-writer of the song, Ric Cartey. The A-side was written by future star Jerry Reed. It came out first on the tiny Stars Records label and then RCA Victor (#6751) in 1956. Neither side charted—yet.

"The Southern Gentleman," Sonny James, released a version of that B-side, "Young Love," the last week of 1956 on Capitol Records (#3602). Just as it started to take off, another version was quickly in the works. Actor/singer Tab Hunter recalled,

> Sonny James recorded the song in Nashville for the country and western market. While in Chicago on a publicity tour, a local disc jockey named Howard Miller suggested I meet with Randy Wood of Dot Records when I returned to California. I followed up on that, and I recorded "Young Love" and the flip side, "Red Sails in the Sunset," at Ryder Sound on Santa Monica Boulevard in Hollywood. We used the

Young Tab Hunter recording "Young Love" in the studio at Ryder Sound in Hollywood. *Courtesy of Tab Hunter*

Jordanaires for the background vocals, and Elvis was none too pleased about that. I was under contract with Warner Brothers, and when they found out that I had recorded for Dot they went ballistic and they started the Warner Brothers record label and eventually brought me over there.

Did he have any formal vocal training? Hunter said, "I sang in the church choir as a kid, and once my recording career got under way, I studied with a vocal coach named Keith Davis."

Both the Sonny James and Tab Hunter renditions of "Young Love" reached number 1 on the Pop charts and both sold over a million copies, earning each singer a gold record. Hunter called his instant recording success "a shock." Hunter also had a big follow-up hit titled "Ninety-Nine Ways" (see the entry for that song).

"YOUNGER GIRL"

Composer: John Sebastian
Original Artist: the Lovin' Spoonful
Label: Kama Sutra Records; *Recording:* Kama Sutra #8050 (LP)
Release Year: 1965; *Chart:* did not chart
Cover Artist: the Critters
Label: Kapp Records; *Recording:* Kapp #752 (45)
Release Year: 1966; *Chart:* #42 *Billboard* Hot 100

"Younger Girl" is a song about "spring fever" and "young love." The singer is infatuated with a young lady, and she "keeps rolling across his mind." Written by John Sebastian, it was a cut on the *Do You Believe in Magic?* album—the first album by the Lovin' Spoonful—but was never released as a single.

The Critters of New Jersey took advantage of that and released a very similar take on "Younger Girl" in 1966 for Kapp Records. It became a Top 50 entry and was used as the title for their only chart album (Kapp #3485). That very same day, the Hondells of Southern California released their single version of "Younger Girl" (Mercury #72563) but just missed the Top 50.

"YOU'RE MY WORLD"

Composers: Umberto Bindi, Gino Paoli, and Carl Sigman
Original Artist: Umberto Bindi
Label: RCA Italiana; *Recording:* RCA Italiana #3235 (45)
Release Year: 1963; *Chart:* did not chart
Cover Artist: Cilla Black
Label: Capitol Records; *Recording:* Capitol #5196 (45)
Release Year: 1964; *Chart:* #26 *Billboard* Hot 100

"You're My World" was written in Italian as "Il Mio Mundo" in 1963. One of the co-writers of the song, Umberto Bindi, recorded the first version. It wasn't a success, but did catch the ear of producer George Martin, who arranged for Carl Sigman to write English lyrics for the song. It's a song about complete and all-encompassing love, thus the title, "You're My World." In 1964, this new Anglicized rendition became a Top 30 hit in the United States for Cilla Black. Black's version also fared well in many other countries.

An even bigger chart version of the song came from Helen Reddy on the Capitol label (#4418) in 1977. It was Reddy's final Top 20 hit in the United States and was also included on her final charting album in the United States titled *Ear Candy* (Capitol #11640).

"YOU'RE SIXTEEN"

Composers: Bob and Richard Sherman
Original Artist: Johnny Burnette
Label: Liberty Records; *Recording:* Liberty #55285 (45)
Release Year: 1960; *Chart:* #8 *Billboard* Hot 100
Cover Artist: Ringo Starr
Label: Apple Records; *Recording:* Apple #1870 (45)
Release Year: 1973; *Chart:* #1 *Billboard* Hot 100

Johnny Burnette was the biggest star of the very musical Burnette family. He and his brother Dorsey recorded some amazing rockabilly under the moniker the Johnny Burnette Trio on the Coral Records label, and both brothers wrote hit songs for Ricky Nelson, but even bigger things were still ahead when the two brothers went solo. "You're Sixteen" by Johnny Burnette on the Liberty label became a Top 10 smash in 1960, and was later included in the soundtrack for the 1973 motion picture *American Graffiti*.

Those same sixteen candles were lit again late in 1973 when the song was remade by Ringo Starr in his solo years. It's interesting to note that Harry Nilsson provided some of the background vocals on the record, and Paul McCartney played kazoo. This time around, the song was even bigger—reaching number 1 on the Pop charts and selling well over a million copies.

The offspring of Johnny and Dorsey Burnette also made their mark in the music world—Johnny's son, Rocky, had a Top 10 hit of his own, "Tired of Toein' the Line" (EMI America #8043) in 1980, and Dorsey's son, Billy, made Top 70 with "Don't Say No" (Columbia #11380) in that same year.

"YOU'RE THE ONE"

Composers: Petula Clark and Tony Hatch
Original Artist: Petula Clark

Label: Pye Records and Vogue Records; *Recording:* Pye #15991 and Vogue
   #1312 (45)
Release Year: 1965; *Chart:* did not chart
Cover Artist: the Vogues
Label: Co and Ce Records; *Recording:* Co and Ce #229 (45)
Release Year: 1965; *Chart:* #4 *Billboard* Hot 100

"You're the One" is a song about someone who, after years of futility, finally
finds "the one" she's been awaiting—the one she loves. Written by Tony Hatch
and Petula Clark, Clark released the original version on both the Pye and Vogue
Records labels early in 1965. It wasn't released in the United States until it was
covered by the Vogues of Pittsburgh, Pennsylvania. It's a total coincidence that
the original Petula Clark version was released on the Vogue label and then covered by the Vogues.

   "You're the One" became the first of four Top 10 hits for the Vogues, and
it was included on the uncharted *Meet the Vogues* album (Co and Ce #1229).

"YOU'VE GOT A FRIEND"
Composer: Carole King
Original Artist: Carole King
Label: Ode Records; *Recording:* Ode #77009 (LP)
Release Year: 1971; *Chart:* did not chart
Cover Artist: James Taylor
Label: Warner Brothers Records; *Recording:* Warner Brothers #7498 (45)
Release Year: 1971; *Chart:* #1 *Billboard* Hot 100

Carole King achieved an incredible comeback in 1971 with the release of *Tapestry*, a number 1 album that went multiplatinum and spent almost five years
on the album chart. The LP was released in April of that year and contained
the original version of one of King's most famous compositions, "You've Got a
Friend," but it wasn't released as a single . . . yet.

   Meanwhile, singer/songwriter James Taylor was seeking a follow-up to his
1970 hit "Fire and Rain" (Warner #7423). He opted to cover "You've Got
a Friend," and two months after *Tapestry* debuted, Warner Brothers released
Taylor's version as a single. It became his only number 1 hit and sold well over
a million copies. It was included on his platinum *Mud Slide Slim and the Blue
Horizon* album (Warner Brothers #2561).

   One week later, Roberta Flack and Donny Hathaway released a duet version
on a 45 (Atlantic #2808). It became Flack's first chart hit.

"YOU'VE LOST THAT LOVIN' FEELIN'"
Composers: Phil Spector, Barry Mann, and Cynthia Weil
Original Artist: the Righteous Brothers
Label: Philles Records; *Recording:* Philles #124 (45)

Release Year: 1964; *Chart:* #1 *Billboard* Hot 100 and #2 R&B
Cover Artist: Daryl Hall and John Oates
Label: RCA Victor Records; *Recording:* RCA Victor #12103 (45)
Release Year: 1980; *Chart:* #12 *Billboard* Hot 100

They began as the Paramours on the Smash and Moonglow record labels without success. While with Moonglow, a California label, Bobby Hatfield and Bill Medley reacted to a shout from the audience during a performance, "That was righteous, brother." The rest, as they say, is history. The Paramours changed their name.

Even as the Righteous Brothers, the duo had only marginal success with Moonglow. It was their move to Philles and Phil Spector's "wall of sound" where magic began to happen. A song composed by Spector along with husband-and-wife team Barry Mann and Cynthia Weil called "You've Lost That Lovin' Feelin'" became their first Philles release. The finished product was almost four minutes in length—longer than any song being played on Top 40 radio stations—so Spector fabricated the time as three minutes, five seconds on the label to fool disc jockeys. The ploy worked, and early in 1965, the Righteous Brothers had their first number 1 hit.

A remake by Dionne Warwick (Scepter #12262) became a Top 20 hit during the summer of 1969. It was included on her *Soulful* album (Scepter #573)—in fact, it was the first cut on the album.

This great song still had more life in it. Like the Righteous Brothers, another blue-eyed soul duet brought it back in 1980. Daryl Hall and John Oates, on the RCA Victor label, reached number 12 on the Pop charts.

The original "You've Lost That Lovin' Feelin'" was included in the soundtrack for the hit Tom Cruise Paramount motion picture *Top Gun* in 1986. It has been designated by BMI (Broadcast Music Incorporated) as the song that received the most radio and TV airplay during the twentieth century.

Z

"ZIP-A-DEE-DOO-DAH"
Composers: Ray Gilbert and Allie Wrubel
Original Artist: Johnny Mercer
Label: Capitol Records; *Recording:* Capitol #323 (78)
Release Year: 1947; *Chart:* #8 *Billboard* Music Popularity Chart
Cover Artist: Bob B. Soxx and the Blue Jeans
Label: Philles Records; *Recording:* Philles #107 (45)
Release Year: 1962; *Chart:* #8 *Billboard* Hot 100 and #7 R&B

This happy little ditty originated in the animated 1946 Walt Disney motion picture *Song of the South* as performed by James Baskett. Because of its very positive message, it has been covered countless times by the likes of Doris Day, Guy

Mitchell, the Jackson Five, Connie Francis, and Steve Miller, but the first true hit rendition came in 1947 when recorded by composer Johnny Mercer on the Capitol label (with vocal backing by the Pied Pipers).

When the song was remade late in 1962 for Phil Spector's Philles Records label it surprised many. Most of Spector's catalog up until then was comprised of original compositions by the up-and-coming talent composing in the Brill Building in Manhattan. With a beat similar to that of "Mockingbird" by Inez and Charlie Foxx, Spector paired Bobby Sheen of the Robins with Darlene Love and Fanita James of the Blossoms and dubbed them Bob B. Soxx and the Blue Jeans. Like the Johnny Mercer version, it peaked at number 8 on the Pop charts. When the song became a hit, Spector released a *Zip-a-Dee-Doo-Dah* album by the group (Philles #4002) with a very colorful album cover. Once again (like with "He's a Rebel"—see the entry for that song) poor Darlene Love had a Top 10 hit under an alias, but she never had one under her own name.

The song was popularized yet again when it was performed by Chevy Chase in the hit motion picture *Fletch Lives* in 1989.

Appendix: Curiosities

Songs Covered by Elvis Presley

"Always on My Mind"
"Are You Lonesome, Tonight?"
"Blue Moon"
"Blue Moon of Kentucky"
"Crying in the Chapel"
"A Fool Such as I"
"I Love You, Because"
"It's Now or Never"
"Love Letters"
"Love Me Tender"
"My Way"
"Suspicious Minds"
"Take Good Care of Her"
"That's When Your Heartaches Begin"
"Unchained Melody"
"The Wonder of You"
"You Don't Have to Say You Love Me"

Songs Originally Known under a Different Title

Known As	*Original Title*
"Apples, Peaches, Pumpkin Pie"	"Ready or Not"
"Beyond the Sea"	"La Mer"
"Blue Moon"	"The Bad in Every Man"
"Come on Down to My Boat"	"Come and Take a Ride in My Boat"

Known As	*Original Title*
"Don't Cry Out Loud"	"We Don't Cry Out Loud"
"Don't Know Much"	"All I Need to Know"
"Get Together"	"Let's Get Together"
"Girl Watcher"	"Boy Watcher"
"I Will Follow Him"	"Chariot"
"Indian Reservation"	"Pale-Faced Indian"
"It's Now or Never"	"O Sole Mio" and "There's No Tomorrow"
"Leavin' on a Jet Plane"	"Babe, I Hate to Go"
"The Lion Sleeps Tonight"	"Mbube" and "Wimoweh"
"Love Me Tender"	"Aura Lee"
"Mandy"	"Brandy"
"Midnight Train to Georgia"	"Midnight Plane to Houston"
"The Most Beautiful Girl"	"Hey Mister"
"Pass the Dutchie"	"Pass the Kouchie"
"Sloop John B"	"The Wreck of the John B."
"Sukiyaki"	"Ue O Muite Aruko"
"Volare"	"Nel Blu Dipinto di Blu"
"Walk Away, Renee"	"Quand un Amour Renait"
"The Way of Love"	"J'ai le Mal de Toi"
"The Wedding"	"La Novia"
"What a Difference a Day Makes"	"Cuando Vuelva a Tu Lado"
"Wooden Heart"	"Muss I Denn"
"Yesterday, When I Was Young"	"Hier Encore"
"You Don't Have to Say You Love Me"	"Lo Che Non Vivo (Senze Te)"
"You're My World"	"Il Mio Mondo"

Songs That Began as Country Music Numbers

"Act Naturally"
"Always on My Mind"
"The Battle of New Orleans"
"Before the Next Teardrop Falls"
"Busted"
"The Chokin' Kind"
"Crying in the Chapel"
"Crying Time"
"Dark Moon"
"Elvira"
"A Fool Such as I"
"Funny How Time Slips Away"
"The Gambler"
"Gone"
"He'll Have to Go"

"I Can't Stop Loving You"
"I Will Always Love You"
"I'm a Fool to Care"
"I'm So Lonesome I Could Cry"
"The Most Beautiful Girl"
"Patches"
"Release Me"
"Rhinestone Cowboy"
"Right or Wrong"
"Ring of Fire"
"Ruby, Don't Take Your Love to Town"
"Sad Movies (Make Me Cry)"
"Stand by Your Man"
"Sweet and Innocent"
"Talk Back Trembling Lips"
"Tennessee Waltz"
"You Are My Sunshine"

Songs Originally Released as Instrumental Works

"Canadian Sunset"
"Cherry Pink (and Apple Blossom White)"
"Ebb Tide"
"In the Mood"
"Love Is Blue"
"Misty"
"Spooky"
"Star Dust"
"A Swingin' Safari"
"Twilight Time"
"Whispering"
"Wonderland by Night"

Songs from Phil Spector

"Ebb Tide" by the Righteous Brothers
"He's a Rebel" by the Crystals
"I Love How You Love Me" by the Paris Sisters
"To Know Him Is to Love Him" by the Teddy Bears
"Unchained Melody" by the Righteous Brothers
"You've Lost That Lovin' Feeling" by the Righteous Brothers
"Zip-a-Dee-Doo-Dah" by Bob B. Soxx and the Blue Jeans

First Name Basis

(Songs in this book with first names in the title)

"Alfie"
"Billy, Don't Be a Hero"
"Cindy, Oh Cindy"
"Danny's Song"
"Donna"
"Elvira"
"Georgia on My Mind"
"Gina"
"Gloria"
"Greetings, This Is Uncle Sam"
"Hello, Mary Lou"
"Johnny Angel"
"Linda"
"Mack the Knife"
"Marie"
"My Maria"
"Ruby, Don't Take Your Love to Town"
"Susie Darlin'"
"Tall Paul"
"Tammy"
"Walk Away, Renee"

"Crying Songs"

"Before the Next Teardrop Falls"
"Cry"
"Cry Like a Baby"
"Cry Me a River"
"Crying"
"Crying in the Chapel"
"Crying Time"
"Don't Cry Out Loud"
"I'm So Lonesome I Could Cry"
"Misty"
"Sad Movies (Make Me Cry)"
"She Cried"
"A Tear Fell"

Further Reading

Gonzalez, Fernando L., ed. *The Discofile*. 3rd ed. New York: Author, 2009.

Whitburn, Joel, ed. *Hot R&B Songs*. 6th ed. Menomonee Falls, WI: Record Research, 2010.

Whitburn, Joel, ed. *Top Pop Albums*. 7th ed. Menomonee Falls, WI: Record Research, 2010.

Index

Note: *Page numbers in italics refer to record label images or photographs.*

About the Author

Bob Leszczak is a native of New Jersey, living in Palm Springs, California. Leszczak's bailiwick is the history of rock and roll, pop, and rhythm and blues music, and almost every job he's ever held has involved that music. He worked in an "oldies" record store in Clifton, New Jersey, while still in college (Seton Hall University); he sang and toured with the 1960s vocal group known as the Duprees of "You Belong to Me" and "Have You Heard" fame in the 1980s; he wrote and produced a weekly five-hour syndicated radio program for United Stations Radio Network called *Solid Gold Scrapbook*; and for the past three decades plus, he's worked as an on-air personality on "oldies radio" stations in great U.S. cities such as Washington, D.C., Boston, Orlando, Hartford, Denver, Riverside/San Bernardino, and Tampa (as Bob O'Brien). While on Tampa radio, he won a coveted Air Award in 1999. He was an extra in the Emmy-winning 2013 HBO biopic about Liberace called *Behind the Candelabra*, directed by Steven Soderbergh.

Leszczak is an avid runner and a lover of baseball and football. His first book, *Single Season Sitcoms, 1948–1979*, reflects yet another of his passions—classic TV. Now Leszczak shares his passion for and vast knowledge of many forms of music in *Who Did It First? Great Pop Cover Songs and Their Original Artists*—a sequel to *Who Did It First? Great Rhythm and Blues Cover Songs and Their Original Artists*.